CARICATURE AND NATIONAL CHARACTER

Humor in America

Edited by
Judith Yaross Lee, *Ohio University*
Tracy Wuster, *The University of Texas at Austin*

Advisory Board
Darryl Dickson-Carr, *Southern Methodist University*
Joanne Gilbert, *Alma College*
Rebecca Krefting, *Skidmore College*
Bruce Michelson, *University of Illinois at Urbana-Champaign*
Nicholas Sammond, *University of Toronto*

The Humor in America series considers humor as an expressive mode reflecting key concerns of people in specific times and places. With interdisciplinary research, historical and transnational approaches, and comparative scholarship that carefully examines contexts such as race, gender, class, sexuality, region, and media environments, books in the series explore how comic expression both responds to and shapes American culture.

CARICATURE AND NATIONAL CHARACTER
The United States at War

Christopher J. Gilbert

The Pennsylvania State University Press
University Park, Pennsylvania

Library of Congress Cataloging-in-Publication Data

Names: Gilbert, Christopher J., author.
Title: Caricature and national character : the United States at war / Christopher J. Gilbert.
Other titles: Humor in America.
Description: University Park, Pennsylvania : The Pennsylvania State University Press, [2021] | Series: Humor in America | Includes bibliographical references and index.
Summary: "Examines wartime political cartoons—with particular emphasis on the works of James Montgomery Flagg, Dr. Seuss, Ollie Harrington, and Ann Telnaes—to examine how, when, and why graphic caricatures serve to illuminate the US national character"—Provided by publisher.
Identifiers: LCCN 2021010039 | ISBN 9780271089768 (hardback) | ISBN 9780271089775 (paperback)
Subjects: LCSH: Flagg, James Montgomery, 1877–1960—Criticism and interpretation. | Seuss, Dr.—Criticism and interpretation. | Harrington, Oliver W. (Oliver Wendell), 1912–1995—Criticism and interpretation. | Telnaes, Ann, 1960- —Criticism and interpretation. | National characteristics, American—Caricatures and cartoons. | Art and war. | United States—History—Caricatures and cartoons.
Classification: LCC NC1420 .G55 2021 | DDC 741.6092—dc23
LC record available at https://lccn.loc.gov/2021010039

Copyright © 2021 Christopher J. Gilbert
All rights reserved
Printed in the United States of America
Published by The Pennsylvania State University Press,
University Park, PA 16802–1003

The Pennsylvania State University Press is a member of the Association of University Presses.

It is the policy of The Pennsylvania State University Press to use acid-free paper. Publications on uncoated stock satisfy the minimum requirements of American National Standard for Information Sciences—Permanence of Paper for Printed Library Material, ANSI Z39.48–1992.

All wars are follies.
—BENJAMIN FRANKLIN, letter to Polly
Stevenson Hewson (January 27, 1783)

---

folly given all this—
seeing—
folly seeing all this—
this—
what is the word—
this this—
this this here—
all this this here—
folly given all this—
seeing—
folly seeing all this this here—
for to—
what is the word—
see—
—SAMUEL BECKETT, "what is the word,"
translation of *Comment dire* (1988)

At the very least, caricatures are responsible for the possibility that they lead willing viewers into accepting transgressions that transform them into society's spectral beings. Caricature has the force to set societies on the sanctimonious path that pits Our Principles against Their Follies, Our Truths against Their Lies, without giving thought as to which introduces the greatest "interruptions" to the social fabric. Under conditions like these, more than one person, group, or nation gets hurt.
—MARTHA BANTA, *Barbaric Intercourse: Caricature
and the Culture of Conduct, 1841–1936* (2002)

Contents

List of Illustrations ix

Acknowledgments xi

Introduction 1

1. Pledges of Allegiance, Sexualized Politics, and Comic Pillories in James Montgomery Flagg's America 26

2. Dr. Seuss and His Wacky War on American Culture 65

3. Children of War in Ollie Harrington's Dark Comedy 100

4. The Battle Rages on in Ann Telnaes's Comic Travesties of the War on Terror 136

Conclusion: Warring Caricatures 183

Coda: Caricature in End Times, or the Future of Caricature 197

Notes 204

Bibliography 217

Index 239

Illustrations

1. Benjamin Franklin, "MAGNA Britannia: her Colonies REDUC'D," ca. 1766 3
2. Marshall Everett, "Ten Thousand Miles from Tip to Tip," 1899 5
3. Editorial cartoon of Brother Jonathan, ca. 1852 14
4. James Montgomery Flagg, "Arrested as a Witch in Salem, 1692" 27
5. Clifford Berryman, "Not in a Position to Give Up the Chase," 1899 33
6. James Montgomery Flagg, "A Call to Arms," 1915 41
7. James Montgomery Flagg, "I WANT YOU," war poster, ca. 1917 43
8. James Montgomery Flagg, "The Cartoonist Makes People SEE THINGS!," 1918 49
9. James Montgomery Flagg, "GET OFF THAT THRONE!," 1917 52
10. Howard Chandler Christy, "I WANT YOU for THE NAVY," recruiting poster, 1917 56
11. James Montgomery Flagg, "A Jill for Jack," 1912 58
12. Dr. Seuss, Vico Motor Oil advertisement, between 1930 and 1940 76
13. Dr. Seuss, "The Lindbergh Quarter," April 28, 1941 81
14. Dr. Seuss, "The End of the Nap," December 9, 1941 85
15. Dr. Seuss, "Quick, Henry, THE FLIT!," December 19, 1941 88
16. Dr. Seuss, "Our Big Bertha," February 18, 1942 93
17. Dr. Seuss, "The Veteran Recalls the Battle of 1943," January 5, 1943 96
18. Oliver W. Harrington, "My daddy said they didn't seem to mind servin' him on the Anzio beachhead," 1960 105
19. Oliver W. Harrington, "General Blotchit, you take your tanks and feint at Lynchville," 1958 117
20. Oliver W. Harrington, lynched school bus, 1969 119
21. Oliver W. Harrington, "Funny how kids' games change with the times, ain't it?," 1958 122
22. Oliver W. Harrington, "Hey, why don't somebody tell these damn starvin' brats that there ain't enough for me and them too!," 1969 127
23. Oliver W. Harrington, kids at the war table, 1977 128

24. Ann Telnaes, Queen Elizabeth and King George, November 19, 2003 140
25. Ann Telnaes, Trump as Queen of Hearts, June 14, 2016 141
26. Ann Telnaes, U.S. war coverage, April 1, 2003 149
27. Ann Telnaes, Americans of the decadence, August 9, 1997 152
28. Ann Telnaes, "You can see these guys wrapped in the flag on TV," October 23, 2003 155
29. Ann Telnaes, "Guide to identifying people by their headgear," September 26, 2001 159
30. Ann Telnaes, pissing contest, January 3, 2018 168
31. Ann Telnaes, the Donald loves a good goose step, from an animation, February 7, 2018 170
32. Ann Telnaes, Emperor Trump has no clothes, February 16, 2017 173
33. Ann Telnaes, the imperial president, June 3, 2018 174
34. Ann Telnaes, Trump's appearance at CPAC, March 3, 2019 182
35. David Rowe, "The Three-Ring Circus," November 2017 195

Acknowledgments

I remember reading somewhere about the writing life as a solitary one in which no writer is ever alone. There are, quite simply, too many interactions with friends, scholars, and mentors, too many conversations big and small, and too many influences on my writing of this book to even begin attaching names to so many tokens of gratitude. I wrote some early ideas for this book while my infant son napped—sometimes on my chest as I typed away on my laptop. I wrote some of this book while riding my bike, pausing on this or that roadside to text message ideas to myself, scribble notes in a small journal stuffed in a plastic bag, or simply think. I wrote some of this book while writing about what I thought then were somewhat unrelated topics, sometimes with co-authors, and always with the benefit of a certain generosity of scholarship and spirit that seems to permeate my fields of study and circles of friends. Quite simply, I wrote this book in various states of solitude, in several iterations, and yet never by myself.

What springs to mind along with the vast catalog of former professors, grad school classmates, present colleagues, mentors past and present, and lifelong friends who contributed in one way or another to my thinking is the feeling that comes with calling any work of criticism and/or creativity complete: what E. E. Cummings once called a sense of "strenuous briefness." It is a feeling of arrival and departure in unison. It is a feeling of dawn dancing with twilight. This book was borne of strange and solemn and sublime and ridiculous imbrications. It was borne of my deep and longstanding interest in how war typifies the Human Comedy pushed to the end of its line, and then again how human beings have since time immemorial charged in and out of the darkness of wartimes with laughter on their breath. I do not know warfare from personal experience. But I do know of it from those who have shared with me how it is that the best of us can be carried away by the worst angels of our natures. I do know that my family motto has always been driven by the notion that there is a sort of comicality at the root of survival, the basis of which is a sense of humor. Cummings wrote of the doggedness that emerges from brevity, from—in his words—all the "solongs" and "ashes." He wrote of this doggedness as someone who saw firsthand the hardships and follies that so often follow when we humans let loose the dogs of war. And yet he wrote of a humanity that found in laughter the best of ways to live and die together.

And so, in brief, I wish to acknowledge mentors and friends like John Louis Lucaites, Stephen Olbrys Gencarella, Jonathan Rossing, Casey Ryan Kelly, Kristen Hoerl, Claire Sisco King, Phaedra Pezzullo, Ted Striphas, Robert Terrill, Robert Ivie, Kurt Zemlicka, Mark Nagle, Will Schiebel, Chris Beyers, Mike Land, and many others who have been supportive in different ways and instrumental in keeping me intellectually sharp. I wish to thank Judith Yaross Lee especially for supporting my work, and Tracy Wuster for providing advice and encouragement along the way. I wish to recognize Ryan Peterson for his gracious editorial guidance. I would be remiss, too, if I did not express my gratitude for the institutional support (i.e., faculty development grants, funding to offset fees associated with reproduction rights) and overall freedom to be the scholar and teacher I am that has been part and parcel of my experience in the liberal arts tradition and in the humanities. Sincere thanks as well to Ann Telnaes (and Sara Thaves), Dr. Helma Harrington (in lieu of Ollie Harrington), and David Rowe for granting me permission to include their wonderful works of comic art in my book. Putting this book together has been strenuous, to be sure, but à la Cummings, it has reminded me just how much "i smilingly glide."

To my parents: steadfast and supportive are descriptors that barely scratch the surface. You continue to bring me up smiling.

To my brother: my best friend, my confidant. Let's ride on.

To my kiddos: living proofs of the comic spirit, of a joyful approach to the world, of pure love, of hugs and kisses aplenty and wits that keep me honest as much as they humor me—and just make me laugh.

To my wife: my partner in carrying our hearts in each other's hearts, my go-to, my lifeblood. You remind me every day how much you love me as I am.

Introduction

Curious reader: it might be said that a solemn lie about national character stands on one leg, a caricature of it on two. In November 1773, Benjamin Franklin wrote a letter to his sister. He was in London as a representative for colonial America, trying to secure peace and commerce between the colonies and the Mother Country without "the Commencement of actual War."[1] Insurrection, after all, more and more seemed to be the most viable route to independence. Diplomacy was not working. In spite of "all the smooth Words I could muster," Franklin wrote, "I grew tir'd of Meekness when I saw it without Effect."[2] So he decided to get "saucy," composing two of his most famous humorous tracts, "An Edict by the King of Prussia" and the companion piece "Rules by Which a Great Empire May Be Reduced to a Small One." Both appeared in a London newspaper, the *Public Advertiser*, in September 1773, as well as in a Philadelphia newspaper of the same name. They were part of Franklin's oeuvre of *jeux d'esprit* (comic witticisms), satires, and political cartoons. The squibs expanded on mockeries of the plain truths and public goods that made up *Poor Richard's Almanack* (1732), establishing a way of seeing America not only for its righteous pursuits of life, liberty, and happiness but also for the foolish idea that war could foster democratic peace. What is more, his literary travesties evinced the rhetorical force of caricature insofar as, in Franklin's words, they "held up a Looking-Glass" for Ministers to "see their ugly Faces," for the British nation to see "its Injustice," and for the rights (and Right) of America to be seen in the distorted reflection of Imperial wrongs.[3]

Franklin is the standard bearer for a mode of particularly American humor that is driven by logics of mordancy, monstrosity, and devil-may-care cheekiness—and by a preoccupation with national character. At the center of these logics are problems of collective identity, public conduct, and national culture.[4] In Franklin's descriptions of squabbling proctors and pettifoggers are resonances of the part-time cartoon artist's Magna Britannia wherein national dismemberment is displayed through a leprous Lady Britain whose body parts (representing the American colonies) have been cut off (fig. 1). Such a grotesque image typifies a deep-seated tradition in American humor of using ugliness and injustice as the rhetorical forces in caricatures of national character. Even so, this book is not about Franklin. Nor is it about the wartime caricatures of this most humorous of Founding Fathers. Rather, *Caricature and National Character* focuses on the comic politics of caricature as they have cropped up in wartime milieus defined by moments of national—and, to be sure, international—disturbance.

Building on the notion that single artists and singular rhetorical artifacts can capture core public attitudes, this book engages the works of particular cartoon artists whose caricatures sift through the madness of America at war. My artists of interest hearken to the Founding Period, but they come from twentieth- and twenty-first-century war cultures in which national character is the point of departure for rather than the endpoint of democratic wrangles and ultimately armed conflict. Franklin's entire political and cultural project was largely the production of a national self-consciousness. This project was picked up by many nineteenth-century political cartoonists and comic artists. Thomas Nast was probably the most prominent purveyor of a comic *ars nationis*. Nast's work, published in *Harper's Weekly*, *Judge*, *Leslie's Weekly*, *Puck*, and more, bears traces of Franklinesque humor, grounded as it was in a growing stock of grotesque imagery for portrayals of strangers and strangeness in the American body politic. US American humor is full of the most prominent fools and knaves as well as the most nationalistic, prideful solons of the age. Both Franklin and Nast were concerned with statecraft. Both, too, presented the United States not only as a nation best understood *through* caricature but also *as a caricature of itself*. Franklin pursued nation building. Nast was drawn to the apparent decline, if not the poisoned well, of a burgeoning republic at the hands of witless warmongers, vicious lords and masters, and corrupt politicians. At the time of the American Revolution, there was not yet an ironed-out American nation to defend. The Civil War era, too, saw struggles over the big ideas of American ideals, and no real emergence of a coherent national image. The American Revolution fomented a war *for* principles,

FIG. I Benjamin Franklin, "MAGNA Britannia: her Colonies REDUC'D," ca. 1766. Engraving. Courtesy of Library Company of Philadelphia.

the Civil War a war *of* principles. By the early twentieth century, the United States was conducting war *on* principle.

The Spanish-American War lurks in this setup. An end of Two Americas (i.e., North and South, Union and Confederate) was, by turns, a precursor to the inception of 100 percent Americanism. The Spanish-American War presaged a sense of national wholeness that remained long after President Theodore Roosevelt's rough riding spirit and rhetoric of the nationalistic frontiersmen led to what Louis A. Perez Jr. calls an "Imperial Ethos," propelling the sort of hyperpatriotism that animated World War I propaganda and pegged Americanism as a cultural good.[5] The quick execution of war for international territories in the summer of 1898 left an indelible mark on images of Americanism. For one thing, armed conflict became an important means of asserting national character in homegrown battles of public opinion amid hostilities on the world stage. Yellow journalism thrived in this context. So did political cartoons of Uncle Sam reaping the glories of military conquest, such as those by Clifford K. Berryman, Rowland C. Bowman, Victor Gillam, and W. A. Rogers. So, too, did a generalized mythos of American exceptionalism that replaced past social, political, cultural, and humanitarian indiscretions with a more plural "Americanness." This mythos circulated a sense "that cultural values inhere in particular racial, ethnic, or national groups."⁶ There are precious few degrees of separation from this mythos and, say, the Know-Nothings, the Chinese Exclusion Act, diffuse anti-immigrant sentiments, eugenics, and America First ideologies. Even Franklin expressed concern about the "Complexion" of the American nation, and thus the "invasion" of non-American "herds." Appropriately, ethnic caricatures tended to emphasize oppositions like superiority and inferiority, Self and Other, Us and Them, thereby provoking humor that derived from cultural stereotypes.⁷ The "Spanish Brute," for instance, represented what an American was *not*, just as portrayals of Filipinos as "The White Man's Burden" stood for a march from barbarism to civilization.⁸

The Spanish-American War also stands as a touchstone for ethnocentric claims to American national character, laying the groundwork for a nativism that rejects indigenous peoples with a blend of xenophobia and nationalism, rhetorics of "foreigners" and "outsiders," and troubled perceptions of what Teddy Roosevelt called "hyphenated Americanism." Given that Americanism presumes its righteousness in the transcendental democratic project, its war powers bring about its global influence, and vice versa. As Paul T. McCartney attests, American national character by 1900 was "the normative standard on which to base the country's actions and measure its successes in global affairs."⁹ Lest we forget, though, the Wounded Knee Massacre occurred less than a decade prior to hostilities in the Pacific and Caribbean. Armed conflict, in both cases, was a recourse for dealing with struggles around cultural identity, civil rights, and self-determination. The one saw embattlements over American imperialism and the Jim Crow empire. The other sowed the seeds of the American Indian movement. The one was an augury for international power grabs. The other was a seedbed for colonialist claims to sacred Native lore and lands. The one, a catapult for a global expansion of the American experiment. The other, a cudgel for US Americanization. Wartime caricatures have long captured what Gillam once drew as Uncle Sam's burden. This burden is made up of the oppressions, brutalities, ignorance, slavery, cruelties, and vices that chisel out a rocky traverse in and through the uncertain terrain on which US Americanism stands.

In these ways and more, the infamous and iconic political cartoon that appeared in the *Philadelphia Press* in 1898, "Ten Thousand Miles from Tip to Tip" (fig. 2), seems to show it all. The bald eagle, once a spirit symbol of numerous Native American tribes, stands on the United States and spreads its wings from Manila to Puerto Rico. Beneath it, a carbon copy of the bird of prey presides over a diminutive depiction of American territories from

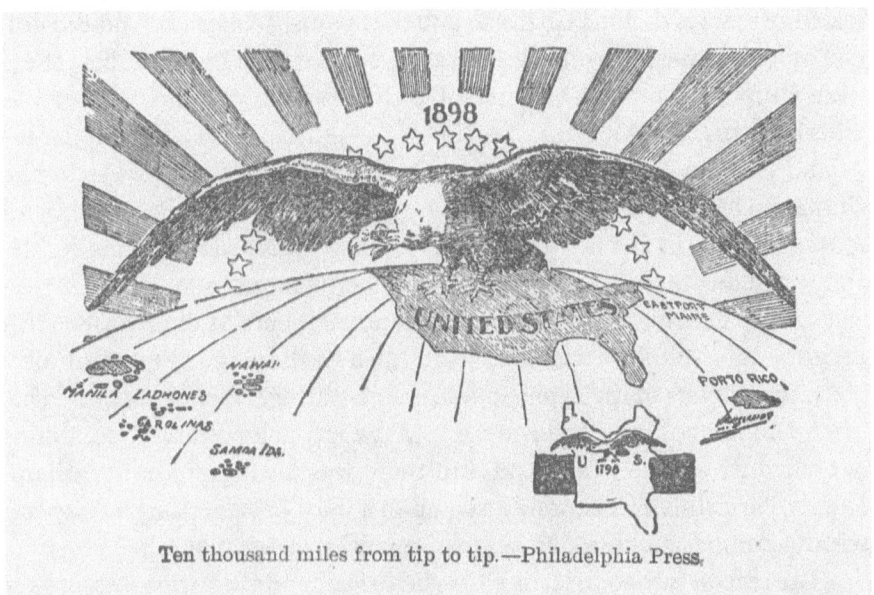

FIG. 2 Marshall Everett, "Ten Thousand Miles from Tip to Tip," 1899. From Marshall Everett, *Exciting Experiences in Our Wars with Spain and the Filipinos* (Chicago: Book Publishers Union, 1899). Cornell University: Persuasive Cartography: The PJ Mode Collection. Photo: Wikimedia Commons.

1798—a testament to the reach of national character from a quasi-war through a civil war, and then again from an assault on the Lakota nation beside a South Dakota creek to what President William McKinley's secretary of state John Hay called a "splendid little war." Warfare had become a defense mechanism for the majesty of America. The figure of Uncle Sam as a compassionate, benevolent protector merged with his personification of a nation breaking away from its constitutional bonds to life and liberty, and forging new nationalistic boundaries with imperialist undertakings. The caricature of an American eagle revels in the view of colonial possibilities abroad, and yet it seems to ask its viewers to take a second look.

The years following the Spanish-American War and leading into the World War I era therefore serve as apt markers for US Americanism, namely in terms of what President Woodrow Wilson dubbed its "leading characters" in a global human drama.[10] The First World War was a fight for transnational democratic tenets that were said to characterize members of—and wannabe adherents to—the US American body politic. It also just so happens that the Great War involved the propagandistic imagery of a war machine in ways that the Civil War and the Spanish-American War did not. Out of it came mad German beasts cast as gorillas with Pickelhaubes. There were Huns with bloody bayonets. Destroyers with missiles rendered as Liberty Loans. The American warrior portrayed as a cross between Hercules and Captain America engaged in combat with the Ghost of Death, the Ghoul of Devastation, the Wolf of Starvation, the Snake of Pestilence, and most glaringly the Unmensch of War. Columbia was an angel of peace. The Statue of Liberty was personified as a divine interventionist of the American creed. Citizens were farmers, dealers, members of the House Wife's League—and soldiers. Excluded from most of these images were thorny domestic matters of racial tension, women's suffrage, the menace of jingoism, ideologies of industrialization, and the warring cultural productions of civic duty and consumerism. But there was plenty of ethnocentrism. Simply, caricature is inexorably tied up in a mess of American militarism, wishful democratic thinking, and nationalistic image making.

The reason is that caricature is a rhetorical mode of variously amplifying, distorting, and even conjuring ways of seeing both personal and public selfhood. It is humorous when a certain hilarity, however dark or gloomy, overwhelms the horror that might otherwise be gleaned from ugliness. It is also ruthlessly historical with its references to past travesties in the trials and tribulations of the present day. Its humor comes from a visual *dédoublement* (duplication), which appears as a comic anamorphosis wherein multiple sides of a character or of a characteristic are reflected in congruency but also in conflict. My primary focus is on editorial cartoons of national character and the humor of comic takes on deep-seated American values. National character encapsulates such values. Caricatures fill out the comic space to engage, exhibit, and redeem what Umberto Eco might call the most "ugly truths" of normative assumptions about collective selfhood.[11] At base, caricature goads a people to look at itself in the comic looking glass, with humor on one hand and an alternative view of history on the other.

To develop and dwell on these critical threads, *Caricature and National Character* concentrates on a handful of caricature artists that animate US American values in war cultures from World War I forward. There is a phrase: "the looking glass." It is a colloquial way of referring to a mirror, and even to that which is normal or expected, and therefore in or out of character. It's an old-fashioned phrase. Yet it underwrites many of the critical threads in this book insofar as it telescopes precisely how some of the ugliest truths of the good and the bad in American national character are caught up in a historical predilection to humor war. So it is that we come back to Franklinesque humor as a basis from which to realize the rootedness of caricature in so many wartime attempts to unmake and then remake an image of America through both international affairs and national issues of things like race, gender, and ethnicity. Franklin's version of American humor developed in the face of war. In the same year that he produced "MAGNA Britannia: her Colonies REDUC'D," which was supposedly printed on cards and distributed to members of Parliament in the shadow of the Stamp Act, Franklin was also testifying before the House of Commons about the "American Interest" and the "force of arms" that would be compelled if imperial oppressions continued to contravene a people of Providence.[12] In other words, the Fates and Follies of American national character align with the humor around its "historiographic fantasies."[13] The American Dream is, in part, an imagination of Americanism itself at the end of history. It is also a rhetorical boilerplate for historical patterns of waging war as a national fait accompli. There are foundations for these patterns in Franklin's America. His politics were born of colonialism. They were born, too, of his time as a military commander during the French and Indian War, subsequent to his years in the Pennsylvania Assembly but seminal to visions of Manifest Destiny and Western (as well as westward) expansion. Franklin was an inventor. He was a postmaster general. He was a diplomat. A writer. A military man. A revolutionary. He knew well the entwinement of war and culture. Franklin's own caricatures of the colonies and of his dream for a new world order imagined civic *and* military engagements as conditions of democratic possibility. They also serve as harbingers for an enduring type of humor about national character that melds aesthetic pleasure, political provocation, and comic effect in an ugly rhetorical standoff of "good" Selves and "bad" Others.

The core point is this: if war is vitally caught up in who Americans are, then caricatures are similarly vital to understanding armed conflict as the catch to a no less democratic *genius loci*. Wars put the strengths (and weaknesses) of national character to the test. War is foundational to US public culture. Franklin observed as much when he gazed through his own looking glass at the close of the American Revolution, recounting the ways to his London landlady's daughter just eight months before becoming a signatory to the Treaty of Paris and seven years after signing the Declaration of Independence. "All Wars are Follies," Franklin wrote. He went on to promote the utterly democratic chances integral to the "Cast of a Dye" over and above the mischievous will to Fight and Destroy. He closed with an appeal to Friendship and Love.[14] Caricatures offer historical resources for interrogating and understanding the deep conflicts in cultural dispositions—toward love, friendship, destruction, and war.[15] In their artistry (and the individuals under study here *are* talented comic artists) is what scholars have increasingly recognized as the rhetorical witness of tensions around collective selfhood in combat zones and in war cultures.[16] Consequently, more important than historiographical veracity is the view of a nationalistic set of images and ideas that make war for democracy look and feel like democracy for war when American national character is seen via caricature, in the comic looking glass.

I write at a compelling moment of both crisis and judgment when it comes to finding humor in matters of national character, war cultures, and cultural warfare. There is an ongoing US military presence in the Middle East and elsewhere despite urgent, and old, calls for the end to endless war. The threat of nuclear war suffuses the global sensorium, never mind the anxieties around an impending barbarism in the face of a global climate crisis. Authoritarianism is on the rise. Democracy is on the decline. The War on Terror lives on. And there is a pandemic wreaking havoc on the globe. At the same time, there is a US president in the Oval Office who comes off as little more than an Ugly American in his unabashed commitment to identitarian politics. President Donald J. Trump represents the worst of flag-waving and political fury, with a worn-out foreign policy of America First and such a loose grip on executive leadership that the social media network Twitter has become a sad site for letting slip the dogs of war. Still, caricature remains the rhetorical outlet de rigueur for dealing with Trumpism and its apotheosis of foolishness, vulgarity, and corruption. President Trump is widely seen as an imperial president on so many warpaths. Trumpism amplifies national character as a theater of combat operations. For Trump, it is a rhetorical prop. But caricature is an age-old centerpiece of this comic stage. It brings rhetorics of humor to the fore in appeals to national characteristics, revealing how express ways of seeing are tied to comic expressions of the war-making conduct that seems endemic to a nation and its citizenry. Additionally, caricature shows forth the structures of wartime feeling that make certain cultural experiences markers of collective temperaments.

This book therefore shows how wartime caricatures are at once a light and a shadow for civic conduct. Todd J. Porterfield argues that there is an "efflorescence" to caricature given its broad reach in the American annals and its participation in the production of visual cultures.[17] I would add that there is a *luminescent* quality to caricature, too, which generates a modality of humor that keeps national characteristics in bloom. But, as caricature reminds us, blossoms fade, flowers decay, and lit objects lose their luster. In 1861, a French writer and close friend of Charles Baudelaire, Charles Asselineau, wrote of caricature as a rhetorical art of humor that looks upon those who fail or refuse to see how and why they are grotesque.[18] Caricature can be an evil flower—*le fleur du mal*. Its shadow appears in a gaze cast on the laughable. Wartime images about the good, the bad, and the ugly of national character thrive in this shadow. As such, caricature is also a basis for grappling with recurring images of the savagery, lunacy, fiendishness, and fanaticism that gets projected onto enemies, both foreign and domestic. To see the light of America is to see its democratic possibilities. To see the shadow beside it is to look upon how ridiculous that light can be when seen for the imperialisms and injustices that reside in its deep surfaces.

America the Ridiculous, or the Folly of War

If the follies of war are at least partly integral to US Americanism, then war footings are at least partly inherent to democratic peace.

But let us back up a bit.

If only the Turkey had been named our national emblem rather than the Bald Eagle. This might seem ridiculous. Yet in a letter to his daughter, Sally Bache, in 1784, Franklin ruminated on this very idea while commenting on a medal drawn up by the Society of the Cincinnati. The Bald Eagle is a thief and a miscreant, Franklin wrote, and "by no means a proper emblem for the brave and honest Cincinnati of America."[19] The Turkey, however, is "a much more respectable Bird, and withal a true original Native of America." And, "though a little vain & silly," it is "a Bird of Courage" willing "to attack a Grenadier of the British Guards who should presume to invade his Farm Yard with a red Coat on." Relatedly, in the lead-up to Independence Day, Franklin hearkened to his 1754 "Join, or Die" serpent (and eventual "Don't Tread on Me" mantra) when he published an anonymous letter in the *Pennsylvania Journal* in defense of the "Rattle-Snake" as the most appropriate emblem, with its allusions to ancient wisdom, defiant attitude, and overall encapsulation of "the temper and conduct of America."[20] At another point he even proposed a picture of Moses parting the Red Sea, encircled by the proclamation that "rebellion to tyrants is obedience to God."[21] Franklin's Turkey manifesto is something of a literary caricature. It is turkey talk. But in this and other bids for fitting national imagery is some potent visual commentary on national character.

The very idea of a "national character" was prominent in the early 1900s and then variously critiqued in the middle of the century by Erik Erikson, Geert Hofstede, Luther S. Luedtke, and others. There is not *a* national culture. Still, there is a tangle of concepts like nation, nationality, nationalism, and national identity.[22] My aim is not to pull off a conceptual sleight of hand in making sense of what Walker Connor calls this "terminological chaos."[23] Instead, it is to engage how these concepts entail images of a people as they relate to systems of government, commitments to a set of common interests, and reactions to social, political, and military conundrums that challenge representations of collective selfhood. In the United States, nationalism tends to typify a sacred creed defined by powerful and ethno-religious ideas of civic duty and the pseudomythological worship of a Revolutionary naissance. Principles of "American belonging," in David Waldstreicher's words, often abide "the prophecy of independence."[24] This prophecy has profound roots in resistance to the Stamp Act, wherein a public (and, importantly, a print) culture of ridicule led American citizens to recognize one another as national selves through the "good" logic of a No True American fallacy. Central to this resistance was a drive "to keep the focus national and to fix the burden of opprobrium on the common enemy."[25] That enemy was the Crown. Its threat was to what Franklin testified as the "civil and military establishment" of America, partially in the wake of the Seven Years' War but also with respect to the will of an American nation already steeped in ideologies of constitutionality and justice.[26] To be American is, in part, to implicate oneself in such narratives, traditions, myths of origins, battles, and—yes—moralistic bromides. America is a characteristically conflicted nation with a fraught nationality, a sometimes chauvinistic nationalism, and a national identity driven by the primacy of the individual. This all makes national character a loaded term.

In acknowledging the loaded nature of national character, it is worth noting just how much matters of race and ethnicity weigh on the supposed comicality of images and ideas. The chapters in this book will bear out these weightings where appropriate. For now, though, consider that history does not repeat itself per se but rather presents so many resources to think through the problematics of bygone eras as they seem to bear some semblance in the present. Race and ethnicity blend, or worse *bleed*, into nationalistic classifications of in- and out-groups, with rhetorical cultures variously playing up or down physical characteristics and character traits as classificatory regimes.[27] As Henry B. Wonham puts it, in the broadest and narrowest of senses, to caricature is to characterize.[28] There is an argument to be made, then, about how nationalisms imply racialized identifications colored by reductive notions of national culture and how *ethno*nationalisms intimate diffuse appeals to blood and soil. In so many caricatures are deep, dark histories of complicity with racist depictions of people of color and with presumptions of white spectatorship. Some have tried to claim that these depictions are due to this or that comic spirit of the times. But in 2020, a combination of the COVID-19 pandemic and the persistent problem of police killings of Black people has revealed once again how character flaws are predicated upon cultural structures of fealty and feeling. Caricatures can be comic lessons in anti-racism and national fellowship. They can also be cruel fodder for white supremacy and nationalistic resentment. One of my primary interests is in paying careful attention to issues of race and ethnicity, as well as other cultural, political, and economic issues as they coalesce in wartime caricatures. Another interest is to attend to the rhetorical potential of caricature for a comic politics of care. Such a politics imagines a cracked mirror when it deals with the mix of bad information, bad feelings, bad faiths, and bad intentions in the most monstrous caricatures. At its best, caricature reminds us how important it is to be ever so vigilant with our ways of seeing.

Yet wartimes do muddy these waters. So many of the rhetorical touchstones of Americanism (or, maybe more aptly, American warism) are virtual clichés. Join, or die. Don't tread on me. The nation must be saved! Respond to your country with dollars. The enemy laughs when you loaf. Wake up, America! Attack on all fronts. We can do it. Are you doing all you can? It *can* happen here. And so on. Then again, there are counternarratives in so many alternative American truisms. War is not the answer. Books, not bombs. Make love, not war. You can't buy freedom with blood. Get out. Give peace a chance. War is folly, a black crime against us all. Resist. In whatever guise, the discourses circulated in such images and ideas embody character judgments, whether in terms of what Michael Billig dubs a "banal nationalism"[29] or in bold anachronisms that revert to a "red-blooded, white-skinned, blue-eyed son of liberty and freedom" in the specter of Uncle Sam.[30] War can bolster a shared sense of belonging. As is seen in caricatures that seem to laugh off the travesties of Americanism, though, it can also lead to what nowadays might be called a rather banal warism.

In some instances, caricatures serve as weapons of comic scorn wielded against nationalistic standards of judgment for wartime conduct. Here they seem to forge fresh, even if farcical, bonds between those images, ideas, individuals, and cultural institutions that influence national character. These weaponized caricatures validate rhetorical warfare with imagined enemies. But they also lead to a humorous regard for the American body politic in a comic looking glass. When I refer to war's follies, I am not simply referring to the futility and foolishness of decades-old American foreign policy.[31] *Caricature and National Character* offers a rhetorical critique of war cultures in the United States according to the humor that caricature draws from images of national character. Contra Henri Bergson, the humor of caricature derives from both rigidity and ugliness.[32] It "walks [a] thin line between pleasurable play with transgression and presentation of frankly unacceptable materials."[33] Furthermore, the humor in caricature exposes a comic frontier wherein there can be no talking with a Boche, never mind a Hun or a Gook, and where no punches need to be pulled with Jim Crow or apologies made for Jap Traps. In this book, caricatures of national character exemplify the unsettled grounds in a warring tradition of, by, and for the US American Way. The weight of this humor, and indeed of this book, therefore lies in the distorted ways of seeing how comic images of national character across modern US history and into the era of late modernism burden us to take seriously a stubborn persistence of war in democratic peace.

My core argument, then, is that what George Washington once called the "plague of Mankind,"[34] war, is deeply connected to what nineteenth-century writer H. H. Boyesen called in the *North American Review* the "plague of jocularity" in American national character. For Washington, a democratic peace is the first commandment of a free people. For Boyesen, an "all-leveling democracy" is the very thing that hedges all bets on judgments of the sacred or profane, war or peace, comedy or tragedy.[35] In characterizing the sacred roots of democracy as the profane outgrowths of war, caricature creates something of an all-leveling humor peculiar to the United States. To say that there is a specifically American humor, though, is sort of like saying that there is a singular American national character. The spirit of a nation is the shadow to a tree, President Abraham Lincoln once said. Its roots are deep. But its look and luster shift shape in the glares of history. No shadow ever stays the same. Nor is there any definitive national character or form of humor that, alone, typifies it. Nevertheless, if dispositional characteristics and founding principles like liberty, freedom, republicanism, and so on constitute a multifarious image of collective selfhood, then caricatures that mingle with repression, strong arm tactics, imperialism, stereotypes, and more stand out in a shadow Self of the nation. Benedict Anderson once remarked on the almost comic effect that nationalistic imaginations can have when they warp perspectives of collective selfhood so much so that *all* peoples, nations, symbols, monuments, and cultural products can somehow appear foolish.³⁶ In some ways, national character is a caricature unto itself. The era of liberation movements, which generally corresponds to the century between 1820 and 1920, witnessed the rise of "visible models" of national character that were otherwise confined to dispersed frames of vision.³⁷ World War I marks a pivotal moment for nationalistic politics of caricature and for US American humor. By World War I, caricatures of national character incorporated humor to counteract gruesome realities of being at war. They also humored war cultures by stoking the tensions that sprang from images of democratic utopia in the dystopia of militarism.

The Founding Period looms large here, particularly with Franklin's early establishment of caricature as a rhetorical resource for transforming foundational principles and folk symbols into comic armaments for wartime enforcements of the "good" and the "bad." By the Civil War era these armaments had become weapons of cultural warfare on the home front. Brother Jonathan, a staple embodiment of the Early Republic and Mad Hatter–like trickster who was also prevalent in British periodicals, such as humor magazine *Punch*, in addition to American periodicals like *Yankee Notions*, was a prime holdover and precursor to Uncle Sam (fig. 3). The earthly goddess, Columbia, was frequently set against the fallen figure of the southern Cavalier, a sort of American Beelzebub and bane on notions of Pilgrim's progress and Revolutionary predestination. By Reconstruction, while Columbia morphed into the nonpareil among images for angels of a better national character, Brother Jonathan came to represent "a devious, crude, corrupt, and violent" aspect of a nation founded not just on freedom and liberty but also on slavery, hypocrisy, and oppression.³⁸ Eventually he was supplanted by Uncle Sam, perhaps the most "affectionate symbol of a democratic government," and yet by the Spanish-American War and even more by World War I, the "stern authority figure, the leader of the nation-state," and the personification of "the war atmosphere."³⁹ During World War II, Uncle Sam became what Brother Jonathan was in his originary guise: an embodiment of the people, in one moment rallying civic troops, in another supplicating for combat soldiers, and then again reconciling diverse expressions of patriotism, dissidence, and duty. Indeed, the cultural milieu of war facilitates a sometimes-righteous, sometimes-ridiculous rhetoric of sense and nonsense in and around national characteristics.

This sense of humor is crucial in my approach to caricature, which is perhaps best gleaned from a metaphor that has been lurking in the story

FIG. 3
Editorial cartoon of Brother Jonathan, ca. 1852. From *Yankee Notions* 1 (1852): 224.

up to this point and that I detail below—the looking glass. Caricature is the bastard child of *ethos*. It embodies a framework for seeing character as a byproduct of identity and activity. Writer and humorist Kurt Vonnegut once portrayed this framework with a mock syllogism that presents itself in three lines of philosophical cum poetic wisdom. It makes up the last words of *Deadeye Dick* (1982) before the epilogue when the book's main character encounters the syllogism as a bit of graffiti on a bathroom wall in Will Fairchild Memorial Airport, where he stops on the way home from work one night to manage a sudden bout of diarrhea. To be is to do, said Socrates. Not so, said Jean-Paul Sartre, when he dwelled on the burden of becoming *what* we will be from the fact *that* we are. To do is to be, he said. Then Frank Sinatra came along and summed up human existentialities with a honeyed tune: do be do be do. Here's the mock syllogism:

"To be is to do"—Socrates.
"To do is to be"—Jean-Paul Sartre.
"Do be do be do"—Frank Sinatra.[40]

We are what we do. We are who and what we see, as a nation. To caricature is to aggravate vital ways of seeing and the characteristics of what is seen. It is to do rhetorical work, and to do so humorously as the burdens of historical weightings play out in characterizations and *recharacterizations*. National character, in caricature, is a sort of *pictura rhetorica* (and, in caricature, a *pictura comica*). What matters is the burden of humor that weighs on how a people pictures who it is and what it does as a nation.

Any image or idea of national character is at least somewhat ridiculous. Caricature is so useful because, as Martha Banta argues, it lays bare the deepest (and darkest) realities about entire cultures of conduct, patterns of cultural expectations in friend-enemy relations, and reference points for getting by in public life.[41] This book builds on Banta's argument but goes beyond a single outlet (i.e., *Life* or *Punch*) or a single artist in order to examine the transhistorical nature of cultural struggles with American national character as they appear in the work of multiple caricature artists over multiple decades. It is therefore as much about the "national" as it is about the "character" in wartime caricatures. Humor is nationalistic "when it is impregnated with the convictions, customs, and associations of a nation."[42] Such impregnations are palpable in *American Humor: A Study of National Character* (1931) when Constance Rourke points out that comic grotesqueries are rooted in caricatures of national character that extend from Yankee Doodle through Jim Crow Rice (the face of Reconstruction-era race conflict) to folk wisdom about the everyday confrontational antics of scalawags and crackers. Still, as Rourke describes it elsewhere, humor is so endemic to the United States because of the nationalistic fantasies caught up in the sorts of mythic embellishments that make up Americanism.[43] Or, as Cameron Nickels puts it, caricature is the counterpart to self-righteousness in the characterological roots of American exceptionalism.[44] Cameron Nickels, Constance Rourke, and others are points of departure for grappling with the humor of caricature by laughing along with deformations that combine the sacred and profane in new visualizations of "old" images and ideas. Caricature pictures "a cruel delight in monstrous deformity,"[45] oftentimes our *own* monstrous deformity, and so re-views our deepest, darkest convictions, habits, institutions, and histories. Caricatures of national character amplify the folly in our rhetorical fantasies about collective selfhood.

The underlying message here is that the rhetorical weight of caricature, and within it a formative mode of US American humor, should give us pause, especially when we are made strange to ourselves. In wartimes in particular, caricatures cast comic projections in the looking glass—clearly, differently, darkly. In 1900, Mary F. S. Hervey remarked on the anamorphosis of the iconic skull in Hans Holbein's famous 1533 painting, *The Ambassadors*, by referring to its "unusual character."[46] In the skull is something familiar, and yet something that requires what Jean-François Lyotard calls an act of "hesitation" when something out of whack needs to be put back into perspective.[47] Caricature replaces the easy work of gut reactions and snap judgments with the more grueling work of recognition. Caricatures provoke pause such that the spectatorial choice to hesitate (or not) is a choice of whether or not to carry the weight of humor. The humor of caricatures in this book demands a willingness to take in a bit more deeply the taken for granted in American national character. War is "as old as the Republic itself."[48] So is caricature. In turning to comic images of wartime national character, I am at once turning to a cultural politics of America the Ridiculous, wherein warism and democracy are all too familiar, albeit strange, bedfellows in the looking glass of US Americanism.

In the Comic Looking Glass

The mirror is a prominent analogue in numerous studies of caricature. Steven Heller and Gail Anderson define caricature as a "savage mirror."[49] Arthur Koestler calls it a "carnival mirror," noting the outrageous exaggerations and monstrous distortions in its basic features.[50] This sentiment is replete in scholarly accounts of looking-glass orientations as much as it is resident in the paroxysms and ordinary jests of everyday life. At the turn of the twentieth century, American social psychologist Charles Horton Cooley theorized the "looking-glass self." Such a self is built on the complex and conflicted relationship between images of selfhood and the judgments derived of interactions with others. "Each to each a looking-glass," Cooley poeticized with words that also appear in a verse from Ralph Waldo Emerson's poem "Astraea." Each to each, says Cooley, "reflects the other that doth pass."[51] We see ourselves in the appearances of others. This cultural praxis amounts to what French philosopher Michel Foucault later proposed as the genealogical work and the cultural politics of historiography to the replay of some imagined, though all-too-real, past in the rhetorical fêtes of a "concerted carnival."[52] Another French philosopher, Gilles Deleuze, followed Alice to Wonderland and approached the looking glass as what I would describe as a rhetorical tool for breaking up linearities and dichotomies, and then locating the good sense of seeing something otherwise by seeing it nonsensically.[53] To see the world via caricatures, for instance through a Lewis Carroll–like imagination, is to live in the Looking-Glass House. Or, to put it in the terminology of another American personage, it is to see the fantastic rhetorical trickeries in our "glassy essence." So wrote C. S. Peirce in 1892 while ruminating on a view of the Self as little more than the symbol of an idea.[54]

Notwithstanding these more scholarly interpretations, the notion that caricature shows forth its object of scrutiny or ridicule as if in a distorted mirror is also standard in so many takes on the humorously grotesque aesthetics of ugliness.[55] This notion goes back to the Carracci brothers, Annibale and Agosto, two revered sixteenth-century Italian painters who sedimented the Baroque style and who saw in the visual burlesque the unique rhetorical capacity to display the peculiar character and particular defects of a person or thing. Early Americans, too, saw the looking glass as a site wherein one could develop deep knowledge of appearances and powerful senses of self.[56] The point is that images of national character as collective selfhood are perhaps most true when seen in the particularly comic looking glass of caricature.

A key element of this looking glass is the humor to be found in the comedy of recognition. A compelling iteration of caricature and its mirror-like qualities comes from sociologist Anton Zijderveld. Humor, for Zijderveld, is a looking glass unto itself insofar as it allows for revelatory glimpses of the world that are nonetheless distorted.[57] That is, it allows for comic opportunities to *re*member, *re*sense, *re*imagine, and *re*think the strange in the familiar, and so to *re*cognize it—with the prefix *re-* here meaning a simultaneous backward orientation and inclination to do something again and again. Caricature is a rhetorical form of humor that mocks the merits of a looking glass as an accurate reflection of reality. Carnival mirrors reveal imaginary selves made of both material and symbolic realities. Caricature is humorous when it expresses a reality as it could be seen otherwise, when it converts a laughing-at-the-world trope into a laughing-in-spite-of-the-self ethos that offers up an alternative way to visualize follies. The disfigurements in caricature demand that we see differently. The humor in distorted ways of seeing dampens the dark depths that come to the surface in deformed images. No conception of caricature, then, can escape consideration of deformations in visual humor.

It is thus worthwhile to reconsider the metaphor of the mirror through a core rhetorical device that drives the humor in caricature: anamorphosis. Anamorphosis is a protoform of distortive portrayal. An anamorphic image is meant to be looked at from a different perspective, or from some oblique angle (i.e., in a mirror), so that what appears distorted can actually be seen properly. Caricature, as a rhetorical mode of anamorphosis, exploits the comic idea that a viewer accepts the realer Real that can come from a transformation in visual form. It developed as an artistic practice at the school of the Carracci and was coincident with a growing artistic appreciation in the sixteenth century of the comic arts and depictions of the ridiculous. An 1842 edition of the *Magazine of Science* pegged anamorphic portrayals as "one of those monstrous projections, which, under ordinary points of view, appears extravagantly distorted and ridiculous, yet seen from a particular situation, the picture strikes the eye as one of complete symmetry."[58] The most famous example is Holbein's *The Ambassadors*, with its anamorphic skull that seems to wear a smile as if in burlesque resistance to the deformation of human flesh in death. The painting combines Deleuzean nonsense with Erasmian folly. The stability of perspective is torn asunder. Ordinary sense is given over to matters of comic nonsense, even as those very matters are so grave as to deal with the core iconography of death. The *haut-goût*, or "high flavor," of regal portraiture is recast as the relish of the ridiculous, with an appeal to the kind of warped imagery that constitutes the humor in caricature.

But anamorphosis does not need to be confined to optical illusions. Holbein's painting is a distorted projection that entails a sort of "perceptual doubling" to "[produce] a rupture in the viewer's gaze and [to disrupt] the stability of the object under view."[59] Lyotard calls them curvatures that throw our grand visions back into our faces. I see them as *comic burdens* on ways of seeing. To caricature is to overload. The Italian verb *caricare* means "to load" or "to exaggerate." Both of the Carracci brothers produced a "Sheet of Caricatures" (Annibale in 1595, and Agostino a year prior in 1594), each depicting various ugly figures whose features (both natural and fantastical) are loaded with comic exaggeration. Annibale defined caricature as a "loaded portrait," more overwrought with reality than reality itself. This is the case for verbal descriptions of folly. It is the case for Fools, the theatrical character of Vice, and the descendants of *mimus*. It is also the case for caricature and its capacity to, say, capture the ugly images of a "whole body of efforts" for articulating "national culture."[60] Caricature reverberates with the consequences that follow from warped perspectives as they appear in lived realities. Furthermore, it puts the weightiness of the looking glass front and center insofar as the prefix *ana-* entails a simultaneous movement of something "up" or "forward" in place or time and "back" or "backward again," the result of which is something seen or made "anew." The suffix, *-morph*, refers to the distinctive character of a thing. These are especially illuminating insights when paired with the knowledge that, in botany, anamorphosis names the strange or *monstrous* development of some aspect of a body. Once again, caricature is monstrous. It burdens ways of seeing. Humor is its morphology.

Seeing the humor in caricature is like seeing the enormities, oddities, and grotesqueries that influence images and ideas about good or bad character. Caricature makes strange truths, or "truthful misrepresentations," from distortions and deformities.[61] These truths pronounce ways of seeing that might not gain prominence in other images or contexts. Caricature, then, offers clarity in the confusion of perspectives, and more specifically in the various viewpoints that are confused (that is, fused in their differences). There is a spectatorial shift from seeing something for what it normally shows to seeing something from different perspectives. Caricature magnifies the view that what is ridiculous from one perspective seems perfectly right, even perversely "true," from another. The compositional elements of caricature therefore matter a great deal in terms of what they suggest about characters and cultural characteristics—the size of visuals and text, the layout of the picture, the angles and scales, the iconographic choices, and the allure of the artwork itself. This composition creates a congruence of deformed and ostensibly faithful portrayals in the comic space of something like an editorial cartoon or illustration.[62] For their humor, what matters most is the fitting *mis*alignment of objects, themes, concepts, beliefs, and other artifacts made manifest in comic imagery.

In so many caricatures of American national character, anamorphic associations between things like people, animals, creatures, and machines are used to re-create realities based on blends of actual histories and imaginations of what could, would, or should be. Caricature lets the *pictura comica* mingle with the *artificiali perspectiva* of collective selfhood. This is why, for Kenneth Burke, caricature is grotesque in the worst of ways: it exploits humor by pretending to respect "categories of judgment, even while outraging them."[63] Humor, says Burke, "pits value against value, disposition against disposition, psychotic weighting against psychotic weighting—but it flatters us by confirming as well as destroying."[64] Where Burke sees a problem in humor that goes too far, or flatters too much, I see possibility.

An overloaded image can compel a second look at how and why seemingly incongruous elements are actually in accordance with each other. Simply, visual humor in caricature does not convert downward. It makes sense of folly. This is the lesson of Samuel Beckett's poem that I reference in the epigraph. Matters of character are so troubling, and yet so terribly trite sometimes, because they contain values, beliefs, convictions, and even civic credos that are subject to competing claims of certainty and doubt. Hence Franklin's drift away from "smooth Words" and toward the comic imagery in crude looking glasses. Beckett's struggle with words is likewise a struggle with ways of seeing. So is caricature. This makes sense. Beckett himself was impacted by his experiences in the south of France during the Second World War. He once told minimalist musician Philip Glass that it is possible to listen to music and simultaneously look at the image it evokes. The same is true of words, and the same is also true in acts of looking at images and seeing the words—the vocabularies, the grammars, the ideographs, the ideologies, the iconographies, the identities—associated with them. The caricatures featured in this book make sense of American national character in terms of their historical situations in wartimes, with humor about Americanism that is as real as it is ridiculous.

A Glimpse of What Lies Ahead

My study is a chronology of exemplary caricatures that capture images and ideas of national character in war cultures from World War I until the early twenty-first century. Even more, *Caricature and National Character* relates how humor mingles with rhetorical cultures in wartimes. Two caveats. First, there is no *singular* character that defines a nation and its people or captures every possible variance. Plainly, no single caricaturist can glean the singular character of a nation, no matter the historical moment. Distribution outlets for caricatures matter. So do ideological predispositions (like those of Western—even Anglo-Protestant—makings, or of a percolating profession of civic faith), not to mention the complexities and conflicts that exist across any number of discourses and among any number of sociopolitical leanings. The study herein features the works of remarkable individuals who foreground the contradictions of national characteristics that get amplified when armed conflict shapes images and ideas of American ways of life. Together, the artworks of exemplary comic artists articulate what Joseph Boskin might call a "comic zeitgeist" just as, following Raymond Williams, keywords can be read as touchstones for talking about larger structures of feeling and experience.[65] Other artists could have been studied. There was Laura Brey, Howard Chandler Christy, Harry S. Bressler, Harry Ryle Hopps, and many more during World War I. There was Bill Mauldin and Herblock during World War II, not to mention Native American cartoonists like Eva Mirabal. There is David Levine's work across the Cold War. And so on down the line of US war cultures, including other Native cartoonists like Ricardo Caté and Marty Two Bulls, Sr., female cartoonists like Etta Hulme, and Black cartoonists like Darrin Bell.[66] What unites the subjects of this book is an overwhelming emphasis on caricature as a vital contact point for grappling with core principles of US national character, like Manifest Destiny, civic duty, and good (and bad) citizenship. Caricatures of national character, in this case, situate public engagements with war as the first principle and the last resort of US Americanism. It has mediated collective identifications and *dis*identifications with ways of seeing selfhood in a distorted mirror, wherein a nation at war can see itself with a sense of humor and so take stock of its own grotesqueries.

Second, while my focus is on humorous characterizations of homegrown images around collective selfhood, I still attend to some of the transnational circumstances that impact competing images and ideas. The image of the United States on the world stage overlapped with Revolutionary sentimentalism, sectionalism, and white supremacy in the Civil War period. During World War I, international alliances were often pegged as pillars of the fight to save the world for American-styled democracy (despite the rampant and countervailing forces of nativism and interventionism). The Second World War, too, saw the United States shrinking in the shadows of isolationism before FDR's hearts-and-minds rhetoric made the international campaign against totalitarianism a nationalistic rendezvous with Manifest Destiny. Throughout the Cold War, foreign adversaries were constantly compared to those in the minority classes seeking freedoms at home, both by domestic commentators and critics looking from the outside in. Many of these adversarial perspectives endure in the specters of America First jingoism, White Nationalist nostalgia, and patriarchal war mentalities today. In each wartime, certain characteristics of Americanism can be identified in the comic play of rival nations, contradictory distortions of civil rights and civic duties, and powerful appeals to the strange truths of character that crop up in the totalizing fictions of caricature. Consequently, the caricature artist stands as a sort of cultural representative for distilling the crises in national character that are catalyzed by armed conflict and attendant cultural warfare. I read caricatures from a rhetorical vantage while relating those readings to the contexts and conjunctures of which they are visual articulations. The result, I hope, is a transhistorical look at a characterology of US wartime public culture as it appears in and through humorous caricatures of how to live out the American creed.

I begin with the First World War. Much of the in-fighting over the nature of Americanism at this point was reoriented toward a mode of Americanization that might facilitate a countrywide inculcation of ideal citizenship. From Allied victory to what Tom Engelhardt terms "victory culture,"[67] and then again from the rise of defeatism and despair during the Cold War to the regeneration of triumphalist mindsets in the War on Terror, caricature provides opportunities to take pause and reconsider how founding principles thrive on tensions between both monstrous and magnificent pictures of nationalistic virtue. It dwells on distorted reflections of patriotism as the last refuge of the scoundrel. In the fog of war, appeals to national character are a sort of American version of the Angels of Mons protecting the body politic. Caricature is a comic demon "[holding] up to God and his creatures the mirror wherein universal individuality dissolves."[68] In the looking glass of caricature is the comic dissolution of national character.

This book unfolds as follows. Chapter 1 considers conceptions of civic duty in the comic underbellies of James Montgomery Flagg's renowned "I Want YOU" poster. Moving away from conventional notions of Uncle Sam as the catalyst to a groundswell of support for the Great War, or of Flagg's infamous poster as purely and simply about American patriotism, the first chapter approaches Uncle Sam's personification of the United States (and the government besides) as a caricature of the nation-state. Uncle Sam is read as a sendup of state-sanctioned "good" character who makes a mockery of US Americanism when his temptations to war footings are coupled with a glaring sexual humor that is unapologetic in its enticement to serve.

These temptations and enticements are rendered even more weirdly and more eerily hawkish in the transmogrifications of some early works by Theodor Geisel, better known as Dr. Seuss. The second chapter examines how Dr. Seuss put his familiar quirkiness and affinity for human-animal imbrications to work during the Second World War in over four hundred editorial cartoons (published in the popular leftist newspaper, *PM*). Uncle Sam figures prominently in Dr. Seuss's *PM* caricatures, which pursue a view of true American character through revisions to tried-and-true national iconography, but even more so through humor in iconography that juxtaposes eagles with ostriches, valiant friends with enemy vermin, and phantasmagoric war machines with all their grit and grime. Dr. Seuss's caricatures constitute a comic abstraction of national character as seen through the looking glass, dirtily, and with a mode of defacement that uses comicality as an ethos to judge the Self. Chapter 2 takes up the Americanism in Dr. Seuss's ridicule of US neutrality, his mockery of pacifism, and his lampoons of the flimsy civic principles for democracy that seem to slacken in the face of self-defense.

That Dr. Seuss's wartime caricatures also relied heavily on racial stereotypes and ethical gray areas makes my turn to Ollie Harrington in chapter 3 all too necessary. Like Harrington, both Flagg and Dr. Seuss homed in on what they saw as the laughable qualities of anyone proclaiming to embody an American character without responding to a call of civic duty. But while Dr. Seuss and Flagg took US goodness for granted in their pleas for political action, Harrington picked apart various discriminations and oppressions as what he came to define as the "hilarious chaos" in his wartime caricatures, many of which appear under the heading "Dark Laughter." Harrington's work spans from World War II all the way to end of the Cold War. I focus on a collection of those from the *Pittsburgh Courier* and the *Daily Worker* (eventually renamed the *Daily World*) in the early 1960s through the mid-1970s. This body of editorial cartoon artwork showcases the civic ills plaguing the lives of Black children on the home front and shows just how much the peculiar tensions between the maturation and decay of American character across the Cold War are so much more potent when they are humored by a Black children's crusade.

The last chapter turns to Ann Telnaes. Like Harrington, a victim of McCarthyism and a self-exile who spent the bulk of his career overseas either in Paris or in East Germany, Telnaes embodies the outsider looking in.[69] Telnaes is an independent cartoonist and Swedish-born emigrant who has made a career of coming to comic terms with prevailing attitudes about race, ethnicity, religion, gender, and class in the United States. For Telnaes, all wars are culture wars just as all cultural warfare is about rhetorical claims to civic identities. Chapter 4 begins with a look at some of Telnaes's caricatures from the exhibition *Humor's Edge*, which ran from June 3 through September 11 in 2004. The exhibition features the works that earned Telnaes a Pulitzer Prize for editorial cartooning, originally appearing in publications like the *Washington Post*, the *New York Times*, and the *Chicago Tribune*. However, while her work became prominent during the George W. Bush administration, it has become perhaps even more potent since the rise of

Trumpism. What many critics and commentators disparagingly refer to as "Trump's America" is driven by a president who embodies American character as if it is a Churchill-like campaign of "ungentlemanly warfare." President Donald J. Trump is a lightning rod for recurrent themes in US Americanism of racism, sexism, misogyny, bigotry, and hypernationalism. In discourses and scholarship about rhetorical presidentialism, the president is often seen as *the* American character. Telnaes utilizes caricature as a way of seeing Trump as the figurehead for an imperial presidency but also as the culmination of perverted democratic (never mind Constitutional) principles. The final chapter of *Caricature and National Character* therefore takes up Telnaes's comic imagery of King Trump as a means of understanding how US American national character in the early twenty-first century seems to amplify warfare itself as a principle of political conduct, from trade wars to actual armed conflict, and then again from newfangled culture wars at home to outmoded notions of neo-isolationism. This is a troubling, yet telling, principle on which to conclude, if for nothing more than its recollection of the idea that democracy—whether stretched to its principled limits or pushed to the end of its lines—is potentially riven by its reliance on a peaceable *bellum omnium contra omnes*, a war of all against all.

It is important to note here that comic images do not necessarily make for "good" visions. In fact, caricature is oftentimes a vicious means of amplifying normative perspectives on selves and others, reinforcing rather than evacuating "stereotypes, prejudices, and narrow horizons."[70] It is also not always a picture or portrait. Sometimes it is a logic of representation, as it was in the containment culture of the Cold War with its officious, and at times official, caricature of East-West relations. To take a caricature seriously is therefore to look carefully at different perspectives as well as perspectives in difference. Additionally, to *become* a caricature, or to act as if another character is a caricature in the flesh, is to, well, humor its limits. The stakes of engaging caricatures of wartime national characters are so high because to study war culture is to see these limits in "the visual construction of national identities through the mythologies that are mobilized to sustain them and to suppress other ways of seeing."[71] In this sense, even "new" images can reinforce "old" perspectives. In this sense, too, Telnaes rounds out a comic tradition in US American humor not only of utilizing caricature to articulate national character but also to consider the very democratic underpinnings of the human condition—or, the Human Comedy. The artfulness of caricatures and their embroilments with ideas of US national character during times of war demonstrate the ways in which pictures can become Pygmalions, and then again personifications that impact real-life experiences.[72] Caricature, in other words, is most dangerous when humor is evacuated from its take on a situation. This book therefore concludes with a rumination on the idea that wartime caricatures goad us not to *dwarf* the magnitude of national character but rather to *dwell* on its details, especially when even the most comic of situations turn dire. After all, the visual humor of caricatures can actually provoke a rhetorical laughter that lets us put our ugliest expressions and enactments of collective selfhood back together with the very burdens of good and bad character that might otherwise stay omitted, if not go without seeing.

Pledges of Allegiance, Sexualized Politics, and Comic Pillories in James Montgomery Flagg's America

I.

To rework a line from G. K. Chesterton, it is one thing to believe in witches, and quite another to understand one's national culture through a rhetoric of the witch-hunt.[1]

There is a squib in *Life* from 1907. Tom Masson, then a well-known humor writer, wrote the mock journalism. Illustrator James ("Monty") Montgomery Flagg supplied the cartoon artwork. The squib is entitled "Our Beginnings," and it provides a sardonic snapshot of Americanism from the infamous Salem Witch Trials to the era of the Constitutional Convention in Philadelphia, including a peek at the framework for William Penn's peace treaty with the Lenape Turtle Clan.[2] Masson's prose is full of anti-woman prosaicisms (i.e., no woman could actually throw spells because no woman can throw), stereotypes of Native Americans (they were superstitious scalpers), and affronts on Jamestown colonists (imbeciles all). It laughs at the judgments of witch-hunters. It jeers Benjamin Franklin's publication of *The Ladies' Home Journal*, not to mention his soubriquet, Poor Richard.[3] It makes fun of Penn's panegyrists. Even more, Flagg's comic pictures portray absurdities in the prides, prejudices, and false progress of Pilgrims. One shows a man who looks uncannily like Franklin standing in the entryway of a locksmith shop and watching as two cantankerous male Puritans

FIG. 4 James Montgomery Flagg, "Arrested as a Witch in Salem, 1692." From *Life* 49 (January–March 1907): 340. Courtesy of Hathi Trust.

ARRESTED AS A WITCH IN SALEM, 1692
A SIMPLER METHOD THAN DIVORCE FOR LONG-SUFFERING HUSBANDS

wrangle a "witch" clad in a long gown, coat, and bonnet (fig. 4). A small dog races away in the foreground with wide eyes and a cloud of dust trailing behind it. The Franklinesque figure smiles wryly, his arms folded across his chest. Another image shows a cadre of Puritan men, women, and children walking to church on a Sunday morning in 1620 with smirks on their faces (the men, at least) and muskets in their hands amid a hail of arrows. Yet another, over the caption "NEXT," displays a Native American leaning out of a tepee. A barber's pole protrudes from his "artistic hair cutting" establishment. A dark-skinned man with long braided hair, a large hoop earring, and a whopping feather atop his head gestures to a line of Puritan men with one hand while wielding a long blade in another. The men urge each other along with trepidation. Each line of Masson's commentary along with each crude drawing from Flagg is underwritten by the conviction that cultural politics can be reduced to the "fads of the day," and that American Providence is part and parcel of a distinctly martial "march of civilization."

The entire historical scene of "Our Beginnings" is laughable. Masson's journalistic temperament is imbued with comic ridicule, and Flagg's caricatures are laced with comical scorn. The Jamestown colonists, Masson ribs, were simple and unscrupulous, as can be gleaned from their propensity to be tricked into getting scalped by Amalek Indians. According to Flagg, the Puritans as Christian missionaries are convinced of their status as the "chosen race," and as war-makers unflinching in the protection of colonial principles. Of course, there is real horror in the humor that accompanies these accounts, just as there is real humor to be extrapolated from the horror behind reigns of cultural terror. Flagg's caricatures show forth some origins of American national character that make any supposed divinity or political predestination behind Manifest Destiny into an all-too-human manifestation of the Devil's work. This is obvious in one of Masson's quips about a nation of nomadic ancient Israelis depicted in the Old Testament, the Amalekites. Some of the humor in Flagg's images comes from this sort of play on exceptionalism. In the comic looking glass of caricature, at least three things stand out. First, the so-called civilized are often more barbarous in their liberatory pursuits than the so-called savage. Second, the character of a people is very much defined by the words and deeds of individuals that are to a great extent recursive across historical moments. Third, and finally, war cultures are integral to conceptions of the nation and its shared sense of selfhood. Flagg's caricatures see national character in monstrous projections of Selves and Others that emerge out of persistent domestic toils, mounting homegrown conflicts, and convoluted foreign relations. The American people of Providence are, from Flagg's vantage, a "people of paradox," more consistent with what Michael Kammen terms an "octopus image" than a sculpture chiseled in stone.[4] Americanism is weird. It has tinges of ideological grandeur and rough edges cut from the niggling trifles of real persons in real historical times. In Flagg's imagery, it is the epitome of a *pictura comica*.

Flagg carried over these paradoxical sensibilities into his wartime artworks just a decade later. In the late 1800s and early 1900s, when Flagg's career was burgeoning, he was drawing political cartoons. Really, he was a caricaturist for *Life* and other outlets, as well as an artist with a reputation for making familiar ideas about the American mind and manner downright strange in illustrated books like *Tomfoolery* (1904) and *If, A Guide to Bad Manners* (1905), and in cartoon serials like *It's Risky to Want Things*. In 1907, he lent his signature pen-and-ink style of comic illustration to matters of US American culture. When he pictured the Pilgrims, the Puritans, and the early Pennsylvanians, Flagg hit on strong threads of obligations to higher callings of country and creed in the American fabric. He hit on deep religious zeal around civil liberties and civic duties that waxes and wanes with political crises and wartimes. On top of these themes, Flagg also touched on what Gershon Legman might see as the decidedly "male approach" to national character and political culture, which is propelled by a masculinistic nationalism that surfaces in so many instances of sexual humor.[5] In "Our Beginnings," Flagg portrays American men who occupy an exceptional position in history that, in Masson's words, is partly due to a "sundry of vices." These vices contributed to the expulsion and massacre of Native Americans. They contributed to a New World Order that was created by the sexual and sex-like exploits of men who struggled to contain both their appetitive drives for inamoratas and power and their dutiful commitments to puritanism. All of these cultural observations and more are condensed in a single, standout image that illustrates Flagg's oeuvre of humor in caricature and serves as the prime contact point for this chapter: the iconic "I Want YOU" rendition of Uncle Sam.

This chapter gets at the formative enigma of national character, and the burdens that caricature places on it, through the historical iconography of Uncle Sam. In particular, I trace his depiction as a kindly force for freedom in the nineteenth century through his transformation into a warmonger in the name of democracy by the onset of World War I. I then turn to the cultural politics of America's Great War, specifically as they are established by the activities of Chairman George Creel and his Committee on Public Information, or CPI. Crucial here is the extent to which national character was melded into ordinary civic existence through insinuations of an (un)civil war over what it meant to support a national cause and thus what it meant to be a "good" American in racial, gendered, and generally patriotic terms. Crucial, too, is Flagg's situation in a larger culture of "new humor" that was sympathetic to Americanization and aggressive toward anything deemed anti-American.[6] Herein, comicality was used to blur boundaries between race, ethnicity, and gender such that contradictions, anxieties, inconsistencies, paradoxes, and dogmas around Americanism became the very makeup of the comic guise. They also became the stuff of "warring ideals" that animated initiatives like the Niagara Movement and ideologies of Blackness that amped up W. E. B. Du Bois and his "soldiers of democracy."[7] A culture of humor accommodated rhetorical judgments about the characteristics of national membership and "the construction of the citizen subject,"[8] with caricatures holding up a distorted mirror for a nation to look upon itself.

Humor, I argue, helped to establish citizens as spectators, and thereby as implicit foot soldiers for state interests. On one hand, pictorial propaganda channeled Edward Bernays's infamous notion that "the engineering of consent is the very essence of the democratic process" in attempts at engineering national character.[9] On the other hand, citizens as implied audience members were drafted as the everyday judges and juries on the conduct of their fellow citizens, urged to police attitudes and actions according to "official" war policy and a structure of shame that typified pro-war communication practices. What is more, they were subjected to a prescription of collective guilt that might serve to mobilize more than debilitate. An examination of how Uncle Sam appears through an anamorphic lens in Flagg's war work fills out these claims, as does my placement of the war on public opinion within a broader pictorial culture of war and humor. Part of this culture entailed the specifically gendered identification of wartime allegiances to the nation-state. Flagg was a major contributor to popular depictions of women before and during the war. He made women into enticements that, much like the United States, urged support for and/or participation in armed conflict. A July 1913 edition of *American Magazine* featured a caricature of Flagg, which the artist sketched of himself, smoking a cigarette with a smirk on his face and straddling a donkey. It accompanied a humorous article entitled, "The Call of the Sex." The appeal was to a "Story of Passion, abysmal, chaotic, typically American, yet virile," and it promised a struggle between "the hairy, primeval, man-in-Khaki" and "the yielding yet submissive Woman." This story is also the first chapter of *I Should Say So* (1914), a book that now looks like comic Americana. I therefore complement my study of Flagg's caricature of civic duty with a view of how his coquettish images of women fed into his renditions of Uncle Sam. In this overlap is a bigger idea of the "stay-at-home" military seductress, and—ultimately—a sense of comic anamorphosis in Flagg's caricature that reveals a nativistic image of Uncle Sam lording over a masculinized nation-state.

War for American Democracy

Look closely enough and you will see that Flagg's Uncle Sam appears to be grimacing. Perhaps it is because deep down he (and Flagg) knows that he is asking a democratic populace to convert ideals of participatory politics and contests of ideas into a coercive and compulsory demand for civic engagement with an armed force, whether through fighting on a battlefield or keeping up the home front. Or, as Cecilia O'Leary suggests, perhaps it is because he reflects a sort of visual segregation of the nation into a populace defined by "a racially exclusive, culturally conformist, [and] militaristic patriotism."[10] Uncle Sam is an image of white male America. Countless all-Black units fought for American freedoms abroad only to encounter racial violence and renewed versions of nationalistic bigotry when they returned home. Women, too, took up many traditionally male roles during the war only to be pressed back into the fight for full citizenship and into the domestic service of men once the war ended. To fall in line with Uncle Sam during World War I, then, was to adopt what a late nineteenth-century commentator described as the "uncanny mingling of the death-rattle and giggle" in American life.[11] Inherent in this mingling is the adoption of a strange and anxious admission that democracy requires war by *any* means and a suspension of normative conditions that can just as soon be reinstated once things get back to "normal." This is no doubt why the chief executive for the Bureau of Cartoons, George J. Hecht, dedicated his volume *The War in Cartoons* (1919) to Uncle Sam, "the child of the cartoonists' fancy, who having gained new stature through the war, symbolizes American manhood and thus embodies the highest ideals of freedom and democracy." Uncle Sam became a glowing, and yet grotesque, caricature of warmongering as a new normal of Americanism.

By the middle of the colonial period, Americanism was *in posse*. By World War I, it had become the stuff of an identitarian, nativistic movement, suffused with wartime spirit and touted by President Woodrow Wilson. The movement was dubbed "100% Americanism," and it reeked of imperial and jingoistic sentimentality. The Salem Witch Trials had morphed into the First Red Scare, the Palmer Raids, and the American Protective League. Jim Crow was alive and stubbornly unwell. Citizens sang of the "Hun." They sang of Johnny, the young "Son of Liberty" in Bill Murray's war tune, which cast American men as sons-of-a-gun, the "gun" being America. Women were recruitment volunteers, on the front as clerks and nurses, in the civil service, in munitions factories, and eventually on strike. Political officials reeled with the felt need to sell Americans on a global fight for the safety and security of American democracy as a transnational good to be sold "over there," and so to sustain the Grand Illusion of democratic idealism. The "Our Beginnings" caricature was a troubling take on colonial history that doubled as a humorous takedown of a misogynistic American custom of doing bad things in good faith, grabbing land, and grafting self-righteousness onto otherwise wicked ways.[12] Flagg's Uncle

Sam stands as a disturbingly related masculine emblem of US American national character, typifying the capacity of war to gloss over crises of gender, race, and nationality in a milieu when combat conquests are akin to cultural victory. What is more, the iconic "I Want YOU" poster is more a comic travesty than a tragic call to arms, betraying an image of a national culture that wages war in the name of a grumpy old man who exists as the laughable symbol of America itself.

The epoch of the Great War was one of nationalistic acculturation. There was in it a widespread realization among the body politic that wars can take interest in people even if they do not have interest in war. After all, war could be waged overseas while being carried out at home in a struggle for "the American mind."[13] During the Spanish-American War, this struggle was staged in the comedies of vaudeville, especially those put on by Edward (Ned) Harrigan and Tony Hart. Comic performances of Self and Other, Us and Them, Insider and Outsider, and Native and Immigrant were designed to display "real" US Americanism. They relied on comic farces that tended to be at once useful and gratifying in their ethnic and racial characterizations.[14] Importantly, these visual character studies in comic stereotypes paved the way to, and played out during (and after), the Spanish-American War.[15] In addition, they made ethnic foundations central to US American humor as well as to early comic portrayals of immigrants availing themselves of a New World amid European (never mind Native) others.[16] No wonder caricatures of "the Whiteman" in so many Native American portrayals reveal an American character who is at best "ludicrous and ridiculous" and at worst guilty of "incompetence and gross neglect."[17] An editorial cartoon by Clifford Berryman from 1899 seems representative of vaudeville's reach in this regard, with its nationalistic, ethnocentric, and imperialistic aura encircling a caricature of Uncle Sam pursuing a hapless Filipino under the title, "Not in a Position to Give Up the Chase" (fig. 5). Racialized, ethnocentric foundations constitute a comic act unto themselves in such an image.

In 1915, Americanization melded with the "melting pot," trading the rhetorical stuff of pluralism for a trope of Us–Them warism tainted by ideologies of "cultural primogeniture."[18] President Wilson himself worried in his address to Congress on December 7 about "malignant creatures" who had been "born under other flags" and yet destroyed the polis by poisoning "the very arteries of . . . national life."[19] The "melting pot" here fosters a nationalistic fantasy that makes the United States a harbinger for racial, gender, and ethnic harmony on one hand and yet full of discord and discourses

FIG. 5 Clifford Berryman, "Not in a Position to Give Up the Chase," 1899. From the *Washington Post*, May 1, 1899. Courtesy of the US National Archives.

of purity on the other. While this fantasy could never have been shared with a straight face in the nineteenth century, it thrived in the culture of World War I. In the pages of *Judge* on January 6, 1917, just months before US entry into the war, an illustration by Flagg of a woman showing the smallest bit of leg in an advertisement for First National Bank (a reprint of a May 1912 cover, in fact) appears right next to a pithy editorial entitled, "A Millennial Forevision." The editorial dubs America a "glorious nation," "thoroughly cosmopolitan and democratic," and "more than ever the melting-pot of nations." As David Quixano says in Israel Zangwill's 1908 play, *The Melting-Pot*, all the contradictions of a culture combine when they are confronted by the darkest ordeals. "The pride and prejudice," says Quixano, "the dreams and the sacrifices, the traditions and the superstitions, the fasts and the feasts, things noble and things sordid—they must all into the Crucible."[20] Interestingly, this is very nearly humorist and caricature artist Max Beerbohm's definition of caricature, which he described in 1901 as the craft of "melting down" the characteristics of a person or thing, "as in a crucible," and then refashioning them in so many comic poses, gestures, and expressions.[21] To borrow language from Zangwill's play, caricatures of character can "look forward" and "backwards, too." Crucibles are receptacles. But they are also burdens, troubles, and torments. As comic crucibles of sorts, caricatures render proportions and perspectives anew insofar as they see their objects of ridicule in their most characteristic moments—for example, wartimes. Flagg's Uncle Sam caricatures Americanism even as it stares sternly in the face of armed conflict.

To understand Uncle Sam's role in the cartoon politics of World War I is at first to appreciate the extent to which the state was collapsed into the US nation as a means of establishing a public culture of war.[22] President Wilson catapulted the United States into a come-to-Uncle-Sam moment on multiple fronts: at the level of civil and military service, the enforcement of correct nationalistic behavior, and the commitment to "100% Americanism." The particularities of any one "YOU" were subsumed into a broader, more universal (even transcendental) nationalism whereby the American body politic was a proxy for national politics, the presidential establishment, and official political order.[23] During Reconstruction and amid the United States' rise to prosperity at the turn of the twentieth century, problems with a particularly plural sense of national character spiraled around concerns over equal rights, racial justice, and social, political, and economic welfare. In many ways, World War I converted such concerns into the dis-ease of an intangible collective image. As George Creel later wrote of the CPI—an agency charged with identifying and influencing wartime public sentiment, and also portraying the distinctive qualities and visual typologies of American-ness—cultural politics comprised "a knowledge of the life and character of the rank and file of the American people."[24] The cartoon became a prime space of characterization for a new nation qua armed force. As in the Civil War era, a war of "nations" became at once a war of pictures—that is, of depictions codifying shared experiences of culture and combat. However, world war required a more marked transition to the wartime unification of *a* nation. Uncle Sam, via Flagg and others, was dragooned into service as a spokesman not for war as politics by other means but rather as a guarantor and guardian of democracy. War *for* democracy was the unifying theme.

Nevertheless, there is a historiographic sense that the horrors of warmaking are perhaps best delineated by humorous imagery. President Wilson's eventual propaganda machine was animated by a dogmatic impression of egalitarian and therefore sovereign people. But support for war has the hazard of restricting this sovereignty in the rhetorical straits of flag-waving and fearmongering. Humor of the people, as Mikhail Bakhtin argues, rejects such "narrow dogmatism (in principle)" by testing it "in the crucible of laughter."[25] It therefore holds images of national character up to a comic looking glass to display the potential monstrosities in portrayals of Self and Other. The humor of caricature is important given the dogmatism undergirding what Christopher Capozzola calls the "culture of obligation" that pervaded much of the public discourse during World War I.[26] Flagg's Uncle Sam is, at base, a caricature of civic duty.

A citizen's responsibility to political community can be defined by certain relations and practices that not only articulate but also actualize a sense of belonging. Such relations and practices require education in civic virtues and vices. Visual imagery has long provided resources for identifying with the duties (not just the individuals) that seem to follow from the very idea of a public as an imaginary community. And it has long offered realistic projections of what appropriate and *in*appropriate public activity looks like. Uncle Sam embodies a grotesque fusion of the realistic and the fantastical. He is often lifelike, his story accords with something like an evolutionary process of political progress, and he is an arbiter for citizenship. More to the point, Uncle Sam—especially at war—shows forth an "accurate" picture of cultural conditions by merging stereotypical American values with the idea that democracy demands occasional acts of violence in its defense. As a *realistic* caricature of wartime national character, Uncle Sam is much less a human subject than an abstract matter, projecting upon a body politic the characteristics (and problematics) of shared responsibility for armed conflict. Flagg's depiction betrays the grotesqueries that emerge when photorealism meets the pictorial distortion of types and topicalities in what appears to be a faithful personification of the nation. Because Uncle Sam is recognizable *as* "an epitome of the nation's character" and *thus* as "a collective caricature,"[27] though, his honest and seemingly unaffected expression of national characteristics comes off as cartoonish. Its cartoonishness is precisely what makes the image a comic look at an American everyman.

Every American and His Uncle

A late nineteenth-century joke, reproduced in the *Railroad Trainmen's Journal* in 1892, gets at the comic paradoxes of character management. As it goes, a bird aficionado often crowed about his ability to coax his parrot into repeating anything he said. One day, with friends looking on, he uttered,

"Uncle." The parrot did not respond. Again and again the enthusiast called out the appellation but received no response from the bird. Angrily, he grabbed the parrot by the neck and shouted: "Say 'uncle,' you beggar!" After earning yet more silence, he twisted the parrot's neck before tossing him into a fowl-house where he should have died in the company of ten prize Dorkings. However, when the aficionado later entered the fowl-house, he was surprised to find nine of his Dorkings dead on the ground, their necks wrung. Atop the tenth was the parrot, twisting the struggling bird's neck and crying out: "Say 'uncle,' you beggar! Say 'uncle'!"

Prior to World War I, the idiom "say uncle" could have been chalked up as a good-humored American idiom, deployed by the presumptive victor of a play fight. By the time the United States entered the "Great War" in the spring of 1917, to say "uncle" was to imply Uncle Sam, and to summon a militaristic cultural politics that surrendered positive civic liberty to negative civil defense. The joke therefore captures the rhetorical impact of coercion on public conduct. It also portrays the consequences of dissenting against authority even as it mocks the voluntary reenactment of brutality. World War I saw such a militarization of Americanism. As Creel said in 1919, the government's domestic agenda was oriented toward "building morale, arousing the spiritual forces of the Nation, and stimulating the war will of the people."[28] Uncle Sam was not only a pictorial embodiment of the state; he was also a mediating authority for the governmental manufacture of "the people." Flagg's "I Want YOU" poster exemplifies both a concern about and solution for a "wartime crucible," in Capozzola's words. "When Uncle Sam jabbed his finger at the American public, he pointed out . . . who was or wasn't an American."[29] Flagg made fun of the finger-pointing ethos by mocking the sublimity of a nationalistic Eros as antidemocratic even as he captured the paternalism behind a democratic culture that was fixing for war.

Half a century earlier, Uncle Sam was not pointing fingers. In fact, he appeared to be pushing up daisies. Uncle Sam was proclaimed dead on June 1, 1861. According to a faux obituary in the *North Carolina Standard*, Jefferson Davis was the surviving family member set to take up Uncle Sam's mantle. That same day, the first battle of Fairfax Court House took place, resulting in the retreat of a small unit of Union cavalrymen and a feeling of pride among Confederates. The Court House soon became a key site for military conferences and for Davis's reviews of Confederate troops. By the end of June, plans were set for the Union army to march on Richmond. And in just over a month, on the Fourth of July, President Abraham Lincoln would deliver a speech to Congress and declare war "a People's contest" over egalitarian versus other forms of government. The choice was clear: either restore democracy as a battle of wits or sustain a tyranny of war wills bent on outmoded conceptions of Southern decency, political racketeering, and the notion that violence is endemic to competing interests. As such, Uncle Sam is a transitional figure, at first an originary icon of popular and willful jocularity in the face of gentility (for example, in the formative guise of Brother Jonathan as the antithesis to John Bull),[30] and later a figure for the strong arm of government.

Thomas Nast is a crucial reference point here. Conventional wisdom has it that he gave us the cartoon image of Uncle Sam. An 1869 engraving portrays him carving a turkey and sharing Thanksgiving dinner in the company of Columbia, an African American family, and a cohort of immigrants from multiple nations. The "common table" signifies freedom and equality,[31] which Nast links in this image to governmental-as-familial generosity. Uncle Sam also appears as "common property," available to all who see him as a "sterling and essentially American type."[32] But he embodies the paradoxes of Americanism in its affordances for freedom and enslavement, civil liberty and oppression, civic duty and engineered consent. Across US history, Uncle Sam oversees segregationism in a world safe for democracy. He embodies white masculinity even as he suffers its consequences. He stands with the suffragettes and the feminized American man. These paradoxes have roots in the War of 1812. Soon after war broke out, provisions were sent to American militiamen. A meatpacker from New York, Samuel Wilson, stamped containers of salted meat with the acronym "U.S." The ellipsis soon inherited a dual meaning: Uncle Sam, the charitable provisioner, and the United States, a nation whose government fed its fighters. The two significations were eventually melded into one, and newspapers began to reference the government as Uncle Sam. By the Civil War era, he was a fixture in nationalistic discourse, taking on a visual appearance complete with the iconic red and white striped pants, blue tailcoat, and starred top hat. During and beyond the Spanish-American War, Uncle Sam was an imposing imperial figure, variously shown as a patriarchal powerbroker in the newfangled praxis of colonial occupation, a political fat cat feasting on the spoils of war, and a military tactician giddy with the idea of expanding US global influence. The principle of protectionism became a characteristic of American selflessness. It also tethered wartime interventions to matters of race, gender, and cultural production.

As one author described him in the early 1900s, on the home front and overseas, Uncle Sam was at the turn of the twentieth century a typification of America and its "genial lineaments" as well as its tendency to be "an avaricious and hypocritical old scoundrel."[33] Visual cultures of humor are replete with these lineaments and tendencies. Consider another cartoon image from *The Public* on January 31, 1902, entitled "Expansion." In it, Uncle Sam is prone on the ground, pinned down by members of the Roosevelt administration who are all rendered as imps. President Teddy Roosevelt, the Archfiend, is standing by the stopcock of a device for water torture, the funnel for which is in Uncle Sam's mouth. American Empire here is figured as the mock "water-cure" for Republicanism. In one of Uncle Sam's clenched fists is a document labeled 1776. In the backdrop of the scene, one little devil is kicking the old man's top hat, and tossing away leaflets variously labeled "American Ideas," "Sumner's Teachings," "Lincoln's Doctrine," "Jefferson," "Adams," and more. An American flag hangs over President Roosevelt, affixed to a large water drum. It has been altered so that its bars contain text that reads "SLAVERY & POLYGAMY PROTECTED SULTAN OF SULU PER ROOSEVELT." Similarly, in the water drum are things like Autocracy, Aristocracy, Plutocracy, Government by Injunction, Repeal of the Declaration of Independence, and Military Despotism. Uncle Sam's belly is bulging. His distension corresponds to the expansion of American warism in the name of national interests and likewise the diminution of democracy. Uncle Sam is decidedly *not* the nation in this comic image, nor is he its leading character; instead, he is a body of principles and practices carried out by the American people and their elected officials. Uncle Sam is a rhetorical vessel for the body politic. Herein is the dark comedy of a new American Empire that followed the Spanish-American War.

Uncle Sam's image is a contradiction in nationalistic personification. While Uncle Sam often takes on an aura of peace and Lincoln-esque righteousness, his national pride comes from armed conflict. In the War of 1812, he was quite literally the hand that fed hostilities. By the Civil War era, Brother Jonathan all but disappeared from American iconography, and his symbolism of the nation and its founding principles was conflated with the image of Uncle Sam as the military arm and executive function of a nation-state. Yet while he was transformed into a "symbol of freedom and union in the northern cause,"[34] Uncle Sam was also made into an icon of condescension and intolerance. Underlying his nineteenth-century façade of frailty and gauntness was a latent aggression that situated Uncle Sam as an object of rhetorical struggle in antebellum public culture and prescribed his role as a governmental authority with the might to wage war and command that peace (i.e., Reconstruction) be given a chance—or not. In Nast's hands,

Uncle Sam went from a peace-offering father figure to the disgruntled parent of a warlike nation. The impish activities of those committed to an early twentieth-century war culture are a natural outgrowth of this expansionism.

The alignment of Uncle Sam with war imagery has long contributed to both gendered subject positions and racialized notions of "good" and "right" citizenship. At the turn of the century, many cartoonists (particularly for humor magazines *Judge* and *Puck*) were fond of portraying Uncle Sam as a displeased schoolteacher, whipping Puerto Rican, Cuban, Filipino, and Hawaiian children into national shape. One cartoon, drawn by W. A. Rogers and published in *Harper's Weekly* in August 1898, depicts Uncle Sam whacking Cuban "guerilla" General Máximo Gómez on the head with a stick. A white man shares a bench with the general but sits at the end, quietly and independently reading a book by Gómez. Two women, one from Hawaii and another from Puerto Rico, mirror the white man on the other side of the room. In the back of the class is Emilio Aguinaldo, the First Revolutionary President of the Philippines, wearing a dunce cap and looking as if the master-slave relationship has been sedimented as that between teacher and student. These latter depictions exemplify the consolidation in caricature of Anglo-Americanism during the Spanish-American War. War relies upon the stigmatization or demonization of an enemy "other." It also relies on a unified albeit divided nation. Uncle Sam embodies the domestic unities and divisions that determine who and what make up the United States. Still, while his image is rife in the visual culture of the Spanish-American War, there is no coordinated message or identifiable pattern other than the "grotesque racialization" of Spain.[35] As such, racial and ethnic typecasts shore up a sense of unanimity built on the occupying force of an interventionist nation "helping" neighboring countries achieve independence (and not pursuing its own colonial land grab). Furthermore, cartoons and caricatures were like catalogs for the actions and outcomes of political officers, military excursions, foreign policies, and homegrown public relations—most of which simply reinforced grandiose assumptions about Uncle Sam as an abstract figure of an inherently righteous Americanism.[36] Prior to World War I, Uncle Sam was a distorted reflection of American national character, a monstrosity of comic (and sometimes tragic) musings. By World War I, he was at the apex of nationalistic self-righteousness.

Hence Flagg's Uncle Sam is as much an example of "self-mocking humor" as it is a picture of nationalistic self-love.[37] Flagg's Uncle Sam is an admonishment about enlistment and duty. But it is also a flippant, self-reflexive mockery of American democracy that makes fun of the role that violence and vigilantism play in its political doctrine. Flagg's poster, in part, apes the iconic Lord Kitchener Wants You recruitment notice. It also pegs national character as a silly, yet severe, form of navel gazing. The nationalism of late nineteenth-century warism is overt in this visage. This nationalistic self-absorption, fitted as it is with a mix of scorn and sufferance, is made even more of a caricature when enlistment is seen as a byproduct of an agnatic death stare—that is, when Flagg's Uncle Sam is seen as an exemplar of *sex*-mocking humor. "Death," writes Esther Fuchs, "lurks not in violence, but in sexuality; love is not the opposite, but the motivating principle of war."[38] It takes a concerted effort to view Flagg's iconic image of Uncle Sam anamorphically if one is to glean the grotesque humor in its superficial warism and almost glib sexual appeal. It takes a comic vantage as well to see that there is, in fact, anamorphosis in Flagg's caricature. Uncle Sam is at once a distorted image of national character and a corrective to a rhetorical culture of disfigured imagery that makes warfare a denuded form of American democracy, or vice versa. Like a crucible, comic anamorphosis refashions familiar images and ideas so that their surface features can be seen for their profound depths. Here, Uncle Sam is a sinister emblem for the perverted consent of the governed. In Flagg's Uncle Sam is a comic portrait of how, decades before the Cold War, Americans might learn to stop worrying and love the battle for democracy. The hysteria and chauvinism behind Uncle Sam's sardonic grin betrays a strange love. It is not without alternative reflections, though. If Flagg's portrayal of Uncle Sam represents the masculine desire of a US nation to conscript an entire body politic, Paul Stahr's iconic depiction of Columbia exemplifies the countervailing feminine directive to "be patriotic" and, consequently, act like a true wartime woman. Stahr's Columbia appears to be a reproduction of a cover illustration on the January 16, 1915, cover of *Judge*, which features a young woman in a white dress adorned with a red and blue ribbon affecting almost the exact same pose (fig. 6). Underneath her is the caption, "A CALL TO ARMS." This cover art is not by Stahr, though; it is by Flagg.[39] Stahr bolstered governmental efforts to conserve food on the home front in order to provide rations for soldiers overseas (not unlike the Uncle Sam of the War of 1812) and so reinforced the gender role of women as those who make homes and prepare meals. But the picture betrays an additional sentiment. Clad in an American flag dress and hat, with amorous blue eyes gazing forward and arms outstretched in a way that both summons and anticipates an embrace, Stahr's Columbia is a woman starved for affection.

FIG. 6 James Montgomery Flagg, "A Call to Arms," 1915. From *Judge*, January 16, 1915.

Women of the First World War were figured as symbols for the love of a nation and, at the same time, as *femmes fatales* that could tempt citizens into a soldier's life through a certain lustful expression of civic responsibilities to warfare.

This image of women reeks of shamelessness. Columbia opens herself to her taker while urging a populace to wage war. Most disconcerting, however, is the extent to which Stahr, Flagg, and others conflated the image of an everywoman with Columbia to suggest that one could flatter her either by enlisting in the military or enrolling in wartime aid programs. For men, combat was a means of indulging in the seemingly lighter side of Uncle Sam's own desire for his "beholder's body and blood and spirit."[40] For women, war—perpetuated on the home front—was a means of publicly identifying with civic womanhood. It was a catalyst to give oneself over to war culture as a resource for shoring up American types. Images of women at war conflate the American body politic with visual characteristics that both insinuate the dreadful desires of men and imply the nationalistic tenets apparent in Uncle Sam's disturbing love of country.

There was thus a public opinion of Uncle Sam as a real force for good and not an *exaggeration* of unfulfilled promises. As one contemporaneous reporter put it, Uncle Sam became "something far more than a caricature" insofar as he had "grown into an embodiment of distinct American traits."[41] He was the central figure of burgeoning warism on the world stage, transmogrifying a democratic social contract into a "social contract of war."[42] On May 28, 1918, the Bureau of Cartoons was established for the purpose of mobilizing and directing "the scattered cartoon power of the country for constructive war work."[43] Uncle Sam was reworked as the figurehead of a state demanding sacrifice for freedom and protection. If the turn of the twentieth century saw Uncle Sam as an embodiment of deep-seated principles, the war culture of World War I witnessed his simplification of complex attitudes and motivations to the ugly truth that war is a guarantor and guardian of democracy. Public opinion was the province of political officialdom, whereby imperialist convictions and militaristic policies led to the criminalization of dissent, the segregation of civilians and soldiers along lines of service, the demonization of "un-American" immigrants, and the "rebirth" of a white, chauvinist America. For these reasons and more, "Uncle Sam lost his avuncular air and became the forceful leader of a world power."[44] To be antiwar was to be *un*characteristically American. It was to disregard war as a civic duty. Wartime caricatures of national character travestied obligatory warfare. Flagg's Uncle Sam promoted civic action in World War I. But he also urged a second look at warlike calls to arms alongside the artifices of democracy. There is humor in the contradictions of a lure that doubles as an ultimatum for democratic citizens to serve, or else. There is, too, a comic appeal in a looking-glass embodiment of the national self in the visage of a blue-blooded martinet, especially one who leaves open the possibility to imagine war as nonconsensual. Accordingly, there are high stakes in humoring Flagg's caricature of Uncle Sam.

Humoring Caricatures of National Character, or the Comic Art of Seduction to War

Wartimes encumber images and ideas of national character. As noticed by "Father of Public Opinion" Edward Bernays, character is often best visualized through "physical metaphors" and the "compact, vivid simplification of complicated issues."[45] Bernays's uncle, Sigmund Freud, saw humor as a resource for characterizing moments of crisis as comic delusions and self-induced states of amusement and drollery. Caricature is effective, says

FIG. 7 James Montgomery Flagg, "I Want YOU," war poster, ca. 1917. Courtesy of the National Museum of American History.

Freud, *because* it distorts reality, *because* it makes the "normal" seem ridiculous. The humor in caricature comes from a certain ugliness that is derived from the frailties and deformities of character. It fosters the makings of comic judgment. Flagg's "I Want YOU" poster is exemplary not only because of its popularity or persuasion but also because of the burden it transferred back to its viewers by making national character a crucible of collective consciousness and public comportment set before the comic looking glass (fig. 7). Uncle Sam coerces action and consent. Nevertheless, he displays a paradox of American ideals in the image of a strong man of democracy gone wild with belligerent leanings.

To see this paradox is to first see that war was an encumbrance to President Wilson's foundational doctrine of neutrality. His own reputation enabled him to position himself as an antiwar president, a peacemaker, and a conscientious isolationist—a position made all the more appropriate in a time when a politics of pacifism predominated. It was only when he could characterize American entry into "a war for democracy, a war to end war, a war to protect liberalism, a war against militarism, a war to redeem barbarous Europe, a crusade" that Wilson could exit the high road and deign to declare the United States a protectorate of the human right to freedom from *Kultur*.⁴⁶ The irony is that Wilson's proclaimed antipathy for supreme and autonomous governing bodies contradicts the vehemence with which he converted nationalism and civic duty into what Creel advertised as "great war machinery" predicated upon the "war-will" of the US government.⁴⁷ This machinery matches a broader sense that humor was conducive to an American narrative of order.⁴⁸ At the center of his war machine, on top of this rhetorical culture of humor, was the CPI—a prime purveyor of Flagg's wartime caricatures.

The CPI conducted pictorial warfare. Established on April 17, 1917, the CPI was chaired by Creel, a muckraking journalist who once composed jokes and comics copy for William Randolph Hearst and his newspapers as well as for outlets like *Puck*, *Judge*, and *Life*. The CPI was charged with coordinating "the campaign for psychological mobilization of the American people," or what Creel approached as a "war for the American mind."⁴⁹ Numerous divisions and bureaus made up Creel's committee, managing news, press releases, editorials, photographs, films, and more. Each division variously worked on recruiting soldiers, soliciting money for war bonds, picturing barbarous and atrocious enemies, and codifying the integrity of friends and families on the home front. The Division of Pictorial Publicity, overseen by Charles Dana Gibson (head of the Society of Illustrators and artist of "Gibson Girls" fame), was in command of visual public relations. Within this division was the Bureau of Cartoons, headed by George J. Hecht, publisher of *Parents* magazine. Along with numerous poster artists, Hecht's bureau was tasked with telling the public what to think about and creating illustrations of *how* to think. As written in an article from the *Philadelphia Inquirer* in August 1917, war had provoked a collective desire for artistic depictions that unpacked the "Great Realities" of national concern. War, in turn, exposed an aporia in visions of the relationship between citizens and a wartime government.

In the rhetorical warism of cartoons, posters, and other illustrations was a public space of humor that promoted support for armed conflict in a way that exploited its horrors much like so-called "trench humor" enabled soldiers to manage the trials and tribulations of combat. Images of Uncle Sam above all crossed over from print publications to propaganda and recruitment placards. One cartoon by popular cartoonist W. A. Rogers, for instance, portrayed the passage of sedition laws in 1918. In it, a foreboding Uncle Sam uses one hand to manhandle a monstrous-looking member of the Industrial Workers of the World (IWW) with a Ketch-All pole and the other to drag a cabal of traitorous fat cats, spies, and provocateurs. The

Capitol building looms large in the background as Uncle Sam rounds up and marches the malcontents out of Washington. Another by Clifford K. Berryman—for whom Uncle Sam was a central figure, often with "T. R." as a teddy bear by his side—was published in the *Washington Evening Star* in 1918 showing Uncle Sam clutching a shovel and spade while shouting into an announcer's megaphone. Text emanating from the megaphone directs people to "speed up the ships" and "spade up the soil." On the shorefront where Uncle Sam stands is a scattering of other messages, including "specifications for ships" and the customary appeal to "buy bonds." Behind him is a cloud of smoke, stamped the "Western drive," and a teddy bear letting loose battleships by the water's edge. Some violent portrayals existed, too, such as Dutch artist Louis Raemaekers's famous cartoon, "The Avenger," which reveals Uncle Sam as a vigilante frontiersman pointing a gun at a German emperor and playing up an idea of American warmaking that traversed international boundaries. All represent national selfhood in terms of the right hand of democracy empowering the left hand of war. All, too, are laden with so many touchstones of caricature. The imagery is grotesque, sometimes ludicrous. Deformations reimagine recognizable symbols and iconography. Representational falsities bespeak nationalistic fantasies. Exaggerations of character types overwhelm ideas about the stakes of war and the defense of democracy with monstrous distortions. In all of them, caricature reigned rhetorically supreme.

None of this is to suggest that there were no dissenting opinions. There were. Hence Hecht went out of his way to portray public opinion as a combat zone. An early cartoon published in the *Chicago Daily Tribune* in April 1916 displays an armless Columbia, perhaps in mock homage both to Benjamin Franklin's view of political dismemberment and his black-and-white demand for citizens to "join or die." Draped around her is an American flag that covers only her bottom half. Her nude torso betrays a sense in which the nation and the dark liberties for which it stands would be laid bare by the exigencies of warfare. She bears the brunt of the rhetorical and material violence that would be carried out in her name. Then there is the even more explicit cover of Emma Goldman's antiwar broadsheet, *Mother Earth*, from June 1912. Its caption reads, "PATRIOTISM IN ACTION." Above it is a masked marauder pinning down a bound and shirtless man while jamming the bottom end of an American flagpole into his mouth. All in all, caricature was embroiled in government-endorsed narratives that justified war as a form of civic renewal and likewise made it a matter of justice such that the characteristics of a national character did not need to be shared in order to be diffuse in war culture; one simply needed to "act as if." This is why one can see in Flagg's Uncle Sam an emphasis on an anamorphic transformation of "the many" into one nation under war. Put differently, Uncle Sam became a means for scorning nonconformists and narrowing the range of possibilities for public conduct. The humor in Flagg's caricature, however, allows feelings of obligation to be turned back on themselves.

Flagg's own war fervor—or, his visualization of the follies of war *in* that fervor—is illuminating given his prewar reputation as a comic illustrator for *Scribner's*, *Judge*, and *Life* as well as *Cosmopolitan* and *Good Housekeeping*. He was known for his "rapier wit," whether in writing brusque editorials or scripting (and even acting in) short satirical films with director and producer Jack Eaton.[50] Flagg drew caricatures of American character and conduct in *personae comicum* like Mrs. Pearl Prunepincher, Matthew J. Pillweather, Stark N. Aked, and others. Perhaps most the rage was Nervy Nat, which was published in *Judge* and portrayed a stereotypical American as "a bibulous ne'er do well and imposter who was living by his wits in Paris" and elsewhere.[51] In one cartoon from 1907, Nervy Nat appears as an aeronaut hammering an American flag into a barren planet. "Well," he says, "I'll just claim this planetine for the U.S.A. and when I go back home I'll spring a few lectures on 'Furthest Up' and make Lieutenant Peary look like a bed-ridden old invalid." In this instance, Flagg mocks the arrogance of those convinced of the moral righteousness of American prospects and yet simultaneously captures the conflicts that animate civic activities relative to civilian-military relations. These and more themes were further developed in Flagg's other cartoons, such as his "Limericks" in *Life*, which included "Tomfoolery," "'If,' A Guide to Bad Manners," and "All in the Same Boat." These titles alone encapsulate much of what accounted for the war mentality that Flagg's Uncle Sam brought to light. Uncle Sam was a man of honor but also a creep and a cad. He was a noble statesman and a buffoon. He was an emblem of republicanism and, as a war maker, an object of ridicule and disgust. Simply, Uncle Sam embodies the American body politic as it is aligned with a particular set of experiences all at a variance with the instabilities and inanities of a democratized war culture.

Flagg's Uncle Sam, at base, is the face of militarism. He appeared on the cover of *Leslie's Illustrated Weekly* on July 6, 1916, above a caption that read: "What are YOU doing for Preparedness?" The Preparedness Movement was a byproduct of Theodore Roosevelt's saber rattling and promotion of war as a necessary evil of twentieth-century democratic self-governance.

Wilson opposed the movement until it became politically imprudent to do so and eventually passed the National Defense Act of 1916 to expand the size and scope of the US military. Flagg's cover image is at once prescient and premeditative, providing a glimpse of the sorts of loaded threats that were to come. It is also premonitory, insinuating that those who were not preparing for war should have felt guilty about (or ashamed of) their inaction. Guilt and shame arise when people are made to feel that they have somehow violated their societal or cultural roles. Flagg's Uncle Sam publicized guilt as a standard for civic judgment. Flagg's posters turned guilt outward by mortifying national character and projecting the idea that people are at fault for antiwar (mis)conduct until they prove otherwise. Capozzola argues that pictorial publicity and cartoon campaigns helped to foment a "citizenship of obligation."[52] For my part, in exaggerating this civic culture, Flagg's portrayals expressed a war culture of *culpability*. Uncle Sam is a bastion of blame.

Guilt and blame have great rhetorical force. Guilt is the result of a negative, even tragic, emotion. It is caught up at the intersections of individuals and cultures, compelling notions of what should or should not be done, by whom, and under what prohibitions and permissions. Unlike shame, which constitutes the reactions of onlookers to some wrongful act, guilt situates attention on self-understanding. As Martha Nussbaum argues, guilt is "unpleasantly stifling and narcissistic,"[53] producing a compulsion in the Self to direct pain and suffering inward in response to some wrong against the privileges or needs of one's community. Guilt entails the management of "good" relations between selves and others based on "bad" feelings in a body politic. Shame is the communication of culpability in character flaws to an audience of watchful eyes. To feel guilt is to feel bad about oneself. To be shamed is to be found out and blamed. In Sara Ahmed's terms, a specifically "national shame" comes about with the publicity of shared wrongs,[54] and it circulates as a sense that each individual has a stake in public-as-personal guilt.

Humor can play a huge role here. Following Freud, when oriented by sexualized circumstances, humor can prompt audiences to feel ashamed or embarrassed if they become aroused when they should be repulsed. Alternatively, humor can establish the possibility to experience and express feelings of guilt or shame *shamelessly*. A comic license is paramount in the potentially guilt-free rhetorical space of caricature, particularly when humor makes one's personal commitment to war preparedness seem ridiculous or the national shame in war itself the foolish predicate of a world safe for democracy. Caricature frequently emphasizes failures. Its humor comes from its deformation of character flaws. It is thus helpful to remember that guilt can also involve a lack of certainty about the Self. Lest we forget that the admonishment to Hail Columbia, which Stahr depicts, has its roots in Francis Hopkinson's oratorio, *The Temple of Minerva*. It was performed in 1781 for President George Washington and couched the "Genius of America" in the deeds of her "warlike sons." Minerva is an ancient goddess of war. Never mind that Flagg's Uncle Sam seems as manly as he is mannish, he is the progeny and the byproduct of impermanent victory in battle. He personifies being prepared by being patriotic and answering calls to participate in nationalistic conquests. He is also a comic picture of male domination that violently *negates* (female) citizenship.[55] Overt allusions to manhood fill out national shaming and the circulation of personal guilt contra civic duty in Flagg's Uncle Sam. All the more reason to see him for his comic androgyny. Superficially, his countenance is stern, his brow is pronounced, and his demeanor is resolute, but his skin is almost fair, his gray hair is flowing out from his top hat, and his lips are ripe and red as fruit. Furthermore, he strongly resembles Stahr's portrayal of Columbia, even if his finger pointing replaces the open arms of an American goddess. Grace and glory blend with gallantry and guardianship. The seduction blends with the adjuration. Shame on men too unmanly to go to war. Shame on women too weak to stand in for their men at home. Shame on anyone willing—and *un*willing—to submit. Caricature sees through these sexualized appeals because it allows the sacred nature of Americanism to indulge its profane grotesqueries, at once encouraging onlookers "to identify themselves with idealized manhood but also threatening them that they would never have the wherewithal to measure up to that ideal."[56] What are you doing? Alter the inflection and you find that this interrogation is suffused with a guilty conscience, and with it a shameless appeal to sexual guilt. This is the comic insinuation in Uncle Sam's flaunts of male fantasy and feminine vanity.

The original rendition of Flagg's Uncle Sam is glaring and insistent, but not yet directive. As a caricature of war culture, he was a comic picture of mobilization. Even though it presupposes the response "not enough" to its accompanying question, there is still a sense of *noblesse oblige* in that viewers are permitted to do what they can. This is less so when the cover is reappropriated as a recruitment poster. By the time it was reproduced in April 1917, Flagg's Uncle Sam was party to a public information operation that had become a propaganda machine. The Division of Pictorial Publicity,

FIG. 8 James Montgomery Flagg, "The Cartoonist Makes People SEE THINGS!," 1918. From *Bulletin for Cartoonists* 20 (October 26, 1918), 1. Courtesy of the Ohio State University Library.

which produced several hundred posters over the course of the war (and over four million copies of Flagg's poster), had secured a cultural institutionalization of poster and cartoon illustrations. Related outfits, like the "Four-Minute Men" speaking troupe, were stirring up pro-war patriotism to buttress other war efforts. What Creel called the "cartoon power" of posters, however, infiltrated public spaces.[57] In fact, it comprised its own front lines through a homeland "poster war," with the country-wide distribution of official war artworks "not just on billboards or walls but also in shop windows, banks, schools, churches, libraries, town halls, factories, recruiting stations, offices, and homes; in cities, small towns, and rural settings."[58] The posters were rhetorical armaments of the war effort, even earning the moniker of "weapons on the wall." Poster imagery was also reproduced as postcards and advertisements in magazines, trade papers, and newspapers. In short, cartoon art and graphic iterations of civic duty were legion—and they demanded allegiance to a national character defined by enlistment.

Uncle Sam was at the nexus of this pictorial apparatus. This is why it is not enough to see Uncle Sam in (or as) a singular caricature, but instead to see him as central to a visual culture of war that relied on the circulation of feelings about national character. A humorous and anamorphic view of the "I Want YOU" image lets one see *multiple* Uncle Sams in the single iteration. And Flagg drew more than one Uncle Sam. On the cover of an October 1919 "Bulletin for Cartoonists" distributed by the CPI is a cartoon by Flagg of an American cartoonist forcing a Kaiser seated before a mirror to see himself for what he truly was: a skeleton (fig. 8). Accompanying the cartoon was the caption "The Cartoonist Makes People SEE THINGS!"

Tellingly, the relationship between Self and Other is pronounced by what each man sees. The Kaiser catches a glimpse of his own dead body, but he would also no doubt see the cartoonist's reflection beside it in the mirror. The cartoonist, too, sees the enemy body as a skinless corpse. The entire scene imbricates war efforts with the life and death of cartoon imagery. The skull appears to be smiling. As a monstrous caricature of Us–Them ontologies, the skull amplifies the consequences we find when we face ourselves and others in the looking glass.

In the "I Want YOU" image, the pointing finger and piercing eyes of a personified US nation followed this logic, forming a forceful interpellation of audience members as the obvious and unavoidable targets of Uncle Sam's petition. The white space around him only adds to the potency of his gesture as he appears to pop out of the poster. One effect is to make the national demand for wartime service more proximate. Additionally, Uncle Sam draws a feeling of public attention to singular citizens—a point that is punctuated by the fact that Flagg's Uncle Sam is also a *self*-caricature: Flagg used his own appearance as inspiration for his illustration. That is, Flagg *is* Uncle Sam, but with the sort of alterations that turn a true-to-life portrayal into an anamorphic commentary on the National Self. To see oneself as the United States personified is to see nationalistic ways of seeing in a different light. To read the poster was to see the caricaturist implicate himself in the comic image. It was also not only to entertain Uncle Sam's call to arms but also to put oneself in the position of being watched by others who either encountered the appeal or were waiting to pass judgment on those who might not heed the call. In this sense, a civic gaze peered through the imagined surveillance of others, making self-governance accountable to the presumed skepticism and distrust of the body politic. To point fingers is to incite blame. At the same time, it is to pass the buck to a guilty or responsible party. The rhetorical purchase here is in the fact that Uncle Sam's gaze burdens a citizenry to see itself for what it truly is (or not), thereby reinforcing the idea of democracy as something that needs to be fought for by "the people" and not simply protected, indiscriminately, by an indiscriminate nation. As a comic abstraction of national character, Flagg's Uncle Sam nominated bodies for war. White bodies. Male and female bodies. Even Black bodies, by their absent presence. Whiteness here as in other rhetorical regimes functions as a universalizing logic, relegating racial and gender identities to the status of disruption and distraction.[59] All of these bodies are colored by the abstraction of an American creed recast in terms of dark yet enlightened American crudity.

This kind of abstraction is in line with a spirit of coerced voluntarism. Creel once likened indifference to warism and civic disaffection as a failure in the domestic "war of self-defense."[60] Flagg's Uncle Sam inflates the fear of consequences for misconduct. Many people responded to recruiting efforts with a form of vigilantism that enlisted everyday citizens as unofficial inspectors of each other's actions. The home front became a combat zone separated from, but nonetheless embroiled in, wartime activities. Those who did not enlist in the armed forces often joined organizations like the American Protective League. One obligation was to investigate "the character and loyalty of citizens and aliens," and so operate as vigilante "vice squads."[61] Unfortunately, a nationalistic guise gave way to bloody shirts when mob violence grew out of a guilt-stricken mindset that led to widespread surveillance, repressions of dissent, and legislative decrees like the Sedition Act. This same watchdog attitude was endemic to poster warfare and inextricable from a broader militarization of ordinary life. Posters were also caught up in the vicious circle of controlling a crowd and letting it loose, revealing even while concealing the ugly blur of boundaries between a nation-state that protects the interests of its members and the cruel acts it requires in its name. This image is what makes Flagg's Uncle Sam that much more cartoonish, since character coerced into being is caricature *in esse*: a truly false, albeit falsely true, impression. It is one thing to be a dutiful citizen. It is another to be a dupe of militaristic seduction. Flagg's Uncle Sam tempts an articulation of its audience not as a democratic polity but rather as a drove of patsies. This makes Uncle Sam the ultimate of tragic, if not pathetic, stooges—an object of humor drawn out by a bodily principle of monstrous travesty. If only he could see himself in the mirror and laugh.

The implication here is that support for war comes in (bellicose) actions, not words. In fact, Flagg's "I WANT YOU" image of Uncle Sam actually makes his December 29, 1917, cover of *Leslie's* surprisingly honest in its self-reflexive rhetorical force (fig. 9). The image is a prima facie warning to the very idea of a Kaiser, if not to Wilhelm II himself. "GET OFF THAT THRONE!" the caption reads. The familiarly disgruntled mien of Uncle Sam portends a call to action that emerges out of earlier calls to arms. This time, however, Uncle Sam is not pointing his finger; he is pointing a gun. One could read this through the eyes of a German soldier and imagine the command that the working end of a Colt semiautomatic pistol might have over an enemy. Or one could read this through the characterological lens of obligatory war service and so regard Uncle Sam as a menace sustaining democratic power through the threat of violent force. Once again, citizens as audiences

FIG. 9 James Montgomery Flagg, "GET OFF THAT THRONE!," 1917. Cover of *Leslie's Weekly*, December 29, 1917. Courtesy of Villanova University.

to Uncle Sam are reflected back as oddly undemocratic if unwilling to wage war, whereas Uncle Sam remains a projection of what author Margaret Sherwood in 1918 variously saw as "the grand national adventure of democracy," "the epic, sometimes comic epic, of republicanism," and the "inheritor and protector of the Rights of Man."[62] The trouble is that this cover art, which represents what the magazine advertises as "THE WAR IN PICTURES," mocks the culpability attached to civic duty with the insinuation that even democratic citizens only respond to calls to arms with a gun to their heads.

The grotesque reminder in this grandiosity appears in the hard lines between what goes with what and who relates versus who does not (and how). These lines are colored by the crookedness of collective amnesia and historical revisionism in a racialized, gendered Americanism. The paradox is that, to commit, one needed to be *recognized* as a legitimate citizen. Despite the participation of Blacks in the Civil War, many white public officials and soldiers alike attempted to ban them from military service even after the passage of the National Defense Act. A main suspicion was that, if Black soldiers proved themselves fit for battle, they could assert their fitness for participation in public life, maybe even compel it through the force of arms. Many African Americans, rightfully, had every intention of leveraging their service with the "ongoing fight for civil rights and social recognition."[63] The CPI—in what little poster propaganda it targeted to potential Black conscripts—demanded sacrifice for the nation rather than for any racial cause. The war was not about making America a safe haven of civil liberties and democracy for all. So, the Black community relied upon commercially produced posters to compete with "official" images that "aimed merely to stimulate African American support for the war without opening up the Pandora's box of American race relations."[64] There was an unofficial pictorial war that widened the national lens to imagine the realization of racial equality in a postwar American democracy. Jim Crow survived in combat divisions. Racial violence and discrimination continued even amid the fog of war and the fervor for national safeguards of American ideals.

Still, there was an almost comic plea that became something of a platitude in its reference to the mistakes made around equal citizenship, and the cultural battles yet to be fought and won or lost. "We return," wrote Du Bois in a May 1919 editorial for *The Crisis*, the official publication of the National Association for the Advancement of Colored People (NAACP). "We return from fighting. We return fighting. Make way for Democracy!"

This cry resonated in Du Bois's description of the sort of laughter that could fend off White Imperial Industry and its cadre of Beasts and Monsters that thrived on "cruel caricatures." It resonated in the miscalculations and misinterpretations around Du Bois's notion that war demands the oppressed to forget their "special grievances."[65] It resonated in his concerns about "democratic despotism" and the tensions between racial identifications and "love" for nation.[66] And it resonated in his idea that the United States was a "jest among nations."[67] But these caricatures break up when a look-and-laugh mentality allows one to "exalt the Lynched above the Lyncher and the Worker above the Owner and the Crucified above Imperial Rome."[68] Flagg's Uncle Sam is a cruel caricature, indeed.

Over and again, Uncle Sam is portrayed as a stalwart white male either coercing his heirs into battle or showing off his own aptitude for a fight. This reaffirms the separation of Black and white soldiers as emblematic of their segregation and further executes an out-of-sight-out-of-mind logic in sustaining the invisibility of Black Americans in popular propaganda. More bluntly, Uncle Sam *wanted* the support of his white troops, but he needed all the help he could get. Such a wartime sentiment is deep-seated in the Wilsonian declaration of war for democracy. Early in his presidency Wilson proclaimed that "the Negro" would no longer be a reason for civil strife, consigning the problem of civil rights to the sort of sectional and segregationist politics that only occurred in the trenches of official policymaking. In fact, Wilson brought a certain "southernness" back to Washington,[69] especially when on March 21, 1915, he entertained a private screening of D. W. Griffith's *The Birth of a Nation* at the White House and so endorsed the relevance of antebellum racism to his burgeoning culture of war. In so doing, Wilson proclaimed not the terrible truth of national caricatures but rather the fact that they upheld images and ideas about democracy as an Us–Them enterprise, whether in terms of enemy relations or racial and gendered lines of demarcation on the home front. A similar discriminatory logic could be applied to the official regard for immigrant populations. While Black men in the armed forces and Black women in the volunteer services faced the fallout of false promises and the misplaced hope for postwar change, immigrants faced the threat of physical internment at worst and the prospects of symbolically (and sometimes physically) violent processes of "Americanization" at best. The CPI's Bureau of Education sought to nationalize nonnatives while regulating the distinction between "responsible" speech and "free" speech. Enemy images coalesced characterizations of wayward combatants with the menace of *any* appearance of opposition to the American Way. Flagg's Uncle Sam projected cultural anxieties that were permitted to cover over the value of social and political differences in the name of combatting a crisis in national character. So it is that I come full circle to an aspect of Flagg's Uncle Sam but also his war artwork more broadly: its galvanization of a gendered combat logic.

Uncle Sam Is Dead, Long Live the Flagg Girl

Along with the war culture of World War I came inceptions of the "New Woman" and its accommodation of Progressive Era reformism. Visions of women at war (en)gender cultural norms of how they are supposed to see and be seen in wartimes and beyond.[70] As many cartoons and cartoonish images of women in World War I attest, traditionalist nationalisms presented the domestic space as a metaphor for the defense of a nation, making private war work in the home a public matter and, in turn, a measure of civic responsibility.[71] Institutions like the American Red Cross, the Women's Land Army, and others provided outlets for female citizens to carry out "soldierly" duties. The US Food Administration even trumpeted the work of "kitchen soldiers" who fulfilled food pledges and conservation efforts in order to alter private habits into public goods.[72] The social contract between the nation-state and its citizens was also a "gender contract."[73] It was a racial contract, too, given that the image of civic womanhood was largely an image of *white* women, even though Black women took on many of the same domestic services and clerical jobs as their white counterparts. The publicity of patriotic hysteria was folded into a sort of seduction to war that perverted the familial relations among male and female citizens. Likewise, it put forth a distortive, carnal conjuncture of feminine images and nationalistic appeals to military service. Consider Howard Chandler Christy's transformation of his infamous "Christy Girl" into a poster girl for combat. In one image, she flaunts a Navy jacket that fits loosely over her skin, baring part of her chest. A white sailor's hat rests atop her head and she gazes beyond the frame while gripping her jacket pockets with both hands. She conveys a sense of longing, which is affirmed by the text beside her: "GEE!! I WISH I WERE A MAN. I'D JOIN THE NAVY." The provocation is unapologetically chauvinistic in both its situation of the Christy Girl as an object of desire and in its less than subtle proposition that a man is not a man unless he enlists.[74] What is more, it appeals to the want of women to service their nation by shaming able-bodied males into a position of inferiority and inadequacy if they have not "volunteered" to serve. "BE A MAN

FIG. 10 Howard Chandler Christy, "I WANT YOU FOR THE NAVY," recruiting poster, 1917. Courtesy of the Library of Congress.

AND DO IT," they are told. And according to the 1918 *Annual Report of the Secretary of the Navy*, Christy's poster was incredibly popular.

Yet this poster suggests that women are best served or serviced by "real" men even though it is the nation itself that stands to benefit. Take a more explicit portrayal of the Christy Girl in full Navy garb, posing with her hands at her hips, an enticing look on her face, and wisps of blond hair spilling out from under her cap. Beside her in red text are the words of Flagg's Uncle Sam: "I Want YOU" (fig. 10). It is plausible to see a progressive image of a woman dressed as a naval officer and able to fight alongside men. However, there is much more in the way of sex appeal in a woman wearing her man's clothing if not engaging in a game of role play, as she beckons her not-yet-military boys to battle, completing the circle of enlisting men to serve their nation if they are ever to be of service to women. Christy's images also demonstrated that when a woman is not seducing men she should be standing up as a public servant in the spirit of America. In Red Cross posters specifically, Christy pictured the national character of womanhood in the body of a beauty who nursed male soldiers. The proper woman either gave in to public service by succumbing to the demands of wartime norms on the home front or did her part behind enemy lines. This war-work of women played into hysterical fantasies that troubled normative conditions of sexuality, vocation, dress, sociopolitical status, and even affective display. It is useful, then, to imagine the Christy Girl as something of a revised version of the Gibson Girl insofar as she was a caricature of femininity and female beauty. The Christy Girl was neither suffragist nor radical feminist. She was a woman who wielded both her sex appeal and her newfound stature as cornerstones for the fatal attractions of armed conflict. As such, she stood as an American type that was unabashedly aligned with the demands and expectations of wartime image makers and the cultural institutions that either influenced them or ended up as their byproduct. Through her and other expressions of female character, American warfare became a measure of what a man would do for a woman, what a woman would do for a real man, and what a woman would do if only she was man enough. The Christy Girl was an ideal type. There was also a "Flagg Girl"—a comic anamorphosis of American womanhood.

The Flagg Girl began as an apparent reference to the "new" womanhood of New Englanders combined with the national stereotype of foolish Americans. She is preserved as sketches in Flagg's first illustrated book, *Yankee Girls Abroad* (1900), with an air of "serenity, kindness, courage, humor, and passion" that might encapsulate "America itself: seductive and courageous, proud and hopeful."[75] She also captures the humor of gender wars and gendered enticements to warfare. Flagg demonstrated the combat imperative to align nationalistic fantasies with the good reasons and common sense so resident in forgeries of the feminine. By the time of his portrayal of Uncle Sam, Flagg was actually better known as an illustrator for women's magazines like *Cosmopolitan* than publications of visual humor like *Life* and *Judge*. Though it would take him until after the war to earn a reputation as a legitimate caricaturist, Flagg made a prewar career of producing "saucy" antitheses to Gibson/Christy Girls.[76] He did this by distorting "traditional" early twentieth (that is, Victorian) images with a modern notion of women as objects of desire, and as American embodiments of vanity, arrogance, and mischief. That Flagg conceived of his own ideal type in the guise of the Yankee is telling. On one hand, the Yankee is a British-made object of ridicule for colonial Americans. On the other, Yankees evolved in humorous fables and cultural folklore from Brother Jonathan through Uncle Sam. According to Constance Rourke, the Yankee is a historical "wanderer, given to swapping."[77] In Flagg's hands, the All-American Girl is a caricature. The aforementioned cover of *Judge* is a case in point, but

FIG. 11 James Montgomery Flagg, "A Jill for Jack," 1912. Cover of *Judge*, October 26, 1912.

so is an even earlier rendering of "A Jill for Jack," which revealed a Christy-esque woman dressed as a sailor and standing as a showpiece for male eyes. Jill here is almost tomboyish, swapping her normal feminine attire for the wardrobe of a yeomanette (fig. 11).

In another cover from the same year, entitled "The Target," Flagg drew Jill holding up a white card with a red heart in the middle. The heart is surrounded by bullet holes. A caption reads, "You'll have to do better than that!" The combination of courtship and live-fire makes a perverse imbrication of sex drives and death drives. Most significant, though, is that these images exist as frontispieces for a satirical magazine, evoking a sense of humor that extends from Flagg's Yankee doodles to his wartime comic pictures. Additionally, they encircle visual caricatures of women as "the identical figures of mistress, wife, and mother,"[78] variously cropping up as the wartime seductress, the companion turned compatriot, and the personification of a new American world order. Flagg therefore reworked the urge to satisfy an oddly sexualized appetite for combat and comradeship. The humor of these comic seductions lies in the caricatures as expositions of contradictions in portraying potential male soldiers as *both* protectors of women *and* as their violators, and then again as the butts of their witticisms about mobilization.

In the visual humor of the Flagg Girl is a caricature of rhetorical courtship. There is, after all, a comic quality to Flagg's "conflation of vamping and prostitution," especially in light of his assertion that "Women *should* be coquettes."[79] Recruitment is a lot like courtship. And courtship, as Kenneth Burke argues, makes propagandistic salesmanship into something like "sexual expressions," entailing "seduction, jilting, prostitution, promiscuity," and even rape.[80] Rhetorical courtship occurs in acts of persuasion—and in what Burke might call the "comic primness" of caricature.[81] Flagg's Girl, like his Uncle Sam, is built on the pretense of being resistant to the vulgar, obscene, and licentious, except that primness is a ploy in his visual humor. Seductive appeals allow for strange communions and comic counteractions to estrangement. Seductions embedded in wartime caricatures of national character exploit the sometimes wanton requirements of war. The comicality of Flagg's sexualized imagery therefore expresses a sense that even the most pronounced claims to national character are wrought by contradictions. The comic looking glass seems to reflect a powerful love of country, but it is just as much a lust for nationalism that betrays the civic impieties of a body politic. Through the popular and pervasive Christy Girls, there is an image of the *femme maison* as a caricature of the *femme fatale*, being drawn into the dangers of armed conflict while getting titillated by the prospect of redefining the feminine. Flagg projects yet another paradox in his caricature of enticement as a *femme fatale*'s means for disarming people and tempting them into sexual activity or other debaucheries. As Claudia Consolati claims, the *femme fatale* "usually represents a threat for the heterosexual, male-dominated status quo."[82] Throughout World War I, militarism was a cultural mechanism for categorizing and marking the roles of individuals, most obviously when women wanted to do "men's" jobs. Flagg mocked armed passions with a *femme comica*.

Ultimately, because Flagg's women are offered up as decoys for what Luce Irigiray might dub "an economy of power and war,"[83] they deform popular conceptions of proper female national character. From the playfulness of his depiction of a Jill for Jack to the gravity of a *femme comica*, Flagg reroutes gendered visions of how war might violate the freedoms and liberties of the nation, and its personifications. This is in part done through images of Columbia and Uncle Sam not as active agents of seduction but as passive proxies to and for whom things are done. It is also in part accomplished through the notion that citizens actually call figures like

Columbia and Uncle Sam into being, and not the other way around. Flagg's caricatures expose the distortions in other pictures that show forth an art of war as an art of sublimation. Caricature was so popular in World War I because it enabled the redirection of images and ideas that were deemed out of character toward the reasoned madness of fostering a national war footing. Its reproduction of rhetorical violence accommodated an aggressive innocence to establish nonconformity as itself a sign of mania, and so as a sign of weakness, infidelity, and depravity. To give in and not to resist temptation was to be firm in one's convictions. This is why, in hindsight, Uncle Sam himself looks like he is looking in the comic looking glass, seeing the contradictions of fights for freedoms in the humor of wars for peace. Behind every man of arms in this look is a woman arming him with the passion to take her up on the offers of rewards promised by military service. Or, following Flagg, masculinity and femininity are coeval characterizations of the good, bad, and ugly activities that convince a citizenry to go to war.

Conclusion: The Crucible of Caricature

Uncle Sam, in many ways, is a consequence of war. Since World War I, he has helped to constitute US public culture from historical states of exception through antiwar demonstrations to the diffusion of his image into everyday depictions of politics, pop art, and commerce. During the Second World War, Flagg's Uncle Sam was revived for selfsame recruitment posters and was complemented with another popular image by Flagg of the nation personified rolling up his sleeves and clutching a wrench amid the proclamation that the "Jap" was next. Uncle Sam was later featured in a poster wherein he holds his finger to his lips while pronouncing that no one should discuss military machinations. Yet another poster has him trading his top hat and coat for a military uniform and cap, conveying with a closed mouth that to "defend American freedom" is "everybody's job." In fact, despite postwar cries for "disarmament, pacifism, and isolationism,"[84] Uncle Sam retained—or at least reclaimed—his rhetorical force as a (comic) picture of US American national character. Uncle Sam's likeness traverses efforts to recruit American hearts, minds, and bodies in the zeal for war. This is evident in the infamous "I Want Out" poster from 1971, which mocks the "I Want YOU" poster by portraying Uncle Sam as a war-weary soldier in Vietnam. It is also evident in the image of a Black Uncle Sam created by civil rights activists in 1976. Surely, the transhistorical, iconic durability of Uncle Sam is worthy of consideration in itself. However, it is important here to dwell on the humorous form of national character for which he stands as an archetypal wartime caricature.

Artist and pioneering chalk-talker Frank Beard pronounced in 1887 that the United States had entered the "Age of Caricature." This pronouncement attended his reputation for creating pictorial monologues by using drawings as substitutes for speech. Similarly, Winsor McCay, a vaudeville artist and animator in the early twentieth century, used these sorts of performances to punctuate his own poster work and newspaper illustrations. Beard's rationale was simple: public culture had so accommodated the role of the ridiculous that character could not be comprehended outside the visual art of distortion. Caricature, wrote Beard, "is the exaggeration of character,"[85] meaning that it is always *ideas* that are caricatured and the *truth* of a matter that gives overemphasis its rhetorical force. This account resonates with Creel's contention that war justified discursive excess and pictorial overkill in order to advertise the "*real* America" with "the carrying power of truth,"[86] and with Walter Lippman's assumption that caricatures and distortions serve as "forms of perception" that enforce "a certain character on the data of our senses."[87] Then, there is Beerbohm's conceptualization of caricature as a crucible, which animates the framework for my argument about Flagg's Uncle Sam, not to mention his American Girl. But, while Beerbohm saw caricature as an art of appearances alone, the depths of character revealed in surfaces make apparent its status as a crucible—that is, as a site for seeing something or someone in a mirror, distortedly. In the spring of 2018, the National WWI Museum and Memorial opened an exhibit entitled *Crucible: Life and Death in 1918*. With the description of what was on display was a definition of the word "crucible," which is taken from the *Oxford English Dictionary*. A crucible is a "situation of severe trial, or in which different elements interact, leading to the creation of something new."[88] It would be hard to offer a better definition of caricature except to say that, in caricature, the change brought about often comes from seeing some self or other differently. It comes from seeing some self or other in the comic looking glass. Caricatures of national character are so compelling because they provide comic looks at collective selfhood, and so alternative views of those core characteristics that define who we are and what we do. They offer insight into how wartime ordeals are contained rhetorically (in and by images and ideas) and materially (in and by the people that make war and its consequences a lived reality). The crucible of war cultures provokes the possibility of revealing our "true" characters.

Uncle Sam in World War I became at once the personification of a nation and the caricature of a model for American citizenship. Instead of drawing on America's emancipatory tradition to express a form of democratic practice worth fighting for, though, Flagg's Uncle Sam revealed the dark underbelly of American democracy in the specter of its character as a nation-state of disgrace. War cultures almost demand that we point fingers so we can deal with the devils we do and do not know. World War I amplified a prevailing nationalistic ideology of self-determination, which counteracted the political philosophy of a burgeoning Soviet Union. It remains in US American memory as a contact point for imagining the stakes of President Wilson's fourteen points for world peace and the eventual formation of American expeditionary forces. As a formative moment in the advertisement of US national character via good intentions marred by bad faiths, it remains a touchstone for Cold War politics and nationalistic cultural mentalities that followed. The war culture of World War I presumed American democracy as a pretext for military interventionism and global policies of containment. If Uncle Sam is a crucial caricature of this culture, then the looking glass of the American Century and its early onset is a dirty, distorted mirror. Perhaps this is why World War I might be seen as constitutive of the "dark age of cartooning," despite Hecht's glorification of caricature in cartoon publicity.[89] Perhaps this, too, is why comic anamorphosis can visualize war as the dark antistrophos to democracy, and the culpability of doing one's civic duty.

It is difficult to keep a sense of humor about Uncle Sam. The conduct of war relies so much on caricatures as cultural fictions for realizing actual realities about a national selfhood and the nation-state that sustains it. Throughout US participation in World War I, Flagg's Uncle Sam insinuated expectations about how to see, think, speak, work, and be. He made nationalism and patriotism into visible characteristics of a democratic citizenry. The problem here is not caricature or even appeals to national character per se. It is the rhetorical mobilization—and, to be sure, sexualization and racialization—of shame and guilt as a collective *objet petit a*, or a special object that lets war renew a nation by travestying (in order to turn on) the tautology that war is war. Humor is an accessory to the rhetorical *objet petit a*, transferring nationalistic desires onto cartoon images that both misrepresent and deliver the truth about the lost object of national character. It is no surprise to find a certain maleness in the fantasies and follies that come with this arrangement. As Walter J. Ong attests, humor tends to imply "the male world," common as it is in images of "gross and boisterous" struggles over identity.[90] Flagg's Uncle Sam resonates with this approach to male-oriented humor, but its gendered appeal is disrupted when considered for its uncomfortable androgynies and its close association to womanhood as the impetus to laugh at real men of war. This disruption is what enables shame and guilt to get projected not onto an Other but onto a Self. It is also what enables us to look upon Uncle Sam as the comic material for reconceiving US American national character vis-à-vis democratic goodness in warmaking.

Uncle Sam is incomprehensible outside of war culture. While he is flexible in his reappropriations, he is quite *in*flexible in his connection to armed conflict, cultural struggles, and combative appeals. He is grounded by the imaginative visual construction of what is not necessarily "there" and those characteristics that are amplified by wartime conditions themselves. On top of this, Uncle Sam does not just speak for, or stand in for, but also speaks *at*, indicating the sort of character that is expected of his audience. This makes him as much a visual articulation as a characterization, connecting historical ideas about national interests to historically situated images of its "true" body politic. The connections that are crafted in caricatures of Uncle Sam enable the sorts of exaggerations of national character laid out in this chapter, which accommodate fanaticism and jingoism, chauvinism and egalitarianism, and latent prejudices that are nonetheless put in full view. Such exaggerations include the notion that audiences should be ashamed to disidentify with a nation at war; that it is un-American to possess characteristics antithetical to officially sanctioned dispositions; that audiences should feel guilty of the cognitive treason entailed in resisting racist, ethnocentric portrayals of enemies without and within; and that a war footing necessitates a warring frame of mind. To see Flagg's Uncle Sam as a caricature is to see caricature as an ur-form of comic re-presentation.

The humor of Flagg's Uncle Sam exposes the imposition of cultural investments on the body of a pictorial image. In resisting identification with a particular person, he transfers the burden of national character to "the people" as both audience and executor of war. Furthermore, he shows forth the comic art of caricature as a means of insinuating that a "true" character lurks in the depths of surface features, and that a distorted looking glass can expose it. Characteristics are not only defining features or peculiar qualities; they are expectations for attitudes, actions, and articulations. They are also propensities of a nation that, when personified, can harbor its own resentments. Perhaps Flagg's Uncle Sam gets at this with his finger pointing. Or perhaps a contemporary illustrator Alex Ross captures it best with his 2009 cover for the *Village Voice*, which recasts Flagg's Uncle Sam with all of his cartoonish realism only rendered anew, now giving the middle finger.

Dr. Seuss and His Wacky War on American Culture

2.

The famed Beat writer, visual artist, and lifelong cat lover William S. Burroughs once wrote about how Nazi SS officers were initiated into the upper echelons of the *Schutzstaffel*. Over the course of a month, an officer was tasked with nurturing a cat. He would feed it, cuddle it, and in effect foster it into a pet. Then, at the end of the month, the SS officer was ordered to gouge out the animal's eyes. The rationale was this: one "achieves superhuman status by performing some atrocious, revolting, subhuman act."[1] In another anecdote, Burroughs made no bones about his feelings for cat haters. "Cat hate," he wrote, "reflects an ugly, stupid, loutish, bigoted spirit. There can be no compromise with this Ugly Spirit."[2] Given Burroughs's penchant for the bleakest of satire, though, one wonders if there is any room for a *comic* spirit in this ugliness.

The wondrous work of Dr. Seuss—pen name for the zany, quasi-surrealist writer and artist and famed children's book author and illustrator Theodor Geisel—stands as a rhetorical embodiment of both the catlike cunning in Burroughs and the comicality of a Burroughsesque cat. Notwithstanding some disturbing scenes from *Junky* (1953) that could make one think otherwise, Burroughs adored cats. He did not just like them for the sake of animal fellowship. He liked their characteristics. He appreciated their beautiful rage. Their awkward grace. Their reputation for so thoroughly cleaning themselves. Their willful abandon in flights of playful fancy. Their killer instincts. Their gentleness. Their independence. Their role as our "Familiars," if not our "psychic companions." And, à la Mark

Twain, their amoral moralism. Now, Burroughs and Dr. Seuss were World War II–era contemporaries, but they were not associates or even friends. If they shared anything it was an affinity for the madcap (and, indeed, the mad *cat*)—and, perhaps, a certain dark humor that for one is manifest as droll saturnalia and for the other shows forth as comic phantasia. I call this reference to mind because Dr. Seuss eventually took on the cognomen "The Cat Behind the Hat," whereby the figure of the cat became something of an alter ego for a man that the president of Dartmouth College in 1955 dubbed "the creator of fanciful beasts."[3] I call it to mind, too, because such fancifulness and beastliness animate the comic abstractions of national character that pervade the caricatures of Selves and Others in Dr. Seuss's entire oeuvre. Dr. Seuss's wartime caricatures deal with the sometimes strange, if not deranged, mergers that must take place for persons to take up nationalistic principles as the ideational analogues to identity politics. Put differently, Dr. Seuss's artwork suggests that if some Other can provide a mirror for Ourselves, then caricature is no less the gritty lenses in ways of seeing collective selfhood.

The figure of the cat is an apt contact point in this setup. Cats have a storied history in myths and metaphors of curiosity, mischievousness, regeneration, and even languor. Dr. Seuss's own Cat in the Hat exemplifies the feline trickster that makes messes but also cleans them up, sometimes for the fun of it and sometimes for the purpose of taking the message to Garcia, so to speak. The humor here also sometimes reworks what Philip Nel describes as Dr. Seuss's "racial imagination," which coalesced the discomfiting stuff of Jim Crow, minstrelsy, and blackface into an "embedded racist caricature in Geisel's unconscious" but nevertheless opened up the possibilities of caricature's comic disruptions.[4] Cats have numerous hallmarks in this sort of comic arena. Behemoth is a shapeshifting, therianthropic, ungodly fiend of a creature at the center of Mikhail Bulgakov's 1937 novel *The Master and Margarita*. But he was also a brazen jokester who regularly played the fool and the beastly "man" of humor among the retinue of Woland, a demonic professor who serves as executor to a cultural grapple with good and evil. Then there is Lewis Carroll's Cheshire Cat, who appears as an illusionist with regard to the rules in Wonderland. In each instance, the cat is an idea attached to an image. The fatuity to be found in Faustian bargains, for instance, brings the comicality of Behemoth's clownings around into sharp relief. The grin without the face invokes the mirth of going mad as well as the power in seeing madness in oneself. The comic displacements inherent to a maudlin mouser and a crazy, discarnating grimalkin also signify a relationship between the thing and the other thing, the Self and the Other. We are what we are not, in other words, just as the Cheshire Cat is Dinah, but in a "world of alter egos and mirror images" that seems to parallel an alternate reality.[5]

In steps Dr. Seuss, who was seen as a weirdo in the World War II era and often rejected as an outsider with an odd sense of humor who dabbled "in far too much fantasy and far too little status quo moralism."[6] Dr. Seuss *in arte* very often seems to be the cat making mischief or serving as the subject of wonder.[7] His art was the art of self-caricature in that it entailed caricatures of the very image and idea of selfhood. The Self is redrawn *as* the Other, recast as a comic abstraction. This was apparent in an illustration Dr. Seuss drew of himself and contributed to the July 6, 1957, issue of the *Saturday Evening Post* in which he is a cat in a hat seen in side profile from the neck up affecting a side-eye.[8] His attention to selfhood is overt, too, in his nonsensical imagery that somehow makes sense of an absurd world. Dr. Seuss's caricatures display a simple wisdom about human conduct and cultural consciousness that can be missed if one gets lost in the rhetorical weight of weirdness.[9] Accordingly, Dr. Seuss follows the line of Twain, channeling the cat as a comic foil for grappling with the "atrocity of atrocities, War,"[10] and its effects (or *defects*) on national character.

Indeed, the Seussian worldview is wackiest in the caricatures that fill out a collection of wartime editorial cartoons appearing in the newspaper *PM*, from January 1941 through January 1943. Philip Nel has argued that World War II occasioned the cultural moment that really made Theodor Seuss Geisel into Dr. Seuss.[11] For sure, Dr. Seuss was inflamed by the rise of Hitler and the escalation of Nazism. Both represented human cruelty and out-of-the-ordinary worldviews beyond even his wildest fantasies. Both also constituted a real threat to the American Way. Equally as true is the disgust Dr. Seuss held for those Americans in whom he saw an Ugly Spirit of anti-warism, which he took as a sign of human failure in the fight against Evil and Folly. So, before he became an icon of children's literature, Dr. Seuss traded in his childlike imagination for a more catlike, or crafty, art of caricaturing American war culture. He did so with what he described as "frantic fervor,"[12] regularly targeting rodent "Japs" and serpentine Nazis and the Devil incarnate Hitler, and thus feeding into rampant, racialized rhetorics of nonhuman animalism (including references of enemy others as rats, apes, and imps) so prevalent in World War II discourse. Dr. Seuss likewise alluded to elements of foreign disease and entomological warfare, especially with images of infectious agents and gross insects. Yet, as ardently, he drew American Others as Appeasers, Isolationists, Weepers, Fifth Columnists, and more. Plainly, Dr. Seuss used the Good War as a bleak occasion to put American national character in the comic looking glass.

This chapter attends to the animal, machine, and foul oddities in the wartime caricatures of Dr. Seuss. The humor in them is uncomfortable. It is based on the rhetorical act of simultaneously identifying and *dis*identifying with national character in the name of War against Evil. Like Burroughs's or Twain's cat, Dr. Seuss uses caricature to look down on his fellow countrymen. He does so first and foremost with bird imagery. Birds are central to US American iconography and ideology. They are providential. The bird is also, in Twain's words, the one creature that inspires a "wriggle" in the cat, provoking the spirit of action most powerfully when the spirit of lassitude seems to prevail. With bird-like creatures as well as other monstrosities, Dr. Seuss caricatures everything from pacifism to nativist politics. In the end, though, the humor in his wartime artwork reveals the idea of going to war as a means of safeguarding US American democracy. His comic alterity urges a way of seeing the world inside out, and of judging people for how they live out their principles in public. Does it sometimes use the comic license to exploit a state of exception in promoting racial, ethnic, gender, and other stereotypical sources of affective zeal in collective selfhood? Certainly. Does Dr. Seuss sometimes come off as a warmonger? Yes. But his humor is ultimately about uniting against the dire consequences of division and defeatism. That the United States should wage war against the Axis powers was a foregone conclusion for Dr. Seuss. Madcap were those who willfully ignored the threat of a mad brute and his *Kultur*. Out of whack were those who ran afoul of foundational principles of freedom and equality, such as people like Charles A. Lindbergh, institutions like America First, and newspapers like the *Chicago Tribune*. With a sense of humor full of rhetorical weight and whimsy, Dr. Seuss was able "to prod an unchecked nation getting too comfortable with itself, and viciously question the principles at its core."[13] The result is a view of World War II–era American national character in the comic looking glass, wherein odd amalgamations recreate even as they disconcert images of This and That, Self and Other, Us and Them. In Dr. Seuss's wartime caricatures, US Americans are cats that have eaten canaries. To see this is to first see 1940s American war culture a bit out of whack.

Seeing World War II Through the Wrong End of the Telescope

Meet Sam-Bird. He is but one of Dr. Seuss's strange caricatures of wartime national character. While his morphology is unclear, he is clearly an eagle that has become just an ostrich by another name, tricking US citizens into believing that democracy at any level is at all noninterventionist. To preserve the democratic spirit, for Dr. Seuss, is to take action, even if through war as a last resort.

This action orientation is the peculiar burden that democracy places on the proposition of war, and likewise the burden that war places on democratic principles. While democracy offers "the best political medium through which to incorporate strife into interdependence and care into strife,"[14] war intensifies the projection of democratic selfhood as itself a site of conflict—in nativistic terms (like those of isolationists who fulminated about American internationalism), racial terms (like those in discourses of "The Jewish Problem" and "Race Hatred"), and so on. Sam-Bird embodies this conflict. In a cartoon from late September 1941, Sam-Bird stares into a carnival mirror—an "Appeaser's Mirror"—to discover that he is a decrepit, battered, and bruised old bird with a long beard and a wooden crutch. "Jeepers!" the bird exclaims. "Is that Me?" Above the mirror is a placard that reads: "Take one look at yourself and despair!" Dr. Seuss makes a direct appeal here to the wake-up call he imagined Americans getting, and the kinds of things Flagg imagined wartime cartoonists making people see, when they realized the consequences of pacification as a *modus vivendi* for attaining peace. He also abstracts an image of the United States nation-state as seen through the eyes of others. The mirror shows Sam-Bird his true self. This was a projection of what could have been. It was also a provocation to consider whether or not an idealized reflection of national character is actually an ugly one. Peace might be the ideal, in other words, but a "good" war might be the only way to take care of a "bad" reality. Dr. Seuss's wartime caricatures disfigure organizing principles. Unpopular as it might be for ideals of democratic agonism as an antidote to armed conflict, Dr. Seuss's point was that entry into World War II would guarantee the continuation of democracy, or at least give it a fighting chance. Differences in opinion be damned when it comes to wartime Americanism, he seemed to be saying. The American Republic comes first.

Something weird happened the month before Sam-Bird saw his distorted reflection. The HMS *Prince of Wales* was moored in Placentia Bay, Newfoundland, alongside the USS *McDougal*. A meeting was to be held between Winston Churchill and Franklin D. Roosevelt. It eventually resulted in the Atlantic Charter. At a certain point on the day of the meeting, "Blackie" walked across the gangplank as if to board the American vessel (and this as the American national anthem bellowed from the decks of the British battleship). Seeing this, Churchill hurried to the footway to prevent Blackie from going aboard. An iconic photograph captures Churchill petting Blackie's head. Blackie was a "ship's cat." Such cats have ancient origins, serving as the spirit animals that were supposed to ward off bad luck. Practically, a seafaring cat can be used for pest control, keeping vermin (like rats) from damaging a ship's infrastructure, getting into the crew's food stores, and spreading disease. Symbolically, cats like Blackie embody a rhetoric of friend-enemy relations, protecting a ship (of state) against being damaged from within while at the same time projecting an air of self-protection. They also embody a comic relationship between humans and nonhuman animals, which Churchill once expressed: "Cats look down on us," he reportedly said while giving the fiancé of his daughter, Mary, a tour of Chartwell Farm. The same could be said of Dr. Seuss's condemnatory caricatures.

Together, this catlike spirit and characters like Sam-Bird establish a basis for seeing Dr. Seuss's wartime caricatures with a sense of humor that combines what George Creel called the "Gospel of Americanism" and the "war-will" of a democratic people. One from October 1941, just a few months after Blackie walked the gangplank in Newfoundland, features a cat looking on in dismay as a woman in an America First blouse reads a book to two young children. The book was *Adolf the Wolf*, with the head of a wolfish Hitler gracing its cover. The woman reads that the fascist wolf "chewed up the children and spit out their bones." This was okay, she assured, because they were "Foreign Children." For the nativist committee that pushed a noninterventionist approach to US entry in the war on grounds of national interest, many critics at the time saw the America First agenda as isolationist at best and pro-Nazi at worst. Dr. Seuss took a different tack, portraying nationalistic selfishness—particularly in the face of a war propelled by the tenets of *Nationalsozialismus*—as self-defeating for both the survival of democracy and the sanctity of American national character. It was akin, in Dr. Seuss's words, to seeing the world through the wrong end of the telescope.

Of course, Dr. Seuss *demanded* the sort of fantastical thinking that sometimes requires "wrongheaded" perspectives. But his view was toward the shortsightedness he saw in those who could not or would not imagine the relationship between a democratic ethos at home (and abroad) and the threat of global warfare. So, he strove to telescope an alternative viewpoint, which is to say that he worked to portray the collisions, mergers, and forces of togetherness that telescoping can also entail. To see through the distorted lens of caricature, then, is to adopt a far-seeing perspective while maintaining a sense that things afar are closer to home than they might appear. Dr. Seuss was goaded on by the prospect of a global order organized by Hitler. He viewed Nazism as the antithesis to Americanism, particularly given its subjugation of a people under the iron umbrella of an omnipotent State and a supreme leader. Fascism embodies a myth of the Nation, lock, stock, and barrel. As Roger Griffin describes it, fascism is a palingenetic form of populist ultranationalism.[15] Before the United States entered World War II, there were fears expressed by some cultural commentators and reporters for the American press (among them, famed minister Halford E. Luccock) that if fascism ever made it to America it would be called not fascism but rather Americanism. Dr. Seuss reflected these expressions. He was fearful that wartime notions of American exceptionalism were doing less to re-enliven the democratic roots of character, civic duty, and nationhood than the scourge of racialized, ethnocentric identitarian politicking. Surely he understood that an American Empire could look and feel egalitarian even as it stirred the body politic into a war frenzy in the name of peace and liberty. However, Dr. Seuss saw troublous predicaments in using the proclaimed foundational characteristics of US Americanism as pretexts for keeping Great Democracy to itself. He therefore saw homespun war politics as tragically farcical when Americans seemed to imagine that democracy is *not* always (if ever) what Henry Hazlitt dubbed in September 1940 an "alternative to war."[16] For Dr. Seuss, entry into world war as a pledge of allegiance to the American Way was what the tripartite of relief, recovery, and reform was for Roosevelt in 1932: "a call to arms."[17] Dr. Seuss's caricatures thus took on the ethos of Burroughs's cat. It was not enough for a person of American character to simply seek safety at home or even, if enlisted in the war efforts, to provide services; one must offer the Self. This is how Dr. Seuss telescoped his view of national character. Before delving into even more details of Dr. Seuss's caricatures, it is worth dwelling on this telescopic view of comic imagery.

The culture of war underwrites such a Seussian comic framework. If US entry into the First World War was predicated on making the world "safe for democracy," in World War II the organizing principle of democracy itself had to undergo a solemn militarization. The official national stance was antiwar. But in a fireside chat on December 29, 1940, President Roosevelt acknowledged that war production was simply "realistic military policy," expressing an unhappy truth that implements of combat could create an "arsenal of democracy." Hence the rise of the America First Committee (AFC) and its principles of national fortification and armed neutrality. The AFC was founded in September 1940. Its most vocal and high profile member was Charles A. Lindbergh, who used his fame from aviation as a takeoff for serving as the advocacy group's chief spokesperson. Other notables included Senators Gerald P. Nye and Burton K. Wheeler, and publishers Robert R. McCormick (of the *Chicago Tribune*) and Joseph M. Patterson (of the *New York Daily News*). These individuals became some of Dr. Seuss's leading stooges, exemplifying the so-called Fifth Column, its subversion of popular opinion, and the antidemocratic orientations of nativist groups. Dr. Seuss sought what James T. Sparrow calls a "warfare state," or a sense of nationalistic readiness and a mass of citizens already initiated in a democratic war culture. For Dr. Seuss, going to war in the name of democracy meant protecting the home front from those anti-war factions who, with their live-and-let-die attitudes, were no better than foreign enemies. In 1941, some newspaper editors such as Benjamin Frazier and Joseph Stanley of the *New York Times* were dubbing isolationism a form of cultural imperialism and civic complacency a manifestation of national betrayal. These sentiments echo those of Herbert S. Houston, executive committee member for the League to Enforce Peace during the First World War, who saw the resolution of war as an agent of Americanism. The kind of patriotism and self-sacrifice that comes with democratic organization is, as the argument goes, also necessary in warfare.

Everything with regard to isolationism changed after the attack on Pearl Harbor (notwithstanding Kristallnacht). In late 1939, public discourse in the United States circled around Roosevelt's "military Magna Carta" and how that might square with the image of a peaceful, democratic America. Roosevelt promised to keep the United States out of war, even though news outlets like *Life* and writers like Henry Luce (who thought that isolationism represented everything wrong with American nationalism) questioned his neutral stance,[18] and even though rumors of a Fifth Column were buttressed by warnings about "espionage, sabotage, and subversion as favored devices of the ruthless Huns."[19] The bombs from the Imperial Japanese Navy Air Service were dropped on Pearl Harbor on December 7, 1941. American isolationism ended on December 8. By August 16, 1942, the head of the Office of Facts and Figures and Assistant Director to Elmer Davis of the Office of War Information (OWI), Archibald MacLeish, proclaimed it dead. World War II quickly became a "new" war for democracy. Armed conflict was a necessary evil.

Dr. Seuss's wartime caricatures appeared in *PM* (1940–48), a left-leaning newspaper that abhorred a print culture built on advertising dollars and shaped its editorial prerogatives toward the public interest. It was backed by investor Marshall Field III and started by Ralph Ingersoll, a former managing editor of *Time*, *Fortune*, and *Life*. Emphasizing drama, storytelling, opinion, and pictures, *PM* combined a nineteenth-century spirit of editorial reporting primarily through "picture news" with "the wit of a magazine and the pace of a daily."[20] Still, it was essentially a medium for supporting labor unions, propounding New Deal politics, expressing a raw hatred of Hitler, and reviling anything or anyone that seemed to trade in democracy for fascism—especially under the guise of a nativist, antiwar doctrine.[21] *PM* promoted a view of national character that countervailed the OWI and its "idealistic characterizations of American life."[22] The OWI shaped public opinion, not unlike the Committee on Public Information. But it also had the burden of ill repute that hung over the comparable propaganda arm during World War I. James Montgomery Flagg's version of Uncle Sam was alive and well, along with its I-Want-YOU appeal. The genre of "picture news," however, had become a cultural industry by the middle of 1942, with cartoons providing a resource for "humoring" the daily chronicle of complex happenings at home and abroad. Caricatures provided a distorted mirror for seeing civic selves in that chronicle.

Caricature made war real for those not on the battlefront and so complemented "the new visibility of the labor of *cultural* production."[23] *PM* was part of the Popular Front. Public artists like Dr. Seuss were cultural workers as much as they were citizens engaged in war work. Dr. Seuss's caricatures channeled a growing nationalistic image of the "democratic character of American culture" in the sense that "democracy begins at home."[24] His caricature campaign was associated with an apparatus of newspapers, film studios, and magazines that converted an idea of "cultural democracy" into a culture of war.[25] Fantastical as they were, Dr. Seuss's caricatures offered a way of showing and telling war culture for what it was. This does not mean that Dr. Seuss avoided the slippery slope into ethnocentrism and racial prejudice. As Richard H. Minear laments, "it is a surprise that a person who denounces anti-Black racism and anti-Semitism so eloquently can be oblivious of his own racist treatment of Japanese and Japanese Americans."[26] Granted. But it is doubtful that Dr. Seuss was oblivious. For one, while he certainly gave himself over to the demonology of Us–Them battle cries, Dr. Seuss came around to the better angels of his nature in making appeals to what he saw as the freedom-loving family of human beings.[27] For two, he made a conscious artistic choice to exploit the rhetorical trappings of comic morphology. The examples that follow make manifest just how powerful depictions of "foreign" others can be for positive depictions of a nonetheless abject national character. Such is the burden of caricature. Such is also the backdrop for Dr. Seuss's development as a caricature artist.

Dr. Seuss has a somewhat strange professional biography. He grew up in Springfield, Massachusetts. After college, he became an illustrator for publications like *Life*, *Judge*, the *Saturday Evening Post*, and *Vanity Fair*. At one point Dr. Seuss did a stint in graduate school at Oxford University but dropped out to become a full-time cartoonist. Soon thereafter he gave himself the title "Doctor" and eventually earned the moniker Poet Laureate of Nonsense. Dr. Seuss was something of a struggling artist until, in the mid-1930s, he dabbled in some nascent political cartooning with a mostly forgotten comic strip, *Hejji*. At the center is a young boy who sails aboard a birdlike creature to a strange place, the Land of Baako, which—as one strip tells it—is essentially shut off from the world and made up of human and nonhuman creatures with "strange ways," like whales that swim in lakes at the tops of volcanoes. But even in its nonsense the strip is not so strange. For instance, upon arriving in the Land of Baako, the young boy is captured by the local people, dubbed a "foreign fool," and brought before The Mighty One who is reputed to be in a "dark, dark mood." The tale ends well enough, and the boy reconciles with the rajah. Still, it amounts to a not so subtle account of how human beings get along with one another. *Baako*, as it happens, is a Hindi word meaning loose tongue. Here, it is a metaphor for the cultural politics of "race, representation, and power."[28] It also bespeaks the comic confusions that Dr. Seuss elsewhere portrayed in paintings like "The Tower of Babble," which was done sometime between 1930 and 1940.[29] This cartoon image encompasses much of the visual imagery of *Hejji* and depicts a confused world full of odd beasts, weird contraptions, bizarre material conditions, and yet all too familiar stratifications. It is almost a metacaricature of caricature itself as a *confusio linguarum*, or confusion of tongues, mocking the sorry state of human affairs in a manner made more significant given its creation in the chiasma of two world wars.

These comic politics of depiction drive Dr. Seuss's storytelling sensibility. About two years before he began his own caricature campaign, in 1939, he published a graphic novella of sorts, *The Seven Lady Godivas: The*

True Facts Concerning History's Barest Family. It was a complete flop, hitting the shelves with little fanfare. But it captures Dr. Seuss's appreciation for being who we are without frivol, froth, feather, or fuss. It was a retelling of an eleventh-century legend that Dr. Seuss made into a story of honor-thy-father sisterly love and recollection of the Peeping brothers (including Tom). The book was full of caricatures made for adults, and it previewed some of the touchstones that typify his famous children's books: quirky nonce words now in common usage, chimerical creatures, zany contraptions, and entire worlds comprised of wit and whimsy. It also exemplified the familial devotion that Dr. Seuss maps onto national politics, especially with its basis in warfare (Lord Godiva, father of the seven ladies, dies after being flung off the horse that was going to take him to the Battle of Hastings), its odd eroticism (the sisters parade around naked, each courting a brother from the Peeping family, though expressly unwilling to marry following a pledge to their late father), and its orientation to the public good (the marriage embargo is stipulated by the sisters' noble quest for "Horse Truths"). To boot, one of the cartoon images features the seven sisters encircling their father, who is splayed out on his deathbed looking unnervingly like Uncle Sam in armor. The grotesqueries here mirror the grittiness of his commercial artwork.

Before getting into children's books and editorial cartoons, Dr. Seuss was known as a wacky adman. Among his many clients were Ajax Cups, Ford, General Electric, Holly Sugar, NBC, and Standard Oil. The most prominent of his ad artwork was that done for Flit, a popular insecticide manufactured by Standard Oil in the late 1920s. A campaign from 1928 made Dr. Seuss "an icon of advertising."[30] It familiarized publics with his witticisms and his quirky worlds inhabited by customers who likely thought, "Quick, Henry, THE FLIT!" when they thought of how to exterminate pests. This slogan accompanied cutesy albeit crude caricatures of insects in what became a standard for humor in print advertising. Dr. Seuss's ad work reveals how indelicate visual metaphors used to sell consumer goods could also be used in caricatures aimed at selling war. A few things therefore stand out in these commercial beginnings.

First, the ads ground his depictions of proper conduct on the home front. In a series of pictures he drew for Holly Sugar, for example, a variety of creatures are faced with a bitter-tasting food item. In one, a frustrated bird chews a cherry. In another, a giraffe plucks a green grape from a woman's hat. In yet another a redheaded human being cringes over a strawberry. The audience is reminded: "All they Need is . . . Holly Sugar" to sweeten

FIG. 12 Dr. Seuss, Vico Motor Oil advertisement, between 1930 and 1940. Dr. Seuss Advertising Artwork. Special Collections and Archives, UC San Diego Library.

any sour deal. A similar sentiment is advanced in ads like those Dr. Seuss created for Standard Oil, which portray the wild glee of Brother Jones as he whips by "onlooking birds and other creatures" after purchasing Pep 88 gasoline or Vico motor oil (fig. 12).[31] These animals later become the wartime voices or eyes of judgment on the blunders of American citizens.

Second, the ads prefigure the sorts of odd monstrosities that Dr. Seuss often used to animate the degeneracy of ostensibly "good" citizens, rotten people or groups, and enemy combatants. In one of his tamer images for General Electric, Dr. Seuss drew the head of a "Bulbsnatcher," or "Domesticus Americanus," which appears as a shamed sculpture sharing wall space with a taxidermal bear, sheep, moose, and lion (all of which are grinning at the human pate). Before them all, two businessmen discuss how just it was to scapegoat the Bulbsnatcher in such an extreme fashion, agreeing that "the Little Neck Explorer's Club went too far in its punishment of the member who persisted in taking lamp bulbs from one socket to fill another." Activities on the home front animate the consequences they arouse. The brashness of these whimsical animals underscores the serious side of a heinous characteristic of the typical, stingy American man.

A third and related point has to do with Dr. Seuss's advertising raid on insects. His entire cartoon catalog for Flit merits sustained attention, but for the purposes of this chapter it is most relevant to highlight how it emphasized the elimination of vermin. This very theme was applied to domestic battles against enemies within and "other" cultures that threatened the American way of life with their "subhuman status."[32] In one ad,

Robinson Crusoe is pictured swimming to the shore of a small island. On it is an indigenous Black man who unequivocally fits the racist and offensive coon stereotype, with big lips, large earrings, and tribal garb. Crusoe seeks safe haven from a sinking ship, which descends into the ocean in the distance. But the Black man turns him away, telling Crusoe to return to the ship and come back with Flit to rid the island of pesky flies. Here, a pesticide is upheld as a symbol of civilization. At the same time, the Black man is a contrarian who forces Crusoe back into a dangerous situation from which he just escaped, and for nothing more than a selfish interest in ridding himself of annoying insects. In another, a tightrope walker comes under assault from a grotesquely large and seemingly bioengineered mosquito with a massive harpoon-like blade for a nose. The funambulist stumbles in horror while a ringmaster gazes up from below in comparable dismay. In large, bold letters that appear above a bug sprayer and a canister of insecticide is the admonishment: "Quick, Henry, THE FLIT!" Both ads capture Dr. Seuss's contempt for complacency and his sense that willful ignorance makes those things right in front of you the hardest to see—perhaps especially when they are buzzing in and around your head.

Then there is Dr. Seuss's machine imagery. In another ad for Standard Oil's Essolube, an oversized, ghastly cat tampers with a car engine as a white male driver looks on in shock. The cat grins widely as he uses his forepaws to abrade the man's motor. A caption above the image advises, "Foil the Moto-raspus!" The Essolube, not unlike Flit, destroys pests. It is also the way for a flock of satisfied birds to fly south in another ad when signs for Essomarine oils and greases line the coast like signposts for a charter. In later wartime cartoons, such machinery indicates a broken body politic, with political solutions as mechanisms for greasing the wheels of war. This machinery, like animalisms and contagions, made enemies and enemy principles into what Kenneth Burke might recognize as "Hitlerite distortions,"[33] exploiting a comic aesthetic of hylomorphism in images and ideas of national character.[34] These rhetorical conventions are everywhere in Dr. Seuss's wartime caricatures, the modus operandi for which is garnering humor from images of an aggregated "us" in the comic space of inimitable tragic farce.

Humor in the Comic Abstraction of Coming to Americanism

There is an undated watercolor painting from Dr. Seuss's secret archives. It is named "Manly Art of Self Defense," and it features a boy squaring off with a cat.³⁵ Both are wearing oversized boxing gloves. Both, too, look utterly awkward. The shirtless boy appears almost dainty, with one gloved fist held out in front of the cat's face. The pugilistic cat is standing on its hind legs, eyeballing the boy's glove with a mix of surprise and unease. The cat's gloved front paws are pointed down but the animal appears ready to pounce, except that "the boy does not grasp the harsh reality of boxing," and the cat realizes it. Together, the cat and the boy make up a sort of doubling with naïve insouciance about combat and self-motivated territorialism. On one side is a boy who is not even aware that he is about to come to terms with his own selfhood. On the other is a nonhuman animal that seems torn between taking the boy down and turning away.

What matters in this setup is comic abstraction. According to Roxana Marcoci, a comic abstraction upsets normative imagery insofar as it is made "to perturb, insinuate, tease, and demystify assumptions."³⁶ Dr. Seuss's approach to caricature is nothing if not perturbing, et cetera, built as it is on a pretension that the Other can and should be seen as a measure of the Self. Furthermore, Dr. Seuss's caricatures abstract imagined characteristics of, say, a category of people (be it a precocious boy or a national body politic) by merging them with the fantastical and absurd. As one art columnist wrote of Dr. Seuss's ad work: "He exaggerates, he distorts, he contrives figures more fantastic than those of the Dadaist or the surrealist."³⁷ Humor emerges out of the pretense that resemblances and distorted mirror images show us more about ourselves than reflections of the "real" thing. It is resident in what is out of whack, especially rhetorical judgment. In Dr. Seuss's caricatures, there is proof for the strange sense in seeing *other*-wise.

The otherness of humor is an important hallmark for considering how the fantastical functions as a sort of comic sublime that at times reroutes and at other times completely refashions more conventional cartoon takes on the war culture of the day. Dr. Seuss was not doing the kind of work so common to that of cartoonists like Bill Mauldin, David Low, and Herblock. Mauldin, for instance, did war coverage for the *45th Division News* newsletter and *Stars and Stripes*, placed great emphasis on the combat experiences of US American soldiers, and—through characters like Joe—chronicled the human element of just war as it was fought on the front lines. Low worked in England. He was widely known as a warmonger who harped on the international stakes of taking on fascism and going to war against the Nazis in order to preserve a liberal, democratic order.³⁸ Low urged American cartoonists to ditch the image of Uncle Sam altogether. He saw realism in caricature as a means of expressing the rationales for war efforts, especially relative to reportage on Nazi ideology, the strongman politics of Hitler and Mussolini, extermination camps, and more. Comicality, for Low, was a way to capture the atrocities of both culture and combat as it emerged out of *Nationalsozialismus*, and to humor a notion of victory at all costs. Herblock was not unlike Low and Mauldin. He was a cut-from-the-cloth interventionist. He won the Pulitzer Prize for Editorial Cartooning in 1942 and drew official cartoon images for the Army. The so-called "Herblock Image" endured throughout the Cold War era. In World War II, this image was over and again one of the evil other. Herblock regularly drew Hitler and the Nazis facing off with US American soldiers or committing atrocities. His realism dwelt on the fact that there is evil in the world, and there are evildoers who justify war production. Dr. Seuss was not indifferent to these orientations. But he took his own caricatures another way.

Dr. Seuss's caricatures set forth rhetorical judgment in the space of the superficial, and humor in the stuff of comic abstraction. Seeing is distorting. Deleuze says something similar when he dubs humor "the art of the surfaces and of the doubles."[39] Deleuze sees in humor, indeed on surfaces, the deepest of human matters. No surprise that he relies on a close reading of Lewis Carroll's tales of Alice in Wonderland to make his case. In Wonderland are multitudinous admixtures of images and ideas. What is more, animals dwell in the depths of the rabbit hole, wherein depth itself becomes surface. Alice's plunge is defined by interpenetrations and coexistences. One sees them not by simply going underground but rather by peering through the looking glass. Dr. Seuss's caricatures amplify an American Wonderland, transmogrifying the phrase "through the looking glass" into a visual metaphor for seeing the depths of surfaces. They are comic abstractions in which human characters become Other by becoming Animal. Nowhere is this more apparent than in his use of so many birds to bring wartime national character to bear, particularly in terms of the cultural warfare that is carried out at home while war is waged abroad.

BIRDS OF A FOLLY

On May 21, 1927, Charles A. Lindbergh flew a solo, nonstop flight across the Atlantic to much fanfare. Lindbergh later became a student of aviation and, by the late 1930s, an outspoken critic of the Roosevelt administration and pro-war factions. He was also widely regarded as a racist (even a white supremacist with Nazi sympathies). In October 1939, Lindbergh delivered a radio address entitled "Neutrality and War" celebrating the racial characteristics of American exceptionalism while laying out a program for nonintervention. Less than two years later, Lindbergh spoke as the proxy for the America First Committee (AFC), condemning "war agitators" like British Jews and New Deal idealists for "subterfuge" and "propaganda" that constituted a plot against America. Dr. Seuss saw it otherwise. In many ways, he foreshadowed Philip Roth's 2004 historical revision, *The Plot Against America*, a novel that reimagines the outcomes of World War II as if Lindbergh ran against Roosevelt in the 1940 presidential election—and won. In Roth's account, the US government signs a treaty with the Nazis, ensuring a peaceless, fascist American nation. For Seuss, a ploy to avoid war in the name of Americanism was itself a plot against America.

Dr. Seuss's wartime birds capture the wayward folly of those who seemed to simply look on—or look away—as war raged on overseas. Lindbergh was an early cudgel for this encapsulation. One cartoon from April 1941 displays Lindbergh in a small prop plane flying above an American city towing a banner that reads, "It's Smart to Shop at Adolf's," with the qualifier, "All Victories Guaranteed." A flabbergasted bird floats in the clouds and looks on as a closed-eyed Lindbergh flies by. The bird is a symbol of freedom, and a countervailing force against the isolationist movement that Dr. Seuss witnessed taking flight in the late 1930s. But Dr. Seuss's birds do not fly. Consider another cartoon, which was published just days later. In it, an ostrich appears on a "Lindbergh Quarter" (fig. 13), stuffing its head in a pile of sand. Above the bird's head, which is plainly visible despite being buried, are the words "In God We Trust (And How!)." A caption reads: "Since when did we swap our ego for an ostrich?"

The ostrich symbolizes the defaced currency of Americanism that is applied to the infamous aviator and his lobbying group. The bird's eyes are closed. Its beak betrays a smile. It is puffed up even with its face down. Dr. Seuss's ostrich mocks those who trade in the cultural purchase of American national character for anti-warism. The sublime meets the ridiculous here. First, the Washington Quarter had not even been in circulation a decade and already its luster was being stained, along with Washington's foundational American sentiment that preparedness for war is preservation of peace. Second, the ostrich stands in stark contrast to the grace and glory of the bald eagle, never mind the stupefaction of the bird left in Lindbergh's wake. Third, the flightless ostrich is known for running away from predators rather than engaging them. The image also exploits the mythic quality of ostriches burying their heads in sand to avoid (or ignore) danger. The Lindbergh Quarter doubles as the Ostrich Quarter. It visualizes the

FIG. 13 Dr. Seuss, "The Lindbergh Quarter," April 28, 1941. Dr. Seuss Went to War. Special Collections and Archives, UC San Diego Library.

"Since when did we swap our ego for an ostrich?"

imprudence of miscalculations in wartimes. It likewise sets the stage for Dr. Seuss's use of caricature to intervene with isolationism and its ethos of cashing in on US American freedoms without paying for them. The ostrich exemplifies a counterfeit national character.

The ostrich is a comic abstraction of civic dispositions. For instance, in his very next cartoon, Dr. Seuss depicted a vendor standing on a plinth fitting white male patrons for "ostrich bonnets." Sharing his platform is a pile of ostrich hats and a sign that advertises relief for "Hitler Headaches," with this guarantee from the Lindy Ostrich Service: "Forget the Terrible News You've Read. Your Mind's at Ease in an Ostrich Head!" Two men wait in line. A third receives his bonnet, and from the foreground into the deep distance of the lower right frame is a row of ostrich-men, all of whom have their heads stuffed snugly in the sand. A caption reads: "We Always Were Suckers for Ridiculous Hats...." Because the vendor is wearing a bonnet himself, it is unclear whether or not Lindbergh is the man behind the mask. What is clear, though, is that the features of both the man and the animal make up the crude madcap. What is also clear is the racial implication in this setup inasmuch as the ridiculous white men only see the world through their own eyes. Theirs is the outward projection of a simplistic, *singular* consciousness. The double-consciousness inherent to Blackness typifies and, in Black bodies, personifies the sort of doubledness that sets Black and white in conflict, never mind war and democracy. Dr. Seuss mocks the single-mindedness that shows itself for what it is in the white gaze of the comic looking glass. Tellingly, the ostrich hat retains the countenance already seen on the Ostrich Quarter.

Wartime miscalculations thus fold into mistaken identity. The Ostrich Bonnet betrays a public show of "unnatural" selection. Each man pretends to be part of the flock. However, the outcome is not so much power in numbers as it is political disempowerment in the self-satisfaction of blissful, even willful ignorance—a point reinforced by the collective loss of identity on display (all the ostriches look the same). A blind eye on the front lines, like a blind eye on the color line, is a losing proposition. What is Dr. Seuss's point? Isolationists are ridiculous human animals, unable to separate themselves from their own egoism in order to appreciate the wider social, political, and cultural contexts of armed conflict and their relation to a more complex, more complete national character. A racial, if not imperial, self-consciousness actually betrays the weakness and cowardice of a purely self-interested nation. This is not confined to individuals. It is a cultural condition. In this context, it is a war culture. Furthermore, the bonnets attribute a certain effeminacy and ethnocentrism to isolationism, allegorizing the "true" character of white isolationist American men even as they hide their faces. As was the case in Flagg's comic abstractions of national character, in Dr. Seuss's early wartime caricatures is an image of comic shame.

Dr. Seuss's ostrich imagery lampoons what it means to be ashamed of oneself in public. Unlike Uncle Sam's "I Want YOU" image, which incites a sense of guilt in avoiding civic-as-military action, Dr. Seuss's ostriches portray the conscious choice to resist war as a shameful vice that masquerades as a virtue. In some of his later cartoons, Dr. Seuss goes so far as to make the ostrich a caricature of fascistic invasion on the home front. Ostriches are an invasive species. Even Roosevelt imagined this possibility, as he said in his State of the Union address on January 3, 1940: "I hope that we shall have fewer ostriches in our midst," he said. "It is not good for the ultimate health of ostriches to bury their heads in the sand." Hence the men in ostrich bonnets. Hence, too, the "GOPstrich," or what Dr. Seuss dubbed in October 1941 the "Offspring of the G.O.P. and the Isolation Ostrich," embodying the official adoption of isolationism by the 1940s Republican establishment. By November 1941, however, Dr. Seuss began depicting the demise of isolationism by situating the ostrich in a museum exhibit. In it, the creature shares space with the skeletal remains of dinosaurs that are acting alive and heckling their new addition. The imagined extinction was portentous. Roosevelt had just enabled American merchant ships to carry armaments, Moscow remained under attack (and the United States had authorized a loan to the Soviets for defense), and the USS *Enterprise* was being mobilized for war. In a week, Japan would grow more belligerent. On December 1, Emperor Hirohito would approve hostilities against the United States as newspapers like the *Seattle Star* announced imminent danger with headlines like "WAR NEARS!" even as others touted the possibility for peace talks. It would not be long until evidence emerged of Japanese activity around Manila, and Hideki Tojo, a general for the Imperial Japanese Army, would ramp up rhetoric about purgation of Americans in the Far East.

Dr. Seuss declared this "GOOD NEWS," and re-upped this sentiment the day after the Japanese attacks on Pearl Harbor, which he celebrated with a cartoon exploding the Isolationism Ostrich sky high. "He never Knew What Hit Him," reads the caption. War, for Dr. Seuss, was the bygone conclusion of what many saw at that time as the ongoing fight to save Democracy by saving the American Way. Dr. Seuss's praise for the "good news" of war was issued by "Sam-Bird," a plump American Eagle with finger-like wings, a long neck, and a beard and top hat combination that codified his congruence with Uncle Sam. In June 1941, Sam-Bird could be seen sitting in a familiar position with eyes closed and finger-wings crossed. He is in a lounge chair, smiling as mortar fire blasts around his "Home Sweet Home." Atop his chair is a tiny umbrella, the only "real" protection against the assault. As bombs burst around him and missiles whiz by his head, Sam-Bird comforts himself with a rhyme: "Said a bird in the midst of a Blitz, / Up to now they've scored very few hitz, / So I'll sit on my canny / Old Star Spangled Fanny . . . / And on it he sitz and he sitz." The whimsical verses imply a churlishness that reinforces the strange suggestion that the bird actually sits in a sitz (a domicile), if not a sitz bath (a treatment for aches and pains). Such a troubling portrayal of complacency evokes a sense that the war wary were doing more to enable the scheming of isolationists than to come up with a good way to intervene.

Across Dr. Seuss's caricatures the eagle is sometimes the governmental apparatus of Washington and sometimes the anthropomorphic animalism of the nation itself. In any case, the eagle (like the ostrich) is a therianthropic shapeshifter that distills the organizing principles of a body politic even as it articulates the possibility of otherness on one hand and the value of seeing differently on the other. Dr. Seuss's fear was that democracy and fascism were two sides of the same coin. On one side was the tragedy of antidemocratic cooperation. On the other, the comicality of democratic farce. His turn to eagles helped Dr. Seuss flip the coin, and the script, on the ostrich.

Here's how: On December 9, 1941, Dr. Seuss's eagle woke up. A cartoon, captioned "The End of the Nap," shows Sam-Bird in a rocking chair (fig. 14). He is enormous, at least compared to five Japanese soldiers that are rousing him into a state of wakefulness. One pulls off his top hat and hits him over the head with a gavel-like mallet, signifying something of a day of reckoning. One is lighting Sam-Bird's feet on fire with a match, while another saws the floor out from under his chair. Yet another shoots a pellet from a slingshot toward the bird's bearded chin. A final soldier drills a screw through the back of the rocking chair and into Sam-Bird's spine. The cartoon is a distorted mirror of Flagg's well-known appeal to "Wake Up, America!" especially with the bird's stern eyes and deep scowl. Even more glaring is the infantilized image of Japanese fighters who appear like children harassing an elder. On top of this is the fact that the soldiers are essentially clones of one another, underscoring Dr. Seuss's racialization of the Japanese as unthinking look-alikes doing the bidding of fascists. The Japanese are a nuisance to Sam-Bird, resembling so many allied depictions of "Japs" as subhuman insects. Insects swarm. Like Dr. Seuss's ostrich bonnet–wearing men, they are one and the same. The eagle, contrariwise, is an always-individuated, always exceptionally singular figure for US national character—until it is infested.

In the prewar period, Sam-Bird was a dodo. He was not unintelligent. He was just outmoded in his assumption that words could thwart war. On May 8, 1941, Dr. Seuss portrayed the American Eagle in his rocking chair with his eyes closed, his wing-fingers crossed across his belly, and his mouth agape spewing "Talk Talk Talk Talk Talk Talk Talk." As opposed to the roused Sam-Bird, this one is much larger than his chair, has an extremely long neck (like an ostrich), and appears happy in his chatter. He is also alone, talking away in puffery that forms clouds about his head. The possible allusions are rife, from references to diplomacy amid Japanese aggression, to talks of trade embargoes and the security of military supplies shipments for European allies, to lend-lease deals, to Roosevelt's closeted racism despite his good talk on race relations (some of his advisors thought it possible that there could be a "Black Cabinet" to counterbalance the "official" one), and even to his efforts to conciliate the prospects of armed conflict in his fireside chats. The eagle might not be Roosevelt.[40] However, it exemplifies Roosevelt's description of war as a matter of public debate. While Dr. Seuss supported Roosevelt and his New Deal ethos, he

FIG. 14 Dr. Seuss, "The End of the Nap," December 9, 1941. Dr. Seuss Went to War. Special Collections and Archives, UC San Diego Library.

aligned himself with strong interventionist factions that had been situating the frights of warfare as the very reasons *to* fight. Freedom, for Dr. Seuss, justified the democratic politics of war. Roosevelt "talked a lot."[41] He was seen as much as a "good neighbor" as a commander in chief.[42] As historian Alfred Whitney Griswold said of Roosevelt in 1938, the president was also a self-proclaimed opportunist—or, what Warren F. Kimball has more recently described as a "juggler" who "reacted, shifted, rethought, and recalculated."[43] His obsession with public opinion polls is thus unsurprising, and with it his request for a "Weekly Analysis of Press Reaction" from the Office of Government Reports. This left far too much wiggle room around a moment that demanded deeds over words. Dr. Seuss made this sentiment painfully obvious when he drew Sam-Bird on a stool, wearing glasses, and using an oversized military sword to literally split hairs with Hitler looking on.

The point is that birds represent Dr. Seuss's caricatures as resources for regarding collective selfhood in a mirror, distortedly. The humor arises out of the comic differences in his bird imagery across its repetition. Humor, à la Deleuze, is an art of creating depth in surfaces. As a prime rhetorical feature of caricature, humor plays with surface features in such a way as to fathom depths. Dr. Seuss's wartime caricatures plumb those depths by showing how American national character had sunk in accordance with a complacency and cowardice in antidemocratic attitudes that festered in the surface features of US Americanism. It is fitting in this regard that humor should also be recognized as a rhetorical "art of consequences and effects."[44] There can be humor in seeing something or someone out of its depths or, in this case, flitting away the conditions of possibility for democratic peace in the folly of world war. Democracy is a veneer that covers the threat of war. Dr. Seuss draws out a deep humor in recognizing how this ugly truth lies just below the surface of America the beautiful.

So it is that on January 1, 1942, Dr. Seuss drew a new image of national character. The eagle is gone (as is the ostrich), and bird imagery is all but flitted away for more realistic fantasies of enemy relations. In place of ostriches and eagles is Uncle Sam, who wakes to the New Year with a hangover. Sitting up in his patriotic pajamas, he rubs his face and finds his bed overrun by two serpents. Another worm-like creature sits atop the headboard. A starred and striped top hat rests at the foot of the bed, while Hitler (with the trunk and ears of an elephant on the body of a snake) sits coiled on Uncle Sam's head. On his pillow is another serpent, most likely representing Hirohito or Shigenori Togo, Japan's Minister of Foreign Affairs. The skin of the Japanese snake is covered in Rising Suns, and his countenance bears stereotypically thin eyes behind a pair of wire-rimmed glasses, which sit on a pig-nose above buckteeth that protrude from a pursed upper lip. Serpentine creatures have invaded the United States' most private of domestic spaces in this cartoon image. Or better, the nation has allowed itself to be assailed by a grotesque political culture. Dr. Seuss's first day is a day of reckoning. It is concerning that Dr. Seuss's caricatures rely so heavily on comic abstractions that both gloss over issues of homegrown nativism, racism, sexism, ethnocentrism, and more, and put "good" use to specifically racial and ethnic stereotypes as nationalistic markers. One can see why he did so, though. Caricature is Dr. Seuss's mechanism for coming to Americanism. It is his vehicle for working through the ugliness that chafes at images and ideas of national character. It is his way of evoking a comic sensibility about the proximities between individual people and their bodies politic, and about rhetorical judgments we make of the unfunny attachments we have to certain modes of organizing ourselves into This or That assemblage. Caricature is, in many ways, a projection outward that doubles back with a comic take on the Self.

Such a doubled projection is apparent in Dr. Seuss's shift from a Self-orientation to a wholly Other-directedness. This shift appears in caricatures that characterize "Jap" culture as an unwitting populace of bugs that cannot be appeased, only exterminated. Surely, there are obvious allusions to Appeasers and Isolationists on the home front, who are seen as infested with wrongheaded views about American democracy in action. But there are even more obvious articulations of American national character gone bad when corrupted by "insect enemies,"[45] and then again by the sorts of war productions that yield cultural waste and industrial cruelties. I therefore turn now to the blighted selfhood that appears in Dr. Seuss's caricatures of otherness—of insects and instruments of war.

BUGS, BILE, AND BIG WAR MACHINES

In shifting his attention to insect enemies, Dr. Seuss altered his orientation from warmongering to the makings of warfare. Eventually, his cartoons encompassed pests and pestilences, smut and muck, and gross implements of armed conflict that traversed enemies at home and abroad. The result, however, was not an image of a tainted Americanism; instead, it was a picture of the disease of war, with caricature as the means of making national deficiencies in character more proximate and unnerving. It began with a move from birds to bugs.

Dr. Seuss was, in many ways, a product of his times even though he was regularly seen as something of a weirdo. A cartoon that appeared in the March 1945 issue of *Leatherneck*—a Marine Corps magazine—advertised a "serious outbreak" of a "lice epidemic." More than mere scuttlebutt, the scourge could be traced back to December 7, 1941, the start of Marine Corps training for "the gigantic task of extermination." The lice had unique, identifiable characteristics: slim and slanted eyes, two large front teeth that jutted out of its wide mouth, what might have been a star of the American Legion on its forehead, six spider-like legs with claws, and a tail with a Rising Sun on the tip. Its binomen was *Louseous Japanicas*, or the Japanese Louse. Dr. Seuss was part of a larger practice of "pseudospecies-making,"[46] with crude animal-human hybrids as syllogisms for classifying and categorizing bodies politic. But this was not entirely a matter of visual metaphor as war allegory. The infamous Unit 731 of the Japanese army "disseminated plague-infected fleas on the Chinese people" as part of its invasion of the Republic of China.[47] Here, insects were literal weapons in an instance of "entomological warfare." The renovation of this concept into a species of rhetorical combat also has roots in the fact that the insecticide

FIG. 15 Dr. Seuss, "Quick, Henry, THE FLIT!," December 19, 1941. Dr. Seuss Political Cartoons. Special Collections and Archives, UC San Diego Library.

dichlorodiphenyltrichloroethane, or DDT, was discovered in 1939 during the production of explosives in Switzerland. A contact chemical, it was described by Rachel Carson as an "elixir of death," because "one of its first uses was the wartime dusting of many thousands of soldiers, refugees, and prisoners, to combat lice."[48] DDT killed bugs. It was only later that the insecticide was found to have deleterious effects on humans. By 1944, Chief of the Chemical Warfare Service William N. Porter expressed his intent to poison German and Japanese troops with the same principles by which one could poison insects.[49] For Dr. Seuss, this translated into the idea that Americans could, and should, take on the rhetorical character of exterminators.

Recall that Dr. Seuss was once the leading illustrator for the insecticide Flit. So when a cartoon appeared in *PM* on December 19, 1941, showing Sam-Bird aiming a manual spray pump filled with the pesticide of US Defense Bonds and Stamps at demonic mosquitos, the association was clear (fig. 15). In the cartoon, two bugs are noticeably larger than Sam-Bird, and each has a long nose that ends in a sharp stinger. One wears an iconic Hitler moustache and a massive swastika on its body. The other is a "Jap." Beside them is another bug, also descending upon Sam-Bird. In the bottom left corner of the frame is the catchphrase, "Quick, Henry, THE FLIT!" In calling for civic action in the form of financial support, the cartoon shifts the valence from public opinion to support for war efforts. It even has crossover with an earlier ad that shows three American soldiers in a tank looking on in horror as a blood-red mosquito dive bombs them from the sky. In the ad, potential buyers are told that it does not cost much to kill flies and mosquitos. Citizens of war, however, were reminded that talk is cheap.

This wartime idea of "Japs" as "yellow vermin" extends beyond insect imagery and into more encompassing concepts of pests as contagions as well as objects of contempt. For Dr. Seuss, it also goads the more explicit incorporation of cats in dealings with the double meanings and alterities of Self. On December 10, 1941, Dr. Seuss showed Sam-Bird under assault by a throng of alley cats. Sam-Bird sits at the end of "Jap Alley," clutching a wooden plank rigged with a nail and strangling one of the feral cats. A swarm of alley cats approaches him. The cultural and characterological foreignness is arrant, with the Japanese pictured as resistant to human socialization, homeless, and stray. They are pests. The cats, like insects, are vermin. A couple months later, Dr. Seuss transmuted the visual metaphor of a swarm into the image of American "Japs" as the "Honorable 5th Column." The cartoon shows a Japanese man as a roadside vendor in an outbuilding situated at the end of an endless drove of Japanese Americans that is making its way from Washington through Oregon to California. As they pass, members of the horde collect a box of TNT. All the while, another Japanese American man stands on top of the hut, holding a telescope pointed to the Far East, "Waiting for the Signal From Home...." The image telescopes the comicality of the Other as a contact point for ascertaining the call to national character. In the same vein, it is a distillation of what was popularly known as the "yellow peril," and so rationalizes the racism and fears of enemies within that led to Japanese internment. Dr. Seuss's response to the disease of armed conflict is therefore the dis-ease of Americanism.

Herein lies a critical ambivalence in Dr. Seuss's war artwork. His caricatures are unapologetically nativist, ethnocentric, and even racist in their merger of Japanese aggressors with Japanese Americans. Combining the two perpetuates the insect narrative and visualizes racial distinctions that are built on value judgments of "the Oriental" as "a discrete specimen of something resembling (but never attaining the status of) a normal—that is, Western and white—human being."[50] The "Jap" is at once the infester and the infested. This is not the place to rehash Edward Said's foundational view of Orientalism (or its hang-ups). But World War II, like so many other wars, was described as a clash of civilizations—of cultures. This clash pitted "the West (which is rational, developed, humane, superior)" against "the Orient (which is aberrant, undeveloped, inferior)."[51] In one sense, there arrives here a "Depression-era xenophobia" that refurbishes the Chinese Exclusion Act and a sort of "blood-will-tell racism" against model enemies.[52] In another, there comes a need for visual assurance that orientalist rhetorics never just describe manners or customs but also deign to depict realities.[53] Caricature is so compelling a visual rhetoric because it so often seems to capture what is actually the case, right there on the surface, right before our eyes. This is the feint of humor in a Deleuzian sense: it is a profound art of taking the superficial seriously. Caricature also distorts and deforms and deranges and draws together strange couplings. In doing so, it makes perceived realities even *more* exacting. Caricature, in this case, reroutes combat treacheries into jingoistic travesties. The ambivalence lies in the domestication of warfare as a comic abstraction of Self and Other. So it is that Dr. Seuss reveals insecticide as a remedy for specifically American mindsets in a wartime context.[54]

In this ambivalence is where the castigations of Dr. Seuss's racism and nativism break down. After all, Dr. Seuss saw the possibility of a human family in the foundational principles of the American idea. Consider a cartoon from June 11, 1942, which displays Uncle Sam wielding an insecticide pump loaded with toxins for killing off the "Racial Prejudice Bug." Uncle Sam smirks in the foreground, treating a white American man by spraying the insecticide into a funnel that is set up to blast its remedy in one ear of its patients and out the other. "Gracious!" says one man receiving treatment. "Was *that* in my head?" Beside him in a cloud of off-gas is a tiny bug. Behind him is a line of white American men, quite similar to the earlier horde of Japanese Americans, waiting to be treated. And above them all is the caption: "What This Country Needs Is a Good Mental Insecticide." The reference here is decidedly *not* to prejudices against Japanese Americans, but rather to the racialized politics that prevented integrated US army units, discriminated against Black Americans in the war industries, and established a separate but equal public policy of military (and civic) sacrifice. Dr. Seuss's point is that "real" Americans do not discriminate against their own, no matter the color or creed. Where this logic crumbles is in the very definition of what constitutes a Real American, as when Dr. Seuss expands on insect imagery to depict persons, groups of people, and values as embodiments of the filth and ordure of a war culture out of whack.

If the "fifth column" typified a foreign enemy, the "sixth column" was the enemy within. The sixth column constituted a collection of individuals that supported subversive activities by propagating the party lines of wartime adversaries. Or, in journalist and media critic George Seldes's terms, it entailed any and all of those "using the means of communication ... to spread dissension, disunity, fear, and suspicion."[55] For Dr. Seuss, it was the appeasers, the Nazi sympathizers, and even the obstructionist politicians who embodied the homegrown uglies of the Second World War. One specific target was the Dies Committee, set up in 1938 by Martin Dies Jr. via the House Committee Investigating Un-American Activities. Organized around suspicions of potential subversives, the committee promised to uphold "true Americanism." Dr. Seuss echoed the widespread critique of the committee as un-American, in large part due to its association of New Deal idealists with Communists and its support of Southern congressmen who detested the Roosevelt administration and its policies. In a cartoon from August 1942, Dr. Seuss recalibrates his insect imagery to suggest how an anti-American contagion had infected certain portions of the US body politic.

Standing before a small crowd of "Just Plain Bugs" is a larger, more grotesque insect. It has a long, lanky body with an oddly ribbed and furred thorax. Its antennas are crooked and bent over its head. Its nose is bladed and sharp. It has a curvilinear tail that comes to a point with a tuft of fur at the end. The appendages of its back limbs are clasped together, and one front limb supports its upper body while the other gestures to the group. With eyes closed, head high, and mouth open, the insect boasts: "I don't like to brag, boys ... but when I bit Col. McCormick it established the greatest all-time itch on record!" The itch was an anti-Roosevelt itch, delivered by "The Anti-Roosevelt Bug." It refers to the contaminated politics of publisher Robert R. McCormick, a target who received the comic wrath of Dr. Seuss like Lindbergh before him. McCormick ran the *Chicago Tribune*, which was well known for calling Roosevelt a Communist and lambasting the New Deal. Along with his cousin, Eleanor M. "Cissy" Patterson, who oversaw the *Washington Times-Herald*, McCormick used his newspaper to decry anything and everything east of the Mississippi River, thinking Washington—and no doubt other East Coast cities—"a Sodom and Gomorrah of sin."[56] As a result, Roosevelt took advantage of many opportunities to dub Cissy a subversive and to refer disparagingly to "the McCormick-Patterson Axis." This forms the basis of Dr. Seuss's alignment of Axis ambitions with the disease-carrying characteristics of mosquitos and germs and the general filth of Japanese imperialism and Nazi propaganda. These alignments were later characterized as "Stalin-itch," "Hitler-itis," "Fascist Fever," and the like, all to the end of seeing comic ugliness in those who were awash with the Ugly Spirit of Americanism.

Take another cartoon, wherein a man representing the AFC sits in an "old Family bath tub" (signifying the "American Hemisphere") overrun by ghastly creatures. The AFC man bathes himself in filth with eyes closed and a smile on his face. Sharing his bath is an anthropomorphic alligator, a menacing (albeit tiny) shark, an octopus, and a cockroach-like insect, all emblazoned with Nazi swastikas. Filth, effluence, and infection overlap in this image and portray an impurification of the very structure of American national character that is punctuated by the claw feet on the legs of the tub. Such impurification is mapped onto the "Jap" stereotype when, in September 1941, Dr. Seuss shows a familiar Japanese character lowering himself into a steaming bath that has been drawn in a clawfoot bathtub. The water resembles sludge and boils over as "War With U.S." Next to the "Jap's" head is an "Old Japanese Proverb" that perverts a foreign tongue: "Man who draw his bath too hot, sit down in same velly slow." Instructively, the man is trying to cool himself with a Japanese hand fan, traditionally a feminine accoutrement that also comes off as an allusion to folkloric devices of ancient East Asian combat. The plain truth that Dr. Seuss travesties is that World War II posed a biotic threat with the capacity to cause US citizens to bathe themselves in the same pollution as "the Japanese character,"[57] and then again to embody the very filth whose surface fetidness betrayed an even deeper evil. Joe Public gone bad, in other words, is just as corrupted as a Jap. Surface meets depth. Good blends with bad. The American Self becomes the Ugly Other. The humor comes from these mergers that indulge even as they inveigh a sorry view of US national character in the comic looking glass.

Dr. Seuss was probably most perturbed by the notion that America had become a citizenry of "cheerful idiots," to use a phrase from Roosevelt. US citizens seemed to lack a capacity to recognize the fragility of its political, cultural, national, and now *inter*national experiment, which could not be kept safe on a wing and a prayer. As such, Dr. Seuss rounded out his caricatures of national character with machines to depict the proper operation of war and to visualize how the United States could understand itself as an operative democratic nation. A few images in particular get at these tensions. The first was published on February 18, 1942. Its message is ironically antidemocratic insofar as it continues Dr. Seuss's sense that U.S. entry in the war meant that the time to stop deliberating had come. In the cartoon, Uncle Sam works a strange contraption that is supposed to be a weapon of war (fig. 16). The "Big Bertha" is something of an American howitzer, only much less a mortar than a mucked-up machine clogged and bunged by "political squabbles," "just plain gas" (the machine's exhaust),

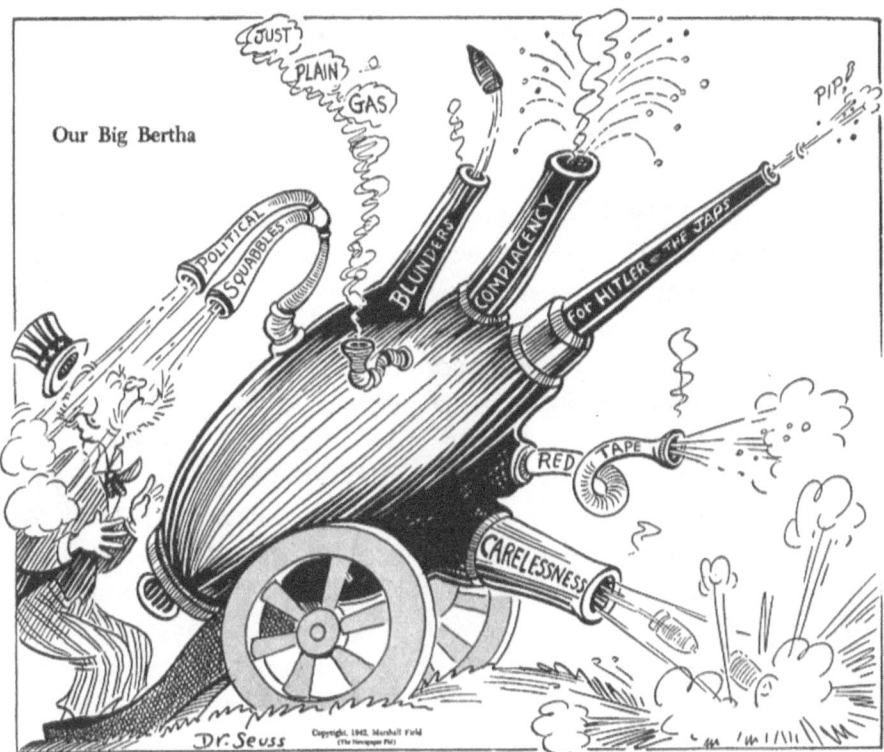

FIG. 16 Dr. Seuss, "Our Big Bertha," February 18, 1942. Dr. Seuss Political Cartoons. Special Collections and Archives, UC San Diego Library.

"blunders," "complacency," "red tape," and "carelessness." This cartoon encapsulates a network of ideas that Dr. Seuss put to work in imaginative portrayals of American incompetence in the conduct of both politics and war. It foregrounds Dr. Seuss's sense that armed conflict indicated the vices embedded in the American Way. The "Big Bertha" is equipped with multiple cannons, all of which fire munitions in a variety of disconnected directions, the most telling of which is the gas from political squabbles that blows back in Uncle Sam's face. In direct equipoise is a "pip" that is fired from the canon "for Hitler and the Japs," intimating the military and political pittance for American firepower.

The politics of war are just as important as the cultural politics resident in this image. In his pull for war production, Dr. Seuss also amplified the racialization of the factory floor, specifically as it disrupted the sort of harmony needed for a nation to succeed in armed conflict. In April 1942, Dr.

Seuss took on the common practice of industrialists denying Black workers either an opportunity to work or equal treatment based on "stereotyped views of their alleged laziness, lack of mechanical ability, and unreliability."[58] The cartoon depicts a "Discriminating Employer" clutching an American flag and driving a tank with two men—one representing "Negro Labor" and the other "Jewish" labor—being towed along in tiny carts. The employer proclaims: "*I'll* run Democracy's War. <u>You</u> stay In your Jim Crow Tanks!" Dr. Seuss's travesty of labor shortages and the "scab race" of industry is unabashed in the depravity of white workers deeming dislikable factions of the workforce inadequate. As important is Dr. Seuss's alignment of race relations and the democratic exigencies of warfare. To sink to the depths of Us–Them relations at home was to feed the beast of Us–Them rhetorics abroad. Racism, like isolationism, hampered the war efforts and corrupted American democracy. New Deal politics offered an ideological anchor for appeals to integration, economic opportunity, and social equality. Organizations like the American Federation of Labor, with its commitment to isolationism, therefore conflicted with the Congress of Industrial Organizations and its history of progressive racial politics, betraying a politics shared by Dr. Seuss and others who declared that to be anti-labor was to be antiwar—and to be antiwar was to be un-American. Isolationist industry leaders tried to avoid alignments with the nation-state and so took little "action to rein in the racist and antidemocratic attitudes and policies of . . . member unions."[59] Dr. Seuss made war a matter of public interest by illustrating labor unionism as important for a united front, complete with equal opportunity and racial justice, to make any aspect of national character based on prewar prejudices antiquated, outmoded, and ultimately unworkable. As he expressed in another cartoon, race prejudice in the United States was akin to "The Guy Who Makes a Mock of Democracy." Such mockery is, for Dr. Seuss, the worst of "wartime blunders."[60]

Given all this, though, Dr. Seuss's rhetorical judgments of wartime national character emerge more subtly, and come full circle, in the image of a small cat. Hammering home the notion that animal imagery amplifies the nature of human conduct, a cat appears in many of the cartoons that specifically target civic engagements with war. In the prewar period, the cat emerged in moments of dismay as he did in May 1941 when he and an American citizen shared in the shock of seeing a woman, representing Fraulein Bund (a German American Federation and organization for American Nazis), pushing a baby carriage with an infantile progeny, the AFC. Toward the end of Dr. Seuss's caricature campaign, the cat adopted the dirty looks of unfit US citizens. The cat is in the bottom right corner of the cartoon showing Uncle Sam cure Americans with a "Good Mental Insecticide." What we find in the cat, then, is "a character without a fixed center," and maybe even "a con artist, a trickster, a character of possibility, aggressively adaptable to the occasion."[61] The cat is sometimes the provocateur, as in Dr. Seuss's depiction of Jap Alley. Sometimes the cat is the cudgel. Consistently, the cat (and catlike comicality) carries the rhetorical load of reorganized principles for sociopolitical communion in perspectives on the American Way that are prodded by the exigencies of war. Following Dr. Seuss, fantastical reimaginations of national characteristics reinscribe matters of wartime civic duty when it comes to the cultural politics of laughing at, laughing off, or laughing last.

Conclusion: Oh, the People We Be

Caricature is a rhetorical art of comic characterization. As a mode of humor, it is also an art of visualizing consequences of character so that in their comic guise they might be seen for the laughingstock that their subjects and objects of ridicule could become once, say, a war has come and gone. The last of Dr. Seuss's wartime cartoons is instructive in this regard (fig. 17). It appeared on January 5, 1943, just two days before he enlisted in the Information and Education Division of the US Army. Dr. Seuss had earned a commission to "Fort Fox," the film production studio of Frank Capra's signal corps unit. There, he worked on propaganda films for both citizens and soldiers until his discharge just over two years later. Dr. Seuss's last cartoon caps off his caricature campaign against those citizens who typified an American nation out of character.

The year is 1973. A small boy sits on the knee of a veteran who recalls the Battle of 1943. "There we were," the man relays. "Japs to the left of us! Germans to the right! Closing in . . . in . . . !" The little boy gapes, his tiny knees held against his chest. "Did I run?" the old man goes on. "I did not! Unyielding, I sat in this chair and groused about the annoying shortage of fuel oil!" The cartoon operates like a joke. Its punch line is anticlimactic, and yet consequential. First, it expresses a veteran's war experience, not with battle but with armchair citizenship. Second, the cartoon alludes to the problems that Dr. Seuss long had with isolationism, appeasement, and complacency—all of which misrepresented the import of war for democratic life and thus misrecognized the sort of national character needed to preserve and protect American democracy. Third, it emphasizes the

FIG. 17 Dr. Seuss, "The Veteran Recalls the Battle of 1943," January 5, 1943. Dr. Seuss Political Cartoons. Special Collections and Archives, UC San Diego Library.

public shame for those who either resisted or disengaged with war efforts. The irony is that the old man is prideful in his embarrassing reminiscence, suggesting that he and others like him would probably go on without ever realizing what it meant to proclaim something like "Uncle Sam I am (not)." And then there is the cat, symbolizing the humor of hindsight rendered before the fact as he sits with his back facing the old man and the boy and his head turned toward them to reveal a look of anguish.

This notion that national character reflects judgments on past actions and on civic responsibility is even more barefaced in a monumental series of cartoons that Dr. Seuss published two years before he enlisted. From January 5 through January 18, 1942, Dr. Seuss created five World War II monuments for American culture. Within this series, Dr. Seuss established the "Society of Red Tape Cutters," a political honor for those like Roosevelt,

Harry S. Truman, Admiral Chester Nimitz, and others who won the reverence of "the Readers of the Newspaper *PM*" for willingness to spur on rather than thwart war efforts. Each monument is a joke on political vice, born out by the wartime activities of *cultural* soldiers on the home front. The first of the War Monuments celebrates John F. Hindsight. It is a sculpture of a white American man in a rocking chair, looking through a telescope that juts out and then circles back to reveal what is behind him. One could easily read this as another travesty of armchair citizenship, and thus of John Q. Public, which Dr. Seuss dubs the "Master Strategist of Yesterday's Battles." The monument recalls Dr. Seuss's disdain for cat-squabbling, as well as his contempt for the types of people he would depict a month later as two small men standing on the edge of a cliff and looking through the lenses of oversized "Rose Colored" glasses to see beautiful bombs bursting in the distance. What they saw was "Our War." Dr. Seuss's first monument was to those who would turn into the apologists of "we coulda" and "we shoulda," the procurers of post hoc visual acuity.

The second commemorates "Walter Weeper," reiterating the metaphor of seeing war through a clouded glass by portraying a man huddled atop a platform as he cries into a pool beneath him. The man's eyes have been plucked out in order to create two holes from which the water pours. A defeated bird contributes to the fountain of tears as it stands on his shoulders and weeps. Attached to the fountain is a placard that reads: "Generously Over-Subscribing His Quota of Tears, He Enabled Others to Furnish the Blood and the Sweat." Mocking ethics of shared sacrifice, the monument upbraids even as it celebrates those who might have loved American democracy but not enough to defend it. What we get, then, is a picture of a *civilian* form of survivor's guilt, underwritten by weak social and political bonds.

The third is for "Dame Rumor." It stands as one of only a few portrayals of American women in Dr. Seuss's wartime oeuvre. When Dr. Seuss did depict women, he tended to emphasize the divisions between home fronts and battlefronts, thus separating the culture of war along gender lines while reinstituting his emasculation of those men who were divested from the war efforts. He also tended to picture American women as well-to-do and stereotypically well-fed—"Mrs. U.S. Waste," for example, who stuffs herself and spoils her pets in a crude display of American consumerism. So it was that Dame Rumor stood out as the "Minister of Public Information," leaning out of a window with her hand to her mouth gossiping with another woman who leans out of her own window, bulges her eyes, and covers her mouth in shock. Between the two is an undergarment strung up on a clothesline. In the backdrop, a woman with a megaphone directs attention to the monument from what looks like a tour by motorcar. She is celebrated for her "inspired words," and, like Dame Rhetoric, is a monument to misinformation with her broadcast of good lies well told. She is also a holdover from World War I and the culture of propaganda replete with stories of horror and high moral grounds. That she also embodies the concomitant consumer culture of war exaggerates the utter publicity of combat as an everyday reality and its constitution of public relations about war and the public's relation to it.

A fourth monument is for John Haynes Holmes, a prominent antiwar pacifist. In Dr. Seuss's cartoon, Holmes's head is cut off by the frame, yet it is held in the hand of a Japanese soldier who has decapitated him. Still, Holmes embraces his slayer, making a grotesque mockery of his many appeals to a worldwide brotherhood of man (referenced in the monument's placard). The image recollects the separation of Japanese from US American character and simultaneously carries out a sort of "I told you so" judgment on those who tricked themselves into thinking that words could serve as weapons against a monstrous enemy. It also reminds viewers of the Japanese contagion and, without the insects, recollects the capacity for "foreign" toxins to contaminate American culture.

So the fourth monument finally aligns with the fifth and final one, which honors "The Wishful Listeners" who were content to wait and wonder whether or not "German Morale" would collapse under the burden of its own bigotry. In the sculpture, a group of four white American men cup their hands to their ears and lean toward Germany as if waiting for the whispers of a distant lover. In this and in the other monumental caricatures, citizen-spectators make up an American typology including "creepers," "weepers," "sleepers," and so on. Some earlier cartoons, such as those aimed at selling war bonds, recall James Montgomery Flagg's aesthetic of implicating "YOU" in the war efforts. However, rather than appeal to the civic duty of potential enlisters, Dr. Seuss caricatures those who in one way or another refused to volunteer either their brains or their bodies for world war. The entire collection constitutes the comic looking glass. War is an exaggerated reflection of a democratic national character, which in turn is caricatured as a warped rule for judging collective selfhood.

This chapter has traversed images of animals, insects, muck, and machines to demonstrate how Dr. Seuss waged a war on American culture early in the Second World War. Before shifting his energies to film production, Dr. Seuss utilized caricature to portray a crisis over what characteristics the US nation and its bodies politic should assume. He therefore became an artistic extension of an approach to both cultural and armed conflict that earned Roosevelt the moniker "Dr. Win-the-War." Dr. Seuss could just as easily have embodied such a cognomen. Notwithstanding his unapologetically racist depictions of Japanese adversaries, or perhaps in light of them, Dr. Seuss offered a comic take on how and why enactments of national character amounted to carrying a heavy cultural load. If anything, Dr. Seuss's caricatures did less to demonstrate the solidity of Americanism as a stable point of identification than to amplify its utter instability. His caricatures were scarcely distractions from the horrors of actual warfare. Instead, they were comic distortions of the horrific burden that war places on a nation that must, at the same time, struggle over how to see itself.

The cat trope typifies the good, the bad, and the ugly of the comic spirit. It provokes considerations of the realities that follow from nationalistic fantasies. In and through Dr. Seuss's comic disposition, and then again in and through the variety of ways in which cats lurk in his wartime cartoons, caricature is a looking glass of visual humor. It transmogrifies members of the US body politic into laughable shadows of who and what they should be, given a set of shared principles that are out of whack when it comes to putting the American Way into practice. Dr. Seuss channeled a catlike rhetoric to display the risks of being a home bird in a little nest, self-satisfied. He looked down on US war culture by providing a bird's eye view of it, with abstractions of bad characters representing the bigger pictures and broader strokes of what was at stake in taking on the Axis Powers. Across his catalog, war is cast as an outcome of human life gone mad *and* as a reflection of humanity just the way it is, as fantastical as it is all too banal. Dr. Seuss's main point is this: if democracy is worth doing, then it is worth fighting for. That there is evil in the world is the unstated assumption behind the Human Comedy that drives this rather straightforward axiom. At the end of the day, Dr. Seuss aimed to keep up appearances, to act as if, and to protect American national character by positing comic images for working through unsmiling ideas about what it means to be a citizen of war, and to be a member of a nation at war with something and someone made out as Other than some larger Self. The comicality of the looking glass matters. Sometimes the Other is Us. For Dr. Seuss, in the face of war and its evils, even democracy can be as ugly as—or uglier than—it seems.

Children of War in Ollie Harrington's Dark Comedy

3.

There is a well-known trickster in African folklore. He is Anansi, the Spider, known as a shapeshifting figure for the Good and Bad spirit in structures of cultural knowledge. Anansi originated in the folktales of the Ashanti of West Africa but eventually cropped up in US American slave narratives. Anansi is cunning. He is clever. He is an embodiment of acumen and its attendant conceits. There is an Anansi parable, however, that demonstrates the trickster out of humor.[1]

Anansi is trying to bottle up all the knowledge in the world and hide it away at the top of a large, bristly tree. He puts the knowledge in a big pot, straps it to his front, and attempts to climb. But the pot prevents him from keeping a good grip on the bark and branches. Anansi slips. He falls. He gets frustrated. Then, from the ground below him, laughter billows up. The laughter comes from his son, Ntikuma. "Tie the pot behind you," says Ntikuma, as if telling a joke. "That way you'll be able to hold onto the tree." Annoyed that his child was right, Anansi fumed and fussed and accidentally dropped the pot. Knowledge spilled out and got swept up in a wind that took it out to sea, dispersing it throughout the world. Humbled on the walk home, and sufficiently humored by his experience, Anansi expressed to Ntikuma, "What is the use of all that wisdom if a young child still needs to put you right?"

In the 1920s, cartoonist Oliver ("Ollie") Wendell Harrington suffered his own experience with the strange fruit of what Jonathan Scott Holloway might call "Jim Crow Wisdom." The adult who bore it was neither trickster nor parent. But she was bigheaded in her bigoted character. "Never, never forget these two belong in that there trashbasket," said Miss McCoy, the sixth-grade teacher of Ollie Harrington and his friend, Prince Anderson. Ollie and Prince were the only two Black students in their class within a South Bronx schoolhouse. It was a few years after the Great War and four decades before Lyndon B. Johnson's dream of a Great Society, haunted as it was by the specter of an Ugly America. As Harrington tells it, Miss McCoy embodied the sort of unabashed racism and nativism that less than twenty years earlier had yielded an exhibit at the Bronx Zoo that featured Ota Benga, a Congolese pygmy who was kept in a cage with his "fellow" monkeys. Harrington's peers reeled "in peals of laughter" at Miss McCoy's comments.[2] Harrington turned to the spirit of Ntikuma.

Ollie took to drawing caricatures of Miss McCoy in the margins of his notebook. One shows Miss McCoy "being rammed into a local butcher shop meat grinding apparatus."[3] Another pictures her simply as the bust of an old maid with a drooping face and woolly-minded eyes. These and other caricatures represent something of a distorted mirror stage in Harrington's development as a cartoon artist. They formed the groundwork for his lifelong portrayal of adult idiocies as they are manifest in "the ordinary problems of ordinary Negroes and the ironic aspects of Negro-white relations."[4] It was Harrington's caricatures of everyday conflicts in race relations that led Langston Hughes to dub him "Negro America's favorite cartoonist."[5] Miss McCoy seemed to have a formative impact on Harrington's caricatures of Black culture throughout the Cold War era, many of which situated children not as audiences or passive victims of race hatred but rather as rhetorical agents in its deconstruction. Many, too, brought the specter of cultural warfare to bear on matters of armed conflict.

Born on Valentine's Day in 1912, Ollie Harrington grew up into nearly a century of war that traversed Jim Crow culture through the Second World War to the Resistance War Against America and the civil rights movement. By 1932, he was on assignment with the *Amsterdam News* in New York. It was in this rag in 1935 that Harrington's most famous character, Bootsie, first appeared in a soon-to-be serial strip, *Dark Laughter*. Much scholarly attention to Harrington dwells on Bootsie, as well as his war correspondence for the *Pittsburgh Courier* and cartoon politics that endured through his own self-exile in 1951 amid McCarthyism and Cold War hysteria. Bootsie is still considered the first nationally recognized Black cartoon character in the United States. A primary reason is that he was "a black everyman of Harlem, an urban dweller who had come to the city during the Black migration and brought with him his southern ways."[6] As such, so-called dark laughter was invoked by "the realistic feel of experienced urban life" that Bootsie embodied. Harrington described this experience as the "almost unbelievable but hilarious chaos" ensnaring and encircling Black culture.[7] In emphasizing the general politics of Bootsie, examinations that mostly skip over Harrington's caricatures from the 1960s miss some opportunities to understand national character with regard to an important gauge of Black experience: children. Put more plainly, there is a need to understand *the whiteness* of wartime American national character through the childlike, corrective attitude that can emerge out of caricatures that put Blackness at the center of cultural politics. Folktales offer moral judgments comprehensible by children. Relatedly, children can offer "folk" judgments on the casualties of war and the adults who cause them. As in Dr. Seuss's work, caricatures in Ollie Harrington's cartoons constitute a sort of childlike wisdom that speaks volumes about adult worlds. Unlike Dr. Seuss, though, Harrington employs the rhetorical force of children *as* caricatures in order to imbue the folly of war and war culture with a sense of humor. This chapter contends that Harrington's caricatures of Black children across the Cold War era demonstrate the damage done by systemic racial prejudice at home and the possibility that visual humor presents real rhetorical agency in the midst of broader crises in national character.

Harrington's caricatures fit in "a tradition of wartime cartoon characters."[8] In the broad history involving cultural politics of caricaturing racial and racialized bodies, Harrington's comic artwork fits in as a contravention to what Rebecca Wanzo calls "visual imperialism," or "the production and circulation of racist images that are tools in justifying colonialism and other state-based discrimination."[9] To be sure, it fits within a complicated historical march of visualizations for "real" Americanism that includes imagery by popular cartoonists like Larry Dunst, Herbert Lock (or "Herblock"), Bill Mauldin, Robert Osborn, Edward Sorel, and even James Montgomery Flagg. An important distinction is that Harrington did not focus on depictions of political figures and members of the establishment class (i.e., presidents and opinion leaders) or readily recognizable abstractions of American-ness (i.e., Columbia or Uncle Sam). Nor did he follow a tendency of Black cartoonists to caricature Southern whites in a form of retributive justice.[10] Instead, Harrington lampooned the links between combat mentalities among those with small-minded, racist attitudes and US war culture. Black children stood in for and reflected ongoing struggles to fend off the otherwise permanent plights of institutional racism and systemic inequality. In other words, Harrington's children of war challenge democratic principles and policies as executors of basic needs like food, shelter, life, and liberty. Harrington's children were not caricatures of dissent from war. Nor were they "beautiful" portrayals of Blackness, particularly given their drift into the "ugly" and the "offensive" as rhetorical forces for "antiracist protest."[11] Rather, they were travesties of domestic discord, amplifying a minority court of public opinion about racialism as the site of homegrown friend-enemy conceptions of US Americanism and American exceptionalism. They constituted a comic tyranny of caricature, working against what Wanzo rightly sees as an imperialism of the very visual field of Blackness (and Whiteness) that "can make everyday lived experience a racial grotesque," then as now.[12] In Harrington's comic travesties is an affirmative, powerful revisionist history of this imperialist bent in the tradition of wartime caricatures.

Childlike humor has long been associated with notions that a child is brutally honest. Children say the damnedest things. They express observations that are sometimes improper, impolite, incomprehensible, or downright rude. Their observations often reflect our unstated assumptions about the world back to us. They exaggerate what we take for granted. They uncover what we conceal in our deepest held, even if superficial, beliefs. Psychoanalytic fidelities notwithstanding, Sigmund Freud once saw in children the faculty for expressing what he called "earnest conclusions" based on "uncorrected knowledge."[13] As a form of humor, such a childlike faculty allows for the correction of perspectives through the "misuse of words, a bit of nonsense, or an obscenity."[14] The humor of Black children facilitates Harrington's construction of *homo rhetoricus liberi* out of *homo rhetoricus Africanus*,[15] born as this figure is out of the witlessness of adults.

To set up the comicality in Harrington's children of war, this chapter begins with a brief outline of Cold War public culture. Included in this outline is a recognition of the very real, very disturbing problems of lynching, rampant unemployment (despite the war boom), unshakable Jim Crow politicking on issues of social policy, housing inequities, and other exigencies that led many to see the close of the "Good War" as a good time for a "Second Reconstruction." The Cold War context of panic, blacklists, and investigations is also accounted for. Calls for civil rights in this context were chalked up to Communist ploys that inspired factions of white Americans to take up a "massive resistance." Some believe that the Vietnam War supplanted the purpose and progress of civil rights. At the very least, a national culture of—and at—war exacerbated the tensions between containment and liberation, separation and excision, whiteness and Blackness. Harrington's children were caught in the middle, especially since "integration" had become a contemptible word to congressional Dixiecrats. If Bootsie embodied Black experience, Harrington's children of war became its unlikely reflections in the comic looking glass. Through an examination of Harrington's caricatures of Black children in the *Pittsburgh Courier* (and the *Daily Worker*, in 1967 renamed the *Daily World*) primarily between 1961 and 1975, I argue that Harrington laughed at the racial character of a US nation that persisted to draw battle lines as color lines, and vice versa.

Old Stories, New Wars

To revise an old Vietnam War era saying: Children without a chance for peace are like a home without a roof. President Dwight D. Eisenhower was not known for his progressive views on race relations. He fumbled implementation of the *Brown v. Board of Education* decision and even sympathized with the interest among Southerners to keep white and Black cultures separate. Still, Ike was an incrementalist who might have been wary about placing the burden of desegregation on children. He was also an outspoken critic of the folly of war, even though he justified its use in the name of preserving the forces of Good over Evil. In a speech before the American Society of Newspaper Editors in April 1953, Ike ruminated on the chance for peace, urging that every war effort "signifies, in the final sense, a theft from those who hunger and are not fed, those who are cold and are not clothed," and most upsettingly those who place the heart of humanity in "the hopes of children."[16] This sentiment rings truer for Black children of war.

On April 2, 1960, Ollie Harrington published a cartoon in the *Pittsburgh Courier* that provided a Janus-faced view of the Cold War era (fig. 18). Two Black boys stand outside a Southern establishment. A large sign in a window reads: "NOTICE: Only white ladies and gentlemen will be seated and served. Members of other races are considered undesirable." Perhaps worse is the welcome extended to leashed animals, but only those "accompanied by desirable clients." One of the boys stares blankly toward the sign while his friend reflects, "My daddy said they didn't seem to mind servin' him on the Anzio Beach-head. But I guess they wasn't gettin' along so good with them Nazis then!" The boy's puerility is as palpable as his petulance.

FIG. 18 Oliver W. Harrington, "My daddy said they didn't seem to mind servin' him on the Anzio beachhead," 1960. From *Dark Laughter*, April 2, 1960. Courtesy of The Library of Congress. Used with permission of Dr. Helma Harrington, Berlin.

The cartoon recollects notions of a "New Negro" that emerged at the close of World War II. This notion is disappointed by overt racism and policed segregation that, even if formally ended in the military in 1948, persisted in the most basic institutions of US public culture. Just imagine that the first question asked of Supreme Court Justice William O. Douglas at a press conference when he visited India in 1950 was: "Why does America tolerate the lynching of Negroes?"[17] This question eventually became a Russian catchphrase for calling out moral hypocrisies and deflecting its own human rights abuses, but it nevertheless encapsulates the dirty laundry in postwar airings of an America that remained racially unwashed and morally unfree. Harrington's cartoon also displays the deep surfaces of a cold culture war that rendered "undesirables" both foreign enemies and domestic contenders for equality in free thought, speech, and action, while simultaneously alluding to the international attitudes of disgust that impacted US political alliances at home and abroad. The Civil Rights Act of 1960 was enacted a month after publication of this cartoon. Yet the next four years saw some of the most decisive activities in the cultural landscape: anti-segregation sit-ins, Freedom Rides, the Albany Movement, the use of US marshals to integrate Ole Miss, Martin Luther King Jr.'s "I Have a Dream" speech, the assassination of President John F. Kennedy, and so on through to another civil rights act. Legislation begat cultural lag, and discriminations continued to run rampant in school systems, labor economies, and housing markets. What is more, another war was afoot. The conflict in Vietnam mirrored a form of homespun militancy that, for many Black citizens and soldiers alike, sparked another two-war front (or, a two-front war) that put the racialism of the American Way in the crosshairs.

There is a deep and complicated history to this ambivalence of US warism. The idea that there could be a federal pronouncement of good civic standing underwrote so many nationalistic efforts during World War II and the corrective measures taken to manage public opinion. This led to the postwar "tensions project" (1949–53), sponsored by the United Nations Educational, Scientific and Cultural Organization (UNESCO), which yielded insights on "aggressive nationalism" and threats to peace. Indeed, what Margaret Mead acknowledged as the "psychological equipment" for winning the war was recognized by UNESCO as the predispositional baggage of national stereotypes, and it facilitated Cold War mentalities as the makings of more generalized conceptions of war as a necessary good when it comes to an all-out defense of US Americanism. The shadows cast by these dark days are long, blending into a nationalistic hubris that fomented the Vietnam War and produced a perverted, top-down, and predacious warrior ethos we now see encircling the War on Terror. Harrington's work pronounces his attention to the impacts of both war footings and culture war orientations. The dark laughter in Harrington's caricatures amounts to a gloomy look at the failures of American democracy in an incapacity to protect all citizens at home even as the United States waged war with international Others deemed a threat to homespun life and liberty. His comic judgment is even weightier given that Harrington's view was that of an outsider looking in—of a citizen unwelcome in his home country.

There is every reason to see the physical and symbolic violence against nonwhite citizens at home as a perverse reflection of the carnage afflicted on nonwhites elsewhere. It is fair to align the racialism driving much warfare with the racism that defines Black–white tensions in the late 1940s and beyond, and thereby to approach the Black children in Harrington's cartoons as caricatures of a US war culture in particular riven by old stories of race relations rewritten for new times. In many ways, these children typify the "struggles for national and racial equality" that "characterize the entire Cold War era."[18] Particularly in the abovementioned cartoon, the two Black children capture confrontations between institutions of racism and everyday rituals of prejudice, thereby reiterating something as banal as the contrast between a racial dialect and the racialized conceit of the faux English pride in Deep Southern values. Consider the vernacular phonology in the child's speech versus the archaism in the sign outside "Ye Olde Dixie Inn." Such is an emblem of "old ways" and "old attitudes" that the Black press and civil rights activists aimed to combat.[19] Harrington waged a battle over national character through caricatures that positioned Black children as the most critical and perspicacious—and indeed humorous— observers of "the ridiculous side of American race relations."[20] This darkly comic side is driven by false premises and false promises in the democratic experiment.

Here again lurks a complicated history. Metaphors and movements around a "New Negro" date back to the Harlem Renaissance. Following the so-called "Father of the Harlem Renaissance," Alain LeRoy Locke, a sense of "newness" signified a cultural reset around the tensions that had long been connected to mattes of racial pride and prejudice, not to mention expressions of Black selfhood and *self*-presentation. From Frederick Douglass and Phillis Wheatley through W. E. B. Du Bois and to the numerous and prominent Black writers, intellectuals, and artists in Harrington's day, one can locate in discourses of the "New Negro" not simply a "rebellion against what has been, but opportunity for what may be."[21] World War II hardly redeemed democracy. Nor did it serve as a racial equalizer. Black citizens were held in limbo as second-class citizens following a relative failure of the Double V campaign. As Mary L. Dudziak argues, a recurrence of troubled race relations—made even more pronounced in times of war—spoils "the image of American democracy."[22] Or, in Du Bois's words, it magnifies the ways that a nation reels and staggers, makes mistakes, and commits wrongs as it attempts to sustain the great and beautiful aura of egalitarianism. Any ideal of democracy in the United States, though, was always already sullied by the institution of slavery, and thereafter the perpetuation of race hatred in the horrible, and horribly festive, act of lynching. In fact, it is the very principle of racism as a mundane way of thinking, speaking, and acting that makes it more of a burden on national character than its manifestation as a pathological monstrosity.[23] Hence the Second World War was fought on two fronts, with racial politics at home and the cultural politics of Americanism at stake in so many military excursions overseas.

The fogs of iron curtains and color lines figure prominently here. An indubitable dilemma in the postwar United States was that commies were cast with much the same die as "colored people" insofar as containment rhetorics situated Americanism "within narrow boundaries of permissible thought and behavior."[24] The motivations for such boundaries were not entirely unfounded. There were, after all, justifiable concerns that the prospect of "Soviet tyranny" looked a lot like the perversions of "Nazi totalitarianism."[25] Yet concerns about the rise of communism in America provoked oversimplified reactions to the "Negro Problem," which by the early 1950s appeared as an extension of ye olde world and a new world reordering averse to anything like Black Reconstruction. The push for civil rights came off as a Communistic ploy. The preservation of US American national character got couched in homogeneous images of collective selfhood.

At the nexus of these rhetorical attempts at containment were matters of Black action in the civil rights movement, iterations of white resistance made grotesquely manifest by an ethos of the Southern Manifesto, and pervasive fears about the Red Menace. Following World War II, there was a popular dispersal of "the delusion that the nation was being overrun by communists" in film, on television, and in print.[26] This was bolstered by anti-Communist national security reports like NSC-68 as well as President Harry S. Truman's "Campaign of Truth," which began in 1950 as a psychological "war of words" in counteraction to Soviet propaganda and in support of postwar sentiments of nationalistic solidarity.[27] One particular concern was that Blacks in uniform had given way to domestic militancy among Black citizens.[28] Black militancy put federal and local governments in a precarious position of needing to deconstruct a system of racial trauma, inequity, and injustice. It pressured ordinary citizens, too, to think hard about what kind of a democratic people the United States should be if the principles of American democracy would be definitive characteristics of a free and equal nation not compromised by the follies of war.

As it was, embattlements regarding national character became outgrowths of "old hatreds."[29] The federal government was burdened with the task of codifying a "Great Society" that was implied by, and finally promoted after, victory in the Good War. The military-industrial complex was transformed into a military-*cultural* complex, which was judged by its successes and failures in nationalistic efforts to secure equal opportunities for all people. The evolution of the Cold War into the Vietnam War, however, all but ensured "the dwindling of official attention to civil rights matters."[30] President Richard Nixon turned away from the civil rights movement. Harrington's modus operandi was to animate "the foibles, the misapprehensions, and the predicaments of African Americans" as they *devolved* from the 1950s through the 1970s.[31] This devolution revolved around "the treatment of black soldiers, segregation, and lynching."[32] The fallout from war, for Harrington, was most evident in false promises around that olden creed about liberty and justice for all, as evidenced by the inefficacy of the G.I. Bill for Black veterans, the continuation of segregationist policies, and targeted racial terror throughout the American South. The droll humor in Bootsie cartoons took on issues of police brutality, antiwar activism, the rise of Black power and Black Nationalism, and the prominence of militant groups like the Black Panthers. Moreover, Harrington pictured Black Americans as rhetorically and materially oppressed by a nation that was more apt to look upon itself in Black-and-white terms rather than for its true colors. Such oppression emphasized a through line from the Red Summer to a Red Scare mentality that urged fears about Black empowerment and a disempowered white America.

Along with communist disquietude, the Cold War era made it so that domestic civil rights were aligned with more international and anti-colonialist movements. For instance, organizations like the Council on African Affairs (which allied with the American Communist Party before its disbandment in 1955) contributed to Pan-African responses to generalized cruelty of whites against Blacks by linking "the struggles of African Americans against Jim Crow" to "the struggles of Africans and colonized peoples for independence."[33] This led to a worldwide ideological union of Black cultures. Another part of this story is the Black press. Following P. L. Prattis, editor for the *Chicago Defender* and later the *Pittsburgh Courier*, the Black press was "an instrument of the embattled minority in action against the repressive majority," as well as a medium for "telling the people the truth, regardless of the corrosive effect."[34] The Black press also "often made common cause with the American Left and, at key moments, with the international Left, including the Communist Party."[35] Especially in the early years of the Cold War, editors of Black newspapers were regularly accused of being in cahoots with Communist radicals and threatened by the economic fallout from publishing subversive content since advertisers were cautious in associating their products or services with anything that could be characterized as extremist. Still, the Black press was a prime source for people of color to track "the changing sense of self, community, and country."³⁶ The Black press is a voice and vision for characteristics of Black culture.

The *Pittsburgh Courier* in particular is integral to the Black press. It was not only among the most popular Black papers during and after World War II (once the leading Black weekly in the United States before being acquired by the *Defender* in 1966). The *Pittsburgh Courier* was also considered "a maverick press" in the fight for racial justice.³⁷ James Baldwin called it "the best of the lot."³⁸ The paper rose to prominence following the Great Migration period. Robert Lee Vann, a successful Black lawyer, was its original editor and progenitor of its fundamental mission to secure the betterment of Black America. In a 1915 editorial, Vann promoted war as an opportunity for "THE NEGRO" to assume "HIS RIGHTFUL PLACE IN THE OPINIONS OF AMERICANS."³⁹ Prattis, who took over editorship during World War II after Vann's death, used his editorship to propagate the "Double V Campaign." The campaign advocated "victory over totalitarian forces overseas as well as over similar forces in the United States that were denying equality to blacks."⁴⁰ As Prattis noted, audiences and artists of the *Pittsburgh Courier* were drawn to "similes and metaphors that lay open the foe's weaknesses," and to "cutting irony, sarcasm and ridicule."⁴¹ This appeal is significant for a consideration of Harrington's work because the *Pittsburgh Courier* had a large section devoted to editorial cartoons and a readership primed for the sting of its biting humor.

The same could be said of the *Daily World* after switching back to being a weekend to a daily paper and then enlisting Harrington in 1968. The paper itself was a byproduct of the Communist Labor Party in 1919, which grew into the American Communist Party. In fact, the *Daily Worker* (later dubbed the *Daily World*) was the paper of the American Communist Party. In the 1930s and 40s, it organized around anti-lynching campaigns, the cultural front of the peace movement, and activism toward civil rights. This made it something of an ally to the Black press, especially considering that the *Daily Worker* evolved into an outlet for denouncing Jim Crow laws and reporting on the racist activities that tormented the Black community. Harrington and other cultural workers aligned themselves with the paper because it supported a more democratic form of Americanism. The *Daily Worker* shut down between 1958 and 1960 due to its embroilments in the Red Scare. However, when it resumed publication in 1968, it did so under the editorship of African American journalist John Pittman, a respected reporter and public supporter of the civil rights movement (including the Black Panthers). The *Daily World* therefore exceeded Bootsie's somewhat parochial politics to delve into issues of class warfare, war profiteering, and the military-industrial complex as a cumulative cultural drain on Black families and their children.

In this context, it is unsurprising that from the early 1950s through the close of the Cold War, "seeing red" was often analogous to seeing black, which "weakened the legacy of civil liberties, impugned standards of tolerance and fair play, and tarnished the very image of a democracy."[42] More to the point, it privileged myopia as a way to win not only the war for US democratic principles but also the culture wars against those who sought to reorder the distribution of public goods. Problems from racial violence to rampant institutionalized prejudice enveloped the "character," "temper," and "cultural makeup" of communities that rendered the Vietnam War a sorry outcome of those Cold War boundaries that so colored public culture.[43] For Harrington and others, critical commentary was better (even necessarily) conducted outside of US borders. After years of publishing cartoons, editorials, and news stories in the *Pittsburgh Courier* (which, incidentally, was monitored under the FBI's "RACON" program), and because of his work with other papers like the *People's Voice* and the *Amsterdam News*, Harrington came under fire.

Harrington's cartoons exemplify the dark ugliness clouding un-Americanism. During World War II, he covered the Tuskegee Airmen from the "safety" of a C-47, combatting the postwar "retrenchment of racist values."[44] At one point he even reported on the activities of the Ku Klux Klan (KKK). While reviving his cartoon campaigns through caricatures of the Black ghetto, Harrington served as a public relations director for the National Association for the Advancement of Colored People (NAACP). As early as the 1940s, Harrington was linked to the radicalism of the Black Left and put on a watch list by the FBI, the CIA, and eventually the House Un-American Activities Committee (HUAC). By the late 1950s, Harrington had become "persona non grata in his home country."[45] So he emigrated with some other African American writers, critics, commentators, and artists. During a stint in Paris, Harrington joined the likes of Chester Himes, Langston Hughes, Claude McKay, Nella Larsen, and Richard Wright. Later, following Wright's controversial death in 1960, Harrington moved to East Berlin while some like James Baldwin, Lorraine Hansberry, Julian Mayfield, and others went to Ghana. Importantly, Harrington brought his own "Vietnam Syndrome" abroad, providing an "outsider's" perspective on American warfare. Like so many in the community, Harrington feared the existential threat that Cold War America posed to Black culture, never mind his own life. He even mused with his brethren about "whether the integration of Blacks would transform and democratize the nation or whether Blacks would be remade in the image of a stultifying, inequitable, and morally bankrupt American society."[46] Self-exile thus developed into an "enabling condition" in that it "symbolized a broader tendency among Black Americans to view the political status and identity of African Americans through African liberation struggles."[47] Harrington remarks in an essay, "Why I Left America," that his overarching goal was to advance Black Liberation.[48] He kept up on happenings on his home front through US news reports,[49] and American newspapers like the *Pittsburgh Courier*, the *Daily Worker* (eventually the *Daily World*, and now the *People's World*, an online newspaper), and the *Chicago Defender* (until 1963) became his organs for caricature. It is in the cartoons he published in these papers that Harrington's emphasis on children of war took shape.

Children are the metaphors for, and the embodiments of, Harrington's comic looking glass. To borrow a few words from a speech delivered by Ralph Ellison in September 1963, "these children" were some of the most discerning "living critics of their environment."[50] They were also quite moving sources of Black humor in caricature given their status as Outsiders of the Adult World who are nonetheless caught up in it. And they took on the subversive quality and critical distance that can empower an outsider to exploit the tensions between those on the outside and those looking in, but with the sort of proximate connection needed to create a distorted mirror image. The children in Harrington's cartoons are vehicles for "caricaturing, challenging, and subverting adult values."[51] These values were the targets for Harrington's revisions of the double binds and double standards that animate race and racism in US war cultures. Harrington's children converse about the mistreatment of Black adults, reflect on policy measures around integration and social welfare, comment on the domestic fallout from warfare, and even wrestle with racial prejudice themselves. At no point are they innocent or ignorant. Instead, they are the unlikely foot soldiers of wartime appeals to a more realistic imagination of the racial impairments in US national character.

Comic Images of Blackness: An Interlude

Before turning to Harrington's caricature campaign for children of war, a brief pause is needed to account for the importance of Black humor as a peculiar yet all too typical vehicle for breaking with traditional views of US Americanism. After all, as literary critic Harry Levin once put it, Black humor provokes reexaminations of rhetorical judgments because it "confronts us literally, as the power of Afro-American blackness asserts itself" in the very comicality of coming full circle amid specific zeitgeists.[52] The very Blackness of Black humor can be found in the ambivalence of absence and presence, of rejoicing and mourning, that shows forth when traditions themselves are "shared, repeated, critiqued, and revised," in vernacular as well as in visual imagery.[53] Blackness exists "on both sides of the existential fence," says Alain Badiou. "As mourning, it makes us cry; as humor, it makes us laugh. And it will make us laugh about mourning itself."[54] Harrington's caricatures appeal to this comic ambivalence.

One thing to acknowledge first and foremost is that comic images of Blackness, and in particular Black Americans, are endemic to—nay, inveterate in—representations of white America, and by extension white citizenship. In the words of Jessie Fauset, Black people are repeatedly seen "as a living comic supplement" to images of whiteness.[55] Or, following Wanzo, there is a rich tradition of Black artists deploying "racist caricatures to mark the citizenship of black subjects in order to show that it is *marked*—by an absence of rights or alienation from the nation."[56] This is why the so-called "Negro Life" was characterized in the early 1900s by some such as poet and writer William Stanley Braithwaite as "a shuttlecock between the two extremes of humor and pathos."[57] It was lightness and darkness. It was the fantastical and the all-too-real. It was freedom and unfreedom. It was, simply, a racial travesty typified by the New Negro as a sort of "comic disparity between the black man and his station."[58] Hence scholars like Henry Louis Gates Jr. and Gene Andrew Jarrett have probed representations of Blacks in the United States for the highest as well as the lowest forms of human life, for the best and the worst of true and false Americanism, for a sense of cultural celebration rather than despair, and thereby for an idea of "blackness as presence" rather than absence.[59] Humor in the Black tradition betrays forms of rhetorical significance that do not require official realms of social acceptance and political enfranchisement. The history of "racial uplift" in Black humor relies on manipulations of imagery to the end of manipulating lived realities.[60] In this manipulation is an image of Blackness laid bare in the comic looking glass.

There is in the humor that comes from such comicality a certain practice of making cultural assumptions about Americanism not necessarily the butts of jokes but most certainly the subject of a distorted perspective. For one thing, insofar as humor is an index of some national or collective character, the Black tradition of humor is a byproduct of the minority status forced upon African American communities for so long, never mind on Africanism. According to Mel Watkins, this status reveals itself in humor as "a tendency toward self-mockery or self-deprecation" that can nevertheless be projected outward and traced from slave times through minstrelsy and vaudeville to the stand-up comedy of Richard Pryor.[61] Yet it also shows forth as a rhetorical mode of usurpation with regard to the longstanding oppressions of dominant white culture. African-American humor is truly Black humor, in both senses of the term. It is the "laugh by proxy," in Langston Hughes's words, cast onto the Other while being boomeranged back to the Self. It is about making Blackness present in order to see selfhood through somebody else's eyes—to look upon oneself as if a stranger, and some other as more familiar than one might like them to be.

The resistances and retaliations endemic to African American humor are similarly about self-liberation in the face of originary subjugation.[62] On one hand, this kind of humor serves as a check on white culture. On the other, it stands to reckon with the (comic) spirit of Black experience.[63] There are clear, albeit discomfiting, overlaps here with what is alternatively characterized as ethnic humor in the United States. At least one has to do with the common sense of insider–outsider relations, centers and margins, simplifications and generalizations, and the habits of identification and division that reveal a "web of ambivalence, cooperation, and anxiety," even more so when humor is used to exemplify these awkward imbrications.[64] All of these and more characterizations reflect the *un*common grounds of foundational principles for the American Way, or what Hughes might describe as the awe—whether awesome or awful—to be gleaned from our own smiles in a mirror. Nevertheless, they remind us of something crucial: "Black American humor began as a wrested freedom, the freedom to laugh at that which was unjust and cruel in order to create distance from what would otherwise obliterate a sense of self and community."[65] If black-and-white (and Black and White) characteristics of US Americanism are gray areas of complex social, political, and cultural histories, then the contingencies of wartimes present even larger points of reference for grappling with the ordinary entailments of any national character. Resistance is a mode of retaliation, just as self-presentation risks self-negation.

Harrington's editorial cartoons are at once exemplary and exceptional in this brief sketch of African American humor. First of all, they embody a comic construction of *proximity*, taking on nationalistic notions of selfhood by combining self-construction and self-understanding with self-criticism.

In part, this meant that during World War II as well as the Cold War he had to openly and explicitly engage "the contradiction between America's fight against the racism of fascism abroad and its own racist practices at home."[66] It also meant that he had to reconsider representation itself as a species of self-delusion, making the rhetorical act of showing and telling it like it is a complicated *comic* art of seeing things differently. Visual humor was a means of making images of Black experience even more complex and nuanced rather than guilelessly liberating. Put differently, Harrington humored Black experience while rendering it comical in order to pursue anti-racism and point out the contradictions, absurdities, and incongruities inherent to racialized travesties. In May of 1942, Harrington was actually criticized by members of the Black community for using his famed character Bootsie to belittle African Americans. He replied that "there are some imbeciles left among us who find time in between bone-pulverizing bombings, mass murder and other sadistic forms of civilized recreation, to laugh."[67] What Harrington was also saying in his unsubtle mockery of foreign warfare and warring dispositions and deeds at home is that, sometimes, it is the one who directs laughter toward oneself who best recognizes the humanity in others.

This is why Harrington's caricatures of Black children are so potent: they strip the machinations of white men and war machines of their "civilized recreation" by proclaiming that the comic spirit is a human spirit.[68] His editorial cartoons are squarely in the Black tradition of humor, especially with their combination of caricature "with a gritty evocation of reality."[69] And yet they make a more universalized humanity even more present by making it into something that exceeds Blackness or whiteness, let alone the complicated issues of ethnicity and race. Harrington goaded Black and white audiences alike to use the misfortunes of wartimes as comic resources for working through the riddles of warring spirits so endemic to US Americanism—or, in the words of poet Georgia Douglas Johnson, to "Unriddle this riddle of 'outside in' / White men's children in black men's skin." Plainly, any self seen in the comic looking glass is at least partly seen in the guise of the other. Children are Harrington's foil for "humoring" such an outlook.

The Black Children of War

To understand Harrington's decades-long use of Black children in caricatures of US war culture is to understand just how much his take stands in stark contrast to the ideas of dread and deference that surrounded images of childhood in white America. Some in the Radical Left viewed children as the last and only hope for egalitarianism. Others saw them as victims of cultural contamination. Discourses of school integration had Communist threads, in which some people argued that *any* kind of mixing "would undermine the fabric of American society."⁷⁰ These threads were tied to everyday consumer activities as well. Comic books. Films. Television shows. Advertisements, like Lyndon B. Johnson's infamous "Daisy Girl" campaign spot preceding the 1964 presidential election. Card games for kids, too. For instance, in 1951 the Red Menace emerged as a visual resource for imagining the Communist threat alongside principles of Americanism. The card set was released by the Bowman Trading Card Company and coupled with packages of bubblegum. There were five in a set. Each contained a graphic image of Cold War conflict (from illustrations of "GENERAL 'IKE' IN COMMAND" to a dour sketch of a "GHOST CITY" overseen by a Grim Reaper in the clouds), all under the aegis of a "Children's Crusade Against Communism." The cards amount to what Margaret Peacock calls "innocent weapons" for young (white) citizens,⁷¹ and they traded in obeisance and fear.

The Black children of Harrington's caricatures are an altogether different stock in trade. They were rife in his cartoons by the early 1950s, and certainly from the Little Rock Nine through *Brown v. Board of Education*. These children were made to look upon the battle for racial separation in view of a more ubiquitous war against Communistic enemies. They were made to see redbaiting as race baiting in the wider context of Massive Resistance. The Supreme Court decision to integrate schools put children on the front lines of cultural conflict at home. Black children were made to understand these conundrums while living out a history of racial terror that had long contributed to the kidnapping of Black children by the KKK and in the lynching programs of white supremacists that animated much of the savagery in early twentieth-century America. These Black children were also urged to see themselves as the pickaninny, or the "mirror image of both the always-already pained African American adult and the 'childlike Negro.'"⁷² However, for Harrington, Black children provided a haunting image of unwitting, yet no less witty and wise, outsiders within a legacy of raced-white labels for American national character.

DIVIDED AND COLORED

A cartoon from 1958 offers an exemplary caricature of Black children as comic foils for Harrington's own crusade. Published under the "Bootsie" heading, the cartoon shows two Black boys walking to/from school amid

FIG. 19 Oliver W. Harrington, "General Blotchit, you take your tanks and feint at Lynchville," 1958. From *Pittsburgh Courier*, 1958. Reproduced from a picture catalogued online for the Prints and Photographs Reading Room by the Caroline and Erwin Swann Foundation for Caricature and Cartoon. The Library of Congress and the National Portrait Gallery. Courtesy of the Library of Congress. Used with permission of Dr. Helma Harrington, Berlin.

a blockade of troops. The soldiers are armed with bayonet-equipped rifles, foreshadowing the paratroopers that symbolized federal enforcement of an integrated Central High in Little Rock just a year later. "Goodness, gracious Gaither," says one boy to the other. "You reckon these fools expect us to run through this hassle every day an' do our HOMEWORK, TOO?" In another cartoon that appeared a few days later, a Black boy, "little Luther,"[73] sits on a stool in the middle of a roadway (fig. 19). He is well dressed, with a uniform jacket, neat tie, and a cap. Behind him a trio of army officers strategizes how to get Luther safely into school. In the backdrop is a collection of soldiers. One officer gives orders: "General Blotchit, you take your tanks and feint at Lynchville. General Pannick, you move into the county seat. And then in the confusion, my infantry will try to take little Luther to school!" The situation of kids in homegrown combat zones is enough to make viewers recoil at the militarization of cultural politics. Yet, as in the first cartoon showing the boys reacting to the Ye Olde Dixie Inn sign, the children speak, and in their speech they mock the relationship between principles and practice. Desegregation, on paper, made all children created equal when it came to schooling. But it did little to remove the war culture that persisted after World War II, which is why—in the second cartoon—the humor is as much in the names of the military men as it is in the image of Luther.

First there are the generals. The surname "Blotchit" is a portmanteau word. It invokes the idea of a "blotch," or a blemish, and is a reference to racism. Then again there is a sense in which this blotch is a cause for desegregation to get botched up, or for the soldiers (to say nothing of the students) to botch it. Or it could directly ridicule the fact that military personnel were necessary because race relations had been mismanaged, bungled, and flubbed in the first place. This resonates with the other surname, "Pannick," insofar as it bespeaks the "blockbusting" and "panic selling" that went along with school integration efforts.[74] Here, however, "pannick" is a mockery, and perhaps even an Ebonic reformulation of racial dread. Such anxiety is highlighted as a "proteophobic expression," amplified by the military measures required to protect a diminutive Black schoolboy and uphold "the dichotomous nature of national boundaries."[75] Finally, there is the overt reference to lynching in the fictitious town of "Lynchville." In one respect, Harrington derides the mob of mass resisters. But the town name also foregrounds the historical endurance of what had become an outmoded, extrajudicial exercise of white power. While the practice of lynching was all but eradicated from public life by the mid-1950s, its corrupted and violent roots were preserved in civic interactions. Harrington pictures how racialized rhetorics are literally inscribed in social systems and socialization processes. He also provides an image of children in need of protection from a domestic aggressor that otherwise might proclaim to engage in warfare, ironically, only in matters of self-defense.

Harrington's early renditions of Black children on the home front therefore tell an altogether different sort of American war story: not one built on ideologies of making the world safe for the American Way but rather one predicated upon a humorous struggle between the white way and the wrong way. According to Tom Engelhardt, this story is "so natural, so innocent, so nearly childlike,"[76] and so ingrained in a historical sense of what victory in World War II would have looked like that the Cold War could only further impede the doing away of racism as a means of putting away childish things. Consider another cartoon from September 1957, in

FIG. 20 Oliver W. Harrington, lynched school bus. From *Daily World*, June 1969. Used with permission of Dr. Helma Harrington, Berlin.

which Harrington laughs at the conceit of some Southern whites who treated Black children as infiltrators in an Americanism to which they supposedly should not have access. The cartoon shows a general awarding "Dixie's noblest medal for gallantry in action" to a foolish-looking ignoramus of a soldier who apparently stood strong "in the face of a suicidal charge by several frenzied Niggra children trying to enter the General Lee Elementary School." If the unapologetic play on the figure of the once-revered Confederate general was not enough, Harrington executed a verbal travesty of an infamous racial pejorative while parodying the Southern drawl right along with Jim Crow mindsets. This travesty lines up with the visual lampoon to portray Harrington's view of "the ludicrous nature of American racism."[77] Furthermore, it captures the backwardness of those who held tight to de jure segregation by treating it as a de facto state of race-based war at home. This backwardness might be most explicit in a caricature that Harrington created of a mob of resisters lynching an entire school bus (fig. 20). A crowd comprised of white men and women, including a Klan member and a sheriff with a cowboy hat, chants, celebrates, and waves Confederate flags beneath a massive, makeshift hanging tree. Suspended in a noose is a battered and partially burned school bus, with its front facing downward and two Black children falling out. Seven stars are carved into the top of the scaffold, along with a few dollar signs down the support beam, which together suggest a Southern Strategy for noncompliance with desegregation.

The image of a lynched school bus is horrifying. But it is reduced to the absurd and amplified to the sublime in a different cartoon that seems to sum up Harrington's child's-eye view on desegregation as a metaphor for nurturing disunity in the American national character. Two Black boys are walking together in the snow. One boy is pulling a wooden sled behind him. The other says: "Man, do you realize that if we was in Alabama it would be against the law fer us cullud kids to walk on this stuff?" The image amplifies the gap between the late 1950s and 1963, a fateful year in which the Southern Christian Leadership Conference along with guidance from Martin Luther King, Jr. rallied, protested, and demanded desegregation of civic spaces as well as public schools in Birmingham, Alabama. Harrington's cartoon reflects on an otherwise raucous and violent series of events that had roots in declarations by some segregationists that the Civil Rights Movement was a Communist intrusion on American institutions. Eugene "Bull" Connor, Birmingham's Commissioner of Public Safety, was chief among those who detested racial integration, and he had since 1958 refused to recognize the civil rights of Black citizens. He even turned a blind eye to the KKK when they terrorized Freedom Riders in 1961. However, in early May 1963, King and others orchestrated what *Newsweek* dubbed a "Children's Crusade," whereby students were enlisted in a march. A number of activists and parents alike expressed concern over King's urgings and even criticized him for converting children into "civil rights kamikazes."[78] Bull Connor ordered police to forcibly remove the children from the streets. In the days between May 2 and May 5, schoolchildren marched and chanted "Freedom . . . Freedom . . . Freedom" before being met by patrolmen and crime dogs. Some were as young as six years old, and among the hundreds of children who were hauled off to jail in school buses. Others were subjected to the brutal blast of water from firehoses. Recall Charles Moore's iconic photograph of a small group of teenagers being pelted against a brick wall, which was widely regarded as a rallying cry for social and political change nationwide. There in the mix but outside the fray were Harrington's two Black boys trudging along in the snow, making the comically perverse observation that whiteness itself established a "dead line." What the boys saw were racial motivations to contain Blackness through both the force of violence and rhetorical force. What they sensed, too, was that children had to bear the burden of war's fallout on cultural battlegrounds.

WAR CULTURE, GAMED

Still, it is in child's play that Harrington really embeds his caricature of the consequences that follow from ugly warring spirits. A cartoon from February 1958 pictures four Black boys bedecked in stereotypically Native American garb wielding hatchets and spears while chasing down three others (fig. 21). Earlier that year, much attention had been paid by *Life* magazine and other outlets to the conflicts between "the Indians" and the so-called "Ku Kluxers." Tribesmen from the latter group had been holding regular anti-Indian gatherings and demonstrations wherein they would burn wooden crosses and rally around bigotry and buckshots.[79] In Harrington's cartoon, the three boys being chased down are wearing white, coned hats with cutout eyeholes. The hats rest on their foreheads, revealing their boyish faces. One boy leads the escape in full stride with a furrowed brow and mouth agape. The boy next to him stumbles to the ground. Trailing behind is a young boy with glasses, fleeing with his tongue hanging out of his mouth. Two Black men observe the play. "Funny how kids' games change with the times, ain't it?" says one to the other. "We used to play cowboys runnin' Indians. Now they play Indians runnin' Ku Kluxers!" The reference here is likely to efforts of the Lumbee to break up Klan rallies in North Carolina. However, it also recollects a colonial heritage in reversing a "traditional" childhood game, "Cowboys and Indians." Following George Herbert Mead's concept of the Self as a collective construction, this cartoon inscribes new agency on Black children "taking the roles of others," and on Indians as a "generalized other" with "organized reactions" to institutional (and vigilante) modes of racism.[80] More glaringly, the impenitence and yet hardly innocent nature of child's play exposes how inurement to civic strife becomes part of the developmental process for those raised to have fun in war games.

This gamesmanship matters a great deal when "role-playing" activities extend from the confines of play to the cultural production of communities. In the company of fellow Blacks, for instance, the Black children in Harrington's cartoon shapeshift to take on different roles based on their own impulses, flights of fancy, and constructed hierarchies. This flexibility and mobility is often compromised, though, once a Black child comes under the rules of play as determined by white children. In another cartoon from

FIG. 21 Oliver W. Harrington, "Funny how kids' games change with the times, ain't it?," 1958. From *Pittsburgh Courier*, February 15, 1958. Used with permission of Dr. Helma Harrington, Berlin.

August 1959, a Black boy dressed as a pirate stands beside two white boys in matching overalls and striped t-shirts. "Hey, Dad . . . ," the boy says to his father, who is puffing on a cigar while pushing a reel mower over a fenced-in lawn, ". . . is these cats tellin' the truth?" the boy inquires. "They say that they don't allow no cullud to be pirates!" There is much irony in this scene. First of all, it belies associations of piracy with blackness. Secondly, it plays on the possible ignorance of the white boys who seem to be unaware (if not proud) of the notion that they are the inheritors of a culture of pioneers and colonizers. While Blacks were so often discriminated against for some form of brutality or barbarism, there is actually a potentially stronger sense in which whites were historically the more barbarous in their own cultural piracy when they "dashed to the sea in their two-sailed barks, landed anywhere, killed everything."[81] The white boys betray the romance of rebel power, looking like children of the American Revolution.

Thirdly, it is not at all clear that the white boys were playing *with* the Black boy. If they were, the Black boy is out of place and unfit for integrated child's play, especially when it is built on conflicting historical imaginaries. If they weren't, the Black boy was clearly disciplined after the white boys witnessed him getting out of line. In either case, even the father figure comes off as an inapt arbiter. The taller, and presumably older, of the two white boys stands straight and stares up at him with a self-satisfied grin. Child's play, like *comic* play, can be a powerful mode of resistance, even if it reinforces Old Ways. Harrington portrays the *de*formative impact on play-as-resistance when US American tradition meets matters of knowing one's role (or place) in the national landscape. The Cold War cultural milieu intensifies this sentiment given that foreign "others" were imaged in terms of mutual and/or unilateral destruction, not coexistence. Harrington's children are "children of Jim Crow."[82] They learned race through cultural warfare, but a type that seemed to do little in the fight against olden color lines. So it is that these children play out and re-create the sort of warfare endemic to Cold War modes of cultural exchange. Resistance for Black children is a struggle against Jim Crow in a wider, more dispersed struggle over multiple forms of oppression and discrimination. Resistance for the white children is, cruelly, self-defense.

The breadth of Harrington's cartoon embattlement is even more striking when it is seen for the history of America it renders in the comic looking glass. An insider's look at American national character, especially during wartimes, would easily find a people of pride. Harrington homes in on what Michael Kammen once called a "people of paradox," namely when grappling with the troubled place of Blacks apropos the white man's historical burdens.[83] One cartoon plays on the familiar theme of characterological allowances when four Black boys are shown in a rowboat, one of whom addresses a boy in the bow. "Well first of all," he says, "you couldn't be Columbus 'cause the white folks wouldn't never let a cullud man discover America!" Here again, heritages are policed according to the realities of the moment, only this time through a Black child's view of acceptable points of national identification. But they are subjected to humor when one of the Black children openly mocks the very idea that white America has been *claimed*, which is to say that it has been both divided and conquered according to the will of a dominant racial group. Nevertheless, at least one of the boys wants to *be* Columbus (or at least a Columbus-like figure) if for nothing more than to occupy a position of prominence in the American story.

All of this is to say that Harrington's 1950s depictions of children form the foundation for his articulation of an American national character in crisis. In 1961, President John F. Kennedy escalated the United States to war. In the process, he championed a brand of nationalism that could not withstand racist treatments of the Negro character (such as the one outlined in the infamous *Moynihan Report* on the "Negro Family," published in 1965) and oversaw the beginnings of his New Frontier. Similarly, while US troops battled through guerilla warfare overseas, citizens (and, at times, the National Guard) combatted racial conflicts alongside images of what Harrington repeatedly showed to be a domestic struggle that deserved a call to sociopolitical arms. Harrington was obviously concerned about civil rights. He was obviously wary of McCarthyism. But his cartoons went even further to offer a window into the cultural structures of race-based ways of seeing the United States as a national Self, taking on the characteristically American institutions of capitalism, war profiteering, social welfare, and others in order to show how the Vietnam War (and the Cold War besides) made, in King's words, "the bombs in Vietnam explode at home." One particular bomb had to do with the problem of poverty.

REFLECTED, POORLY

In 1960, the KKK used a Confederate flag to extinguish the fire in the torch held up by the Statue of Liberty. At least this is what Harrington suggested in a cartoon. The United Klan has been a powerful force in the Southern states and in the US imaginary ever since the *Brown v. Board of Education* decision in 1954. Harrington's cartoon is a visual commentary on the KKK. As prominently, it is a remark on the fact that the Statue of Liberty was erected in part to commemorate freed slaves, and so to symbolize the universality of American freedom. There is a broken shackle and chain on the platform next to Lady Liberty's foot. This imagery assimilates easily into the narrative of immigrants who are themselves looking to break free from the bonds of tyranny and oppression. The Klan co-opted the symbolism of liberty as an emblem of white freedom. Harrington took it back to draw a crooked and colored line from impoverished American values to actual penury.

That President Lyndon B. Johnson had to declare war on poverty while serving as commander in chief of a foreign jungle war is a telltale sign of his sense that, with munitions or metaphors, "war is always the same."[84] King reflected on this in March 1966 when he wrote that the "assembled armies" of civil rights activists fought over the configuration but also "the content of freedom."⁸⁵ King focused on the enduring issues of employment, housing, and urban distress that sustained socioeconomic battles and the revolving door between public culture and (armed) conflict, not to mention conflicts of national interest. This is why King declared "an all-out war on poverty," not just in the ideals of a "Great Society" but also in the ground operations carried out on American city streets. As US involvement in the Vietnam War amped up in the years between 1965 and 1968, Harrington drew attention to the casualties of the War on Poverty. The Black children in his cartoons from 1969 through 1975 reveal a sense that America is a poor reflection of its own ideals when it actively neglects, let alone represses, entire communities. More generally, Harrington's Black children are evidence that the United States was fighting the wrong fight in Vietnam. The plight of the young at home represented a need for moral over military rectitude. In April 1965, during his "Peace Without Conquest" speech at Johns Hopkins University, President Johnson identified the materials of armed conflict (guns, bombs, rockets, and warships) as the "necessary symbols" of human folly. Tellingly, he transitioned to this sentiment by way of a statement about poverty as the index of disorder.⁸⁶ Harrington's cartoon of Lady Liberty is a necessary symbol. His Black children are unfortunate manifestations of American folly—and failure.

While more and more attention was paid to battles overseas, less and less was done to ensure that equal civil rights were actually operationalized. The so-called wars against poverty and drugs typified the increasingly transactional nature of race relations as a line item in the "welfare state regime."⁸⁷ It eventually folded into a broader policy of "Vietnamization" whereby public responsibility took on a form of pacification in place of political priority. For Harrington, this meant the disarmament of important programs and a disproportionate picture of what Eisenhower once called "just relations"—two conditions that Harrington approached with Black children no longer as weapons but rather as casualties of war. Following Joseph Boskin and Joseph Dorinson, the humor in the depictions of these children is as much about survival as it is about subversion.⁸⁸ The humor is replete with a realism that chides a majority white culture, and it emphasizes racialism as the lens through which one might expand the looking-glass view on US cultures of war.

Crucial to Harrington's even sharper cultural criticism is the publication of his work by the *Daily World* in 1968, wherein the tenor of his caricatures increasingly appealed to racial warfare as a byproduct of legislative maneuverings and war as an exemplification of the national interest.

In April 1969, President Johnson's attempts to "Americanize" the Vietnam War with a broadened military campaign and a domestic agenda that emphasized civil rights had done little to secure victory on either front. By many accounts, the War on Poverty had not been won. Johnson's outgoing State of the Union Address was thus in part an admission of defeat. "Urban unrest, poverty, pressures on welfare, education of our people, law enforcement and law and order, the continuing crisis in the Middle East, the conflict in Vietnam, the dangers of nuclear war, the great difficulties of dealing with the Communist powers": all of these problems persisted.[89] However, when President Richard Nixon took office, he converted the War on Poverty into something of a covert war, conducting law enforcement, welfare programs, and so on with little fuss or fanfare in order to devote his attention to ending the Vietnam War. Yet his own "Vietnamization" tactics represented an overall ideology that pitted deficiency against dependency, meaning that capitalism was the antidote to Communism just as free market economics was the corrective to paternalistic forms of protectionism. It was to be a mode of so-called peacemaking through widespread withdrawals of support.

The irony is that this policy was accompanied by assaults on Cambodia and a general escalation of bombing operations in northern Vietnam. Consequently, Harrington zeroed in on the role of US military generals as figureheads for the military-industrial complex. In a cartoon from April 1969, this figure appears in full dress uniform, with an actual warhead for a head, sitting at a table on which a steaming spread of food waits to be consumed (fig. 22). The figure personifies the spoils of preparing for and waging war. And, not unlike Uncle Sam, it provides a picture of the nation. Each food item from an enormous steak to a pile of vegetables to a bottled drink is branded with a dollar sign. On a wall behind him is a framed picture of an American eagle. On the other side of the cartoon, standing behind General Warhead just beyond an open door, is a pair of young children, a boy and a girl. Together they hold each other as well as an empty bowl and look upon the Rabelaisian scene with despair while their knobby knees support malnourished bodies. Interestingly, these children seem to be white and thus defy the racial implications of social welfare programs that many at the time would have come to expect. Harrington, though, seems to make a bigger statement, which is that combat orientations cloud thinking, and lead to circumstances where battle provisions (whether on a literal battlefield or in policies of economic warfare) circumvent the will to provide for the nation's children. Here, the boy and girl

FIG. 22 Oliver W. Harrington, "Hey, why don't somebody tell these damn starvin' brats that there ain't enough for me and them too!," 1969. From *Daily World*, April 13, 1969. Used with permission of Dr. Helma Harrington, Berlin.

'Hey, why don't somebody tell these damn starvin' brats that there ain't enough for me and them too!'

typify the welfare of *all* children of war and thereby allude to the Statue of Liberty and its implication of a poor, huddled mass. This is most apparent when one considers the hawkish words of the talking warhead: "Hey, why don't somebody tell these damn starvin' brats that there ain't enough for me and them too!" As much could be said of the stake in American pride and principles that Harrington's cartoon implies.

With hints of aversion to the war industry and even to US imperialism, as well as intimations that mistreatment of children amounts to war crimes, Harrington homed in on what political activist and social democrat Michael Harrington called in 1962 "the other America." The Otherness in this one of Two Americas is defined by the tension between "the right war at home" and "the wrong war in Southeast Asia."[90] Consider a cartoon from the *Daily World* in July 1969 (which was reprinted a number of times from 1971 through 1977). The cartoon features two emaciated Black children reaching out for bread and milk that sit atop a tall table (fig. 23). Missiles, emblazoned with the acronym USA, stand out as the table's legs that keep

FIG. 23 Oliver W. Harrington, kids at the war table, 1977. From *Daily World*, April 2, 1977. Used with permission of Dr. Helma Harrington, Berlin.

a tabletop towering over the children. The image is emblematic of the imbrication of a culture of poverty and a war culture. It captures the idea that everyday life was sustained by the right of military might, that even if war was provisionally swept out of public view it still propped up the table, and that various forms of political force determined access not only to basic needs but also to democratic principles—the very stuff of a free and equal existence. In addition, the cartoon channels the popular antiwar sentiment of bombing for peace, an almost laughable notion positing that the same practices and policies that were put in place to support the national interest were the very things that could also destroy it. This went for the Vietnam War. It went for segregationist and prejudiced ideals in government programs, too. And it impacted both foreign children and Americans.

As horrific as the image of children starved of a human right appears to be, there is humor in the ugliness made plain by the warring impulses of the American Way. It is humorous because it reverses the standard approach of making the grisly luridness of a situation seem ludicrous in order to ease the anxieties of children by making children the embodiments of inhumanity. As Wanzo notes, many of Harrington's caricatures relied on a "realistic aesthetic" that put "a perverse twist on stereotypical representations of the black child."[91] The bodies of suffering Black children are comic images of *real* bodies. Still, the fantastical prominence of missiles over meals for children appears as a cruel joke on this very aesthetic, a self-reflexive gesture to uncertain futures to be built on painful pasts that subjects adult onlookers to an image of national selfhood as an abject object. The children are pitiable. The adults who make their plight possible are loathsome. For readers of the *Daily World*, such an imbrication of horror and humor would no doubt have been met with feelings of freedom and relief. Blackness is not buffoonish here. It is the epitome of bathos. If laughter is the only weapon humans have against an absurd world largely of their own creation (as Mark Twain once said through the mouthpiece of Satan), then it is borne of black humor in this caricature, and its laughter is dark, indeed. Still, as with much humor that emerged out of the Civil Rights Movement (and slave cultures before it), humor makes it so that matters of *cultural* famishment can be put on the table as topics of both American warfare and the American democratic experiment. Bulging armaments juxtaposed to gaunt little bodies create an abject scene. Even worse is the inkling that both are the consequences of perverse war mentalities, feeding into a national character that might treat Black children as collateral damage at worst or, at best, as mere "brats" unworthy of table scraps.

There is a compelling merger of the nation-state with national character here in the image of two children who are twice bitten by the hand that does not feed them. At this point, the nation-state had begun to move away from policies around social and racial justice. Even before he was president, Nixon was against "forced integration" of either schools or neighborhoods. In keeping with a general sense that different races occupied different communities, he therefore kept a relatively low profile vis-à-vis civil rights after 1970. When he did speak out on the issue, he tended to align antiwar protestors (whom he even called criminals) with Black power leaders. Moreover, Nixon appealed to the "silent majority" in suggesting that enough was enough with civil rights, inciting a general attitude among those opposed to him that the two-front war was a white man's burden but a Black man's fight. The national character, in kind, was characterized as caught in a state of exception. This was apparent in President Nixon's burial of the civil rights agenda in policies of "Vietnamization," which resulted in a sort of "Americanization" of Black culture at home. We are not One America. We are at minimum Two Americas. This much was black and white in the folly of Nixon's interest in forcing an already-deprived population to fend for itself.

In a cartoon from August 1971, the humor in Harrington's caricatures of Black children turns the tables. It shows a US military plane at the top of the frame. As it flies from right to left, the plane drops both bombs and supplies to an undisclosed location below. It is patently ridiculous, on first glance. Who would use carpet-bombs to drop off aid? Harrington is critiquing the bombing campaigns that characterized the US air war against the North Vietnamese. He is clearly placing children in a proxy war with the United States abroad and children on the home front. However, there is also bare reality in the cartoon's indication of governmental dealings with civil rights, which were often approached through a lens of military campaigning. Along with the bombs in the 1971 cartoon are boxes containing "Diet Tips," "Anti-Baby Pills," medical supplies, and, perhaps most disturbingly, "Kid's Books." In many ways, Harrington insinuates that this is precisely the manner in which federal support was provided to Black communities. First, given the clear allusions to food stamps, child welfare programs, and crime prevention, Harrington links state repression to the Vietnam War by showing the men, women, and children who suffered from policies that left cities and schools in ruin. Second, the cartoon mocks the idea that any work against "the system" was either un-American or antiwar since the United States aimed to destroy certain living conditions and replace them with a new way of life. Third, and finally, Harrington demonstrated an official policy of dealing with problems from a distance, and furthermore making them utterly transactional. The cartoon closes the loop between armed conflict abroad and domestic culture wars.

At the end of the day, for Harrington, the welfare of children is a contact point for understanding the character of a nation. The United States' participation in the Cold War generally and the Vietnam War in particular displayed a national character that largely ostracized Black culture. Caricatures of children have such comic rhetorical force here because children are the most vulnerable outsiders within an otherwise wealthy and well-off nation. Consider, then, a cartoon from April 24, 1973, that shows a grotesque Cold War vulture gripping a diminutive Black boy in his talons and carrying him out of his urban environment. Inscribed on the inside of the vulture's left wing are the words "WILD PROFITEERING," and on the white shirt of the Black child are the words "OUR KIDS." Later, Harrington built on this image of a false promise of freedom from war by tracing Nixon's follies to President Jimmy Carter's subsequent failures. In 1977, this meant drawing Black and white children under a table eating leavings while an enormous fat cat with a bib labeling the arms industry feasted on a bowl of the "BIGGEST BANG, BANG, BANG, BUDGET EVER!" President Carter continued America's military build-up, investing in NATO while putting stock in neutron bombs. For Harrington, this meant the continuation of wartime policies that had long put children of multiple races against "military fellers" who starved the young so that the national defense could thrive. It meant that pigs—which in earlier cartoons had symbolized police, "corporate monsters," and financiers chaining up the "free" world—became the symbol for "HIGH-FINANCE GLUTTONY," with one seen gulping down a city hospital alongside a kindergarten, church, and university building. And it meant that, by the end of February 1978, the Cold War vulture had transmogrified into a "CAPITALIST CRISIS," feeding a rat of "RACISM" to its young. There would be no "lasting peace," in President Carter's words, so long as war was the best of a bad lot for securing American values. Casting the country's lot with armed conflict across the Cold War meant over and again exposing the follies and failures of American national character. For Harrington, these follies and failures were generational things.

Conclusion: American Children, or Cartoon Progenitors of the People

It is fitting that the Vietnam War is now regarded as a campaign of Lost Innocence.

The Cold War era confirmed war itself as an American pastime. It codified the homegrown humbug in cultural warfare. In Harrington's cartoons, it generated images of US American national character in terms of what Twain might call "high-grade comicality." The absurdities and grotesqueries in Harrington's caricatures of Black children gave way to the truths and consequences of living in the adult world. These children were drawn as the Fathers and Mothers of wisdom, given their wartime experiences. They were the embodiments of a nation in *and* out of character, living down its racist legacies while living up to its reputation for waging war on the basis of democratic principles and the collective self-interest. In Harrington's cartoons are primal scenes of self-loathing that emerge when Black children of war are the images reflected in the comic looking glass.

Children make so much sense in Harrington's cartoon politics because they typify the capacity for taking amusement in messing around with the rhetorical materials of dark realities. Children provide a vehicle for portraying an odd delight in the conveyance of worldviews and real-world existentialities that are patently unfunny. They are the comic effects—for sure, the very progeny—of war and its aftermath. This is why the humor, like the lifeworld it situates before a rhetorical mirror, darkly, is irresolvable. Black children are Harrington's mechanism for portraying the unintended comicality in caricatures that capture the Self in the Child by mirroring the horrendous wrongs of the adult world. Yet they partly right American wrongs by making war for the sake of democracy look like a corruption of the good sense in nonsense. They make the foundational principles of liberty and justice educe the peculiar institution of racism, too, and Doomsday Machines betray the madness of a national character built on the heat of battle. Harrington's children mock white America as a body politic replete with orchestrators of an O.K. Corral approach to the Free World. At the same time, they empower Black culture by rewriting the American war story according to the dark heritage of laughing at the jangle of chains. Old Ways cannot be the fetters in new days of freedom, Harrington seems to suggest, if the United States is to avoid becoming what historian Ernest May once dubbed the "imperial democracy," or the nation of endless warfare. Following Harrington, a nation of children, by children, and for children can be a nation of peace.

The road to Black Reconstruction, as a path to a new birth of US American democracy, is a long one. The stretch of Harrington's cartoon struggles evinces as much. Through 1987, when the *Daily World* became the *People's Daily World*, Harrington kept up his deployment of caricatures to lash out on issues of institutional racism, systemic inequality, racial profiling, poverty, hunger, unfair housing, police corruption, apartheid, the War on Drugs, the War on Poverty, urban squalor, rampant capitalism, and more. He also continued to foreground Black children as both quarries and cudgels in the divers wars of containment. It is helpful to remember here that, as early as 1945, Harrington's *Jive Gray* series drew allusions to the racial grievances that would fold into postwar culture, which easily comport not only with the children of "mammies" but also with the contemporaneous population of "brown babies" (or *Negermischlinge*) in Germany and the United States. Harrington's long roll of dark laughter also presaged the transformation of Black children from mini-Sambos of the nation-state to so-called "superpredators," a term denoting the myth of violent, antiestablishment juvenile delinquents of the Black youth. This coincided with the war in the Persian Gulf, and the retroactive label applied to the "Superpredator Scare," which stinks of Cold War imagery. Perhaps most importantly, though, is that Harrington never lost sight of how children in particular could be figured as the fallout or the fomentation for war cultures during and after formal wartimes. Cold War culture incited a sort of public hysteria around the idea that children were being primed for crime. Race conflicts, but also more widespread worries about American youth, revolved around media reports of "crime time bombs," "kids who kill," and generalized "moral panic." By the early 1990s, when James Davis Hunter infamously defined a "culture war" as a "struggle to define America," the national characterization of Black children had devolved into notions that they went from being hapless victims to brutish perpetrators. It thus fulfilled the rather racist prophecy that self-responsibility for personal failings had always been the defining factor of racial injustice. The *People's World*, and Harrington's work therein, was caught up in this late twentieth-century postwar milieu, but it suffered from financial instability that led to an eventual reversion of the Communist-inspired newspaper from a daily to a weekly. By 1994 Harrington was back in the United States as an artist-in-residence in the school of journalism at Michigan State University. He died in 1995.

What lives on in Harrington's caricatures of Black children is a powerful notion that children are the progenitors of "the people." First, when viewed as caricatures of wartime national character, Harrington's cartoons featuring children provide a revised sense of "fourth-generation warfare" such that war becomes indistinguishable from the politics of cultural formations, and enemy combatants signify the most vulnerable and the most vicious of our "fellow" citizens. There is much talk today about next generations of war, with references at home to "soft war" cultures and "military Millennial problems." Alongside this is a healthy discourse around the indoctrination of children into Islamic and other forms of extremism overseas. More recently, a coronavirus pandemic has reinforced cultural wars in terms of class divisions, social distances, and civil liberties (i.e., to wear or not to wear a mask in public) and of deep-seated race relations (i.e., to get a vaccine or not). These sorts of standards of judgment for cultural politics enable warfare to be used as a rhetorical weapon with children as fodder for the continued reliance on old stereotypes and outmoded images of national character that reinforce friend–enemy relations. Harrington's point, though, seems to be even more elemental. If one can look upon a child, any child, and not see humanity, then there is something wrong with one's way of seeing. For Harrington, war is the right way to see US Americanism, most pressingly because it is wrong.

Second, the importunity of Cold War thinking discloses a certain politics of containment that thrives in cultures of fear and false impressions so resident in the era of a War on Terror and, maybe more relevant, a simmering Cold War between the United States and China. More than this, though, it shows forth an imbrication of childishness and cruelty, animating the types of "grotesque imaginings" and "distorted caricatures" that John Spargo once saw in early anti-Communist depictions of "foreign" adversaries.[92] There is humor in caricatures of these imaginings. It lives in the child's play of war games, and in the impoverishment of rhetorical cultures that takes place when the free play of democratic comportment gets cordoned in "well-guarded playgrounds."[93] Children traffic in such imaginings because they do not know better. Adults do so because they know all too well. Play can promote subversion, especially when playing on the types of aggressive, nationalistic compulsions that characterize us–them, black-and-white classificatory systems for Selves and Others. Children are such a compelling aspect of caricature because they can amplify a comic license to play with what it means, in James Baldwin's words, to be a "stranger in the village." They are even more interesting as featured subjects when national character is nurtured as a rhetorical storehouse for characterizing what is really a collection of strangers.

Of course, if national character offers images and ideas of *homonoia*, or a unity of hearts and minds, of sociopolitical concord, and of opposition to strife,[94] then caricature offers the requisite sense of humor for upsetting delusions about this unity. Caricature is ultimately driven by *heteronoia*: otherness, difference, and disruption. Here, it is a rhetorical iteration for the Otherness of Childhood. Children view the world with *open* hearts and minds. This openness, by adult standards, amounts to lunacy. Children are prone to acts of folly. In the hands of Harrington, Black children portray a form of lucidity in the lunacy of war culture. Harrington's caricatures encapsulate the good sense, and the good humor, of seeing wartime national character through the eyes of a child. Toward the end of his life, Harrington had difficulty drawing cartoons—in part because he was increasingly ill, and in part because he might have harbored a bit of a bad conscience over his incapacity to spawn measurable change from a lifetime of cultural work.[95] In his time, Harrington witnessed the transformation of the Cold War into a so-called "war of ideas," which grew out of the New Right in the 1970s and proclaimed a colorblind commitment to the public good. Through the 1980s and '90s, the New Right flourished. Since the 1990s, it has developed into animus over how national values can and should be articulated in an argot of political correctness, which as of the early twenty-first century transformed again into a generalized air of barefaced (white) nationalism, among other modes of partisanship and privilege. The coinage of Ugly Americanism, the perpetuation of a

War on Terror, the resurgence of America First—these are but some of the elements ensnaring the brave new worlds and bigoted old guards that have been born out of the protracted undoing of American national character. The last chapter takes up this undoing.

For now, Harrington's caricatures can leave us with reminders of the dangers lurking in predilections to fall back on racial stereotypes while preaching the march of American progress. They also remind us of the danger inherent to picking away at these predilections, in good or bad humor. Battle lines over the American Way are almost always color lines. All war is *cultural* warfare. These are some of the most crucial truisms in Harrington's cartoon oeuvre. They are crucial because they encourage critical imaginations of the next instance of racial tension as an outgrowth of combat mentalities in war cultures and culture wars.

There is some more Ashanti folk wisdom, and it filters through Harrington's recourse to vulturine imagery in the later stages of his career. It comes from a tale that tells of a vulture with a taking spirit. In one telling, the Vulture and a Crow are slaves to the same master. While in a market doing their master's bidding, the creatures happen upon two untended boxes, one bigger than the other. In a fit of self-indulgence, the Vulture pushes the Crow aside and snatches the big box. He opens it to find nothing but trash. The small box, which the Crow opens, contains beautiful garments, with which he later adorns himself. Once beautiful, the Vulture from then on was doomed to dwell in rubbish and filth.[96] Here is an Ashanti proverb: "When children see an eagle draggled by the rain, they say it is a vulture."[97]

Harrington warns of what might come when vultures nest, when vultures circle, and when vultures live with other vultures. Such warnings are apt metaphors for the war-torn American spirit. Harrington urges a childlike wisdom, and thereby a view of US national character through the comic looking glass as a better way to witness children of war. With regard to war's follies, Harrington implies, what use is the wisdom of adults?

The Battle Rages on in Ann Telnaes's Comic Travesties of the War on Terror

4.

War is a rabbit hole. So, too, is democracy.

    Chaos and confusion are, in many ways, endemic to democratic action. To approach it through ideals of deliberation, decision making, and good public judgment is almost a fool's errand. Many of the American Founders were wont to profess that democracy at best is messy and muddled. Democratic institutions are there to guard against political bedlam and to promote a spirit of democracy despite the specters of faction and folly—and war.

    The march to war can be similarly cast as a march of folly. In Andrew Bacevich's words, the drift into endless war betrays a certain "madness lurking just beneath the surface" of the American Way.[1] President George W. Bush's decision to invade Iraq in 2003 followed a false trail. It was a response to the September 11 terrorist attacks, to be sure, but it is now seen as one of the biggest missteps since the Vietnam War. That the ensuing Iraq War was a blunder based on bad intelligence is even more the case nearly two decades on, especially given what Bacevich further describes as "the strangely circular and seriously cuckoo Alice-in-Wonderland nature" of the War on Terror.[2] A core problematic is that the War on Terror relies on fears and nationalistic fantasies, both of which have led to a pervasive mode of Americanism that equates democracy with dominance and wartime exigencies with cultural warfare. The looking-glass world of Lewis Carroll's imagination was one of warring factions. It was a world of black-and-white kings and queens and chess-like soldiers. It was riven with identity crises and seen through the eyes of those who really looked at themselves in the mirror to see the wisdom and folly of their lived realities.

These are precisely the sentiments of Pulitzer Prize–winning editorial cartoonist Ann Telnaes. Her work is featured in the *Washington Post*. However, it has been syndicated in outlets like the *New York Times*, the *Los Angeles Times*, the *Chicago Tribune*, and elsewhere since her career took off in the late 1990s. Her cartoons traverse media, appearing in traditional print as well as online in animations, visual op-eds, and live sketches (i.e., of political debates, congressional hearings, and news conferences). While she has long attended to homegrown matters of concern like domestic civil liberties and more global human rights, after 9/11 Telnaes shifted her attention to nationalism and the militarization of democratic politics. Throughout the War on Terror, Telnaes has caricatured the relationship between American national character and the so-called Forever War. Central to her caricatures is an image not of "the people" per se, as is common in so many war caricatures in the editorial cartoon tradition, but rather an image of leadership. War, in many ways, is a litmus test for democratic praxis. For Telnaes, the protracted War on Terror presents an opportunity to understand the chief executive—the commander in chief—as a distorted reflection of the US body politic. If the Cold War is partly responsible for the imperial presidency (however imperiled by constitutional separation of powers), then the post-9/11 milieu has bred the imperialistic *president*. The president, Telnaes suggests, is the national character par excellence. In the United States, the president is burdened to retain an image of the National Self that does not abrogate "the people" for a preemptive warpath to keep that world safe for democracy in the Age of Terror. Telnaes's concern is that the ongoing march to war in the early twenty-first century has been part and parcel of a death march for democracy. Furthermore, that march has stirred up presidential politicking along lines of distastes for democracy and brazen imperialist commitments. Yet it has also betrayed an American imperium as American idiocy.

In the run up to 9/11, the United States enjoyed something of a victory culture. The Cold War was over. Operation Desert Shield was a success. There was a perception that the 1990s presented a decade of Great Prosperity. Then two planes hit the Twin Towers in New York City, and the sitting president set in motion a newfangled "war fought in freedom's name that had the look of an atrocity."[3] The members of al-Qaeda who carried out the attacks were likened to Japanese dive-bombers at Pearl Harbor. After World War I, the United States made a notable attempt to "escape down the rabbit-hole of . . . isolation and neutrality."[4] President Woodrow Wilson initiated the "America First" slogan prior to the Great War, and President Warren G. Harding used it as a framework for backing away from the international stage. In the interwar period, the rabbit hole was an endgame. It constituted a politics of escape. World War II changed the game. So, too, did 9/11, which provoked a presidential approach to Americanism that might be reduced to the phrase "It's the War on Terror, stupid." With this reduction came a sort of King-and-Country dilation of war powers and executive dominion that recast American values of life and liberty in terms of nationalistic pride, prejudice, patriarchy, xenophobia, racism, sexism, and bigotry—all of which have a discomfiting resonance given the resurgence of a reductive America First ideology under President Donald J. Trump. The very decision by George W. Bush to make his presidency about war and terror also reduced his role to the simplistic tensions between "good" and "evil." The principles and plans behind the 2003 invasion of Iraq were widely seen as dumb, foolish, reckless, and even criminally idiotic. Like the president. The war-a-day politics of President Trump have approached sheer lunacy and have been downright maniacal in response to global flare-ups. This was made worse by the outbreak of a coronavirus pandemic that put President Trump's self-indulgences, tendencies toward economic absolutism, and predispositions to wartime presidentialism on full display.

Here's the hook: if an olden logic of using militarism to make the world safe and right for American democracy once animated the Great and Good Wars, the ill logic of battling for Americanism with perpetual warfare defines a post-9/11 culture of war. At the very least, a *rhetorical* warism will shape the post-COVID-19 world, especially given President Trump's insistence on declaring the novel coronavirus a "foreign virus" and the principal enemy in "our big war."[5] All wars are tragedies. Following Telnaes, warfare goes beyond tragedy when it is revealed as a farce. Her presidential caricatures in particular show forth a comic travesty of the War on Terror by demonstrating the notion that combat mentalities comprise the biggest character flaws of national character when the ship of a democratic state is given over to warmongering fools. From the tenure of George W. Bush through the presidency of Donald J. Trump, there is a cumulative image of American democracy itself as the collateral damage of war measures. Some have identified terroristic attributes in the fear and anxiety attached to COVID-19,[6] and then again to the decay of democratic institutions in the rise of authoritarianism. Telnaes is on the front lines for sorting out these death dealings in the *élans vital* of democracies the world over by laying out a view of the Ugly American turned Jingoistic Ignoramus.

Telnaes has focused a lot on President Bush and President Trump. This is not to say that she was uncritical of President Barack Obama's perpetuation of the Bush Doctrine, which operated on an ethos of preemption and preventive self-defense against "terrorist enemies." For instance, in a cartoon from November 2014, a caricature of President Obama is seen walking toward the Tomb of the Unknown Soldier with a wreath of dollar bills signifying his recommitment of troops to Iraq and his codification of drone warfare. This is also not to say that Telnaes was unconcerned with the cultural fallout of the Obama presidency, which was riddled with legitimate outcries about executive overreach and covert drone wars to the same extent that it was plagued by what I have elsewhere characterized as festive racism.[7] It is to say, however, that Telnaes sees President Obama as set between two dangerously foolhardy presidents. President Obama was often demeaned as the professor in chief. He was intelligent, calculating, capable, and shrewd. In contrast, President Bush was sometimes labeled Dumbo, and he was infamous for his senseless gaffes, dubbed Bushisms. President Trump, too, has been variously called a dope, a moron, and, by North Korean dictator Kim Jong-un, a dotard.[8] Whereas the Obama administration was purposeful and deliberate (even if, for some, cunning), the Bush administration was conniving but senseless much as the Trump administration has been characterized as utterly slipshod. On either side of President Obama is a chief executive who embodies the American Idiot.

The trouble is that these two presidents are also widely regarded as would-be despots.[9] Bush II, as he was called (with all the echoes of political dynasty), bore the nickname King George, too. Telnaes captures this cognomen in a cartoon from November 2003, which situates President Bush next to Queen Elizabeth II during a state visit to England (fig. 24). It followed King Bush's excursion in Iraq to have Thanksgiving dinner with troops, and to meet with members of the Iraqi Governing Council. The state visit exposed a palpable tension between royal pomp and antiwar protests that took place in London. While there, President Bush affirmed his notion that freedom and liberty are coextensive with war, and that the United States' own righteousness was partly due to its might. In a return-of-the-king mockery, Telnaes depicts President Bush as a kingly aspirant, standing tall with his hands behind his back and a crown atop his head.

FIG. 24 Ann Telnaes, Queen Elizabeth and King George, November 19, 2003. Used with the permission of Ann Telnaes and The Cartoonist Group. All rights reserved.

Of course, the crown jewel is a missile, and the queen is giving the president a sideways glance.

President Trump, for many, is also a king *in loco*. He has been hailed, despairingly, as King Trump. He has been cast as an emperor with no clothes. He has been caught up in debates about the fascistic tendencies inherent to Trumpism, the ripeness of the United States for tyranny in the early twenty-first century, and the express sentiment that—à la Sinclair Lewis—it *can* happen here. Within weeks of his election in November 2016, Telnaes rendered King Trump with a diminutive crown atop his notorious red Make America Great Again (MAGA) hat. Before he was even elected, Telnaes caricatured candidate Trump as Carroll's Queen of Hearts (fig. 25). In Carroll's words, the queen is "a sort of embodiment of ungovernable passion—a blind and aimless Fury."[10] The presidential candidate, at the time, was already being forecast as a president who would abuse his executive powers. A *Time* contributor proclaimed that the ancient Greeks would have labeled Trump a *tyrannos*, or an unfit ruler of a polis.[11] In Telnaes's cartoon, the president appears in the iconic red dress of the queen, holding a heart scepter emblazoned with the word "ME," wearing a tiny crown on his head, and screaming "OFF WITH THEIR HEADS!!" to a wee male sovereign, appearing as a caricature of then house speaker Paul Ryan. A caption suggests that Trump ran with the silly assumption that he'd be elected "absolute monarch." Tellingly, President Trump worked hard to cast himself as a "generous monarch" after botching the federal response to the coronavirus by signing off on stimulus

140   CARICATURE AND NATIONAL CHARACTER

FIG. 25 Ann Telnaes, Trump as Queen of Hearts, June 14, 2016. Used with permission of Ann Telnaes and The Cartoonist Group. All rights reserved.

packages and shipments of medical supplies from the Strategic National Stockpile.[12] He even went so far as to dragoon the Treasury to print his Brobdingnagian signature on people's Economic Impact Payments, colloquially referred to as stimulus checks, in a miserly move to act as if he were using his own money and not that of the taxpayers. Such are the self-referential exploits of an imperialistic "wartime" president who, in the words of the rabbit, has lost his head.

Herein lies the substance of Telnaes's comic travesties. That things like kingliness and egotism and despotism can be so readily applied to democratic leaders is less a sign that a dissident American democracy is alive and well than it is a *warning* sign about the perpetual warism of US presidents. In a dissent of the 1944 ruling on *Korematsu v. United States*, Associate Justice Robert H. Jackson warned that the potential for an imperial presidency "lies about like a loaded weapon."[13] War was raging. In echoes of an early twenty-first-century parlance, American culture was divided. Lurking in Justice Jackson's remark is a sentiment from Federalist 69, which warns of the risk that the highest servant of the people could deign to become an autocrat if propped up by the follies of factionalism. In Telnaes's caricatures are distortive pictures of presidents who have picked up the loaded weapon, but with far more foolish pride than democratic principles. These caricatures are wrought with humor that blends the possibilities of "becoming-mad" with the predictions of "the unforeseeable," yet in light of that which has come before and left residues of attitudes and histories.[14] Such a blend is the province of Wonderland. It is the provocation to dredge the depths of collective identification when their dark profundities are apparent in the surface features of leading characters. It is in the tenets of warring for war's sake, or for the sake of saving one's own political skin. If war is a tragedy of American democracy, the farce is war culture's confusions worse confounded.

This chapter is therefore about the Wonderland of American war culture that Telnaes makes of the relationship between post-9/11 presidentialism and predictions about war (and the war mentality) as a merchant of democracy's death. I do not tackle issues of military strategy, party politics, and foreign policy, important as such issues are for the presidents under consideration in Telnaes's work. Instead, I examine what presidentialism during the War on Terror—and, by extension, in the Age of COVID-19, with its rampant discourses of enemies and weapons and battle plans and fighting spirits and front lines—shows and tells about national character, namely when the president is conceived as *the* public face to, and of, the nation. Even more, I weigh how comicality serves as a uniquely apt mechanism for imagining the consequences of seeing a president as the embodiment of an American nation "at war with itself,"[15] and thereby suffering certain fates of its own making—fates scarcely worse than democracy's death. The War on Terror represents a conjuncture of people and public officeholders who are unable and/or unwilling "to discriminate between metaphoric and literal expressions, distinguish jokes from factual statements, real threats from bluff, real war from rhetorical war."[16] Caricature is so powerful in war cultures because it affords combinations and crude mixtures that imagine what "true" character looks like, what are its consequences, and why it matters, not beyond the surface appeals of something like Americanism but rather *in* those appeals. Telnaes has her partisanships, no question. She has her predilections. Like Ollie Harrington, she is something of an outsider. She was born in Stockholm, Sweden, and attained US citizenship as a teenager in the mid-1970s. In other words, she has her critical distance as well, using caricature to articulate the connective tissues of rhetoric and reality with regard to the ugliness of warism. I dwell on this ugliness.

To do so, I first outline what it means to go down the rabbit hole of post-9/11 war culture. I then detail my view of comic travesty over and against the concept of presidentialism, which provides the framework for analyzing cartoons from Telnaes's oeuvre of President Bush and President Trump. That analysis is carried out with an initial look at cartoons from the Pulitzer Prize–winning collection *Humor's Edge*.[17] This is followed by an examination of *The Lyin' King*, a compendium of Telnaes's take on

President Trump's antidemocratic deportment, in addition to a series of cartoons portraying his up-in-arms approach to everything from geopolitical diplomacy to the novel coronavirus. Ultimately, this chapter accounts for Telnaes's comic travesties of the folly that can be found in freakishly self-minded American presidents letting a democratic nation—nay, leading it to—wander into imperial waters on the tides of war.

Down the Rabbit Hole of War (Again)

To borrow some thinking from the Queen of Hearts, there is a first principle for fighting terror that urges the disposition to impose sentences first and verdicts afterward. When this principle is applied to democratic action or cultural politics, things—as Alice might say—get curiouser and curiouser. In January 2010, Senator Joe Lieberman called President Obama's anti-terrorism methodologies an Alice-in-Wonderland approach to the War on Terror. Such a pronouncement would not be as noteworthy if it did not reiterate a notion that the Obama Doctrine was essentially the Bush Doctrine, aligning terror wars with American-style democracy. War, terror, democracy—each typifies a sort of Humpty-Dumpty argot for characterizing post-9/11 Americanism. This is even more true in the time of the Trump Doctrine, with the war of all against all serving as a principle for intensifying the forces of nationalism and what Naomi Klein might call a "shock doctrine" in response to the public health crisis of COVID-19.[18] What is more, the tripartite of terrorism, war (with visible and *in*visible enemies), and the increasingly critical conditions for global democracies has led to imperial thinking as the groundwork for the American Way. The most public paragon of this imperialist turn is the US president.

Telnaes's corpus of wartime caricatures flies in the face of this turn, like Alice's burst of laughter in the Queen's croquet-ground. It also provides a few apt resources for viewing post-9/11 war culture as a mix-up of presidential politicking and Washington-in-Wonderland policymaking. For example, a cartoon from August 2003 turns some of the rhetorical materials and literal accoutrements of President Bush's wartime approach into a set of action figures and accessories. Vice President Dick Cheney, the puppeteer of presidential power, clutches a martini with a dollar-signed cocktail pick. Secretary of Defense Donald Rumsfeld, whom British writer for the *Guardian* Tristram Hunt dubbed "a Puritan on a warpath,"[19] is clad in doublet, breeches, and wide-brimmed hat with a copy of the US Constitution in one hand a Zippo lighter in the other. Accessories include a surveillance camera, a crude oil barrel and gas pump, and an American flag with a Christian cross for a pole. Post-9/11 Americanism is a war game in this cartoon, the baits and switches and bunkos of which appear as political damage in a comic looking glass.

Over a decade-and-a-half later, Telnaes sent President Trump down the rabbit hole. A cartoon from October 2017 displays a white warren. The ground on either side of it is purple, rocky, and filled with bugs. The roots, visible at the top, are a deep green. Some things going down the hole are scales of justice, a Ku Klux Klan hood, a gas mask, squawking Twitter birds, a baby bottle, a framed photograph of Russian President Vladimir Putin, a pair of stilettos, and a roll of toilet paper. The insinuations are legion. President Trump's appeal to white supremacists. His racial and ethnocentric and misogynistic talk. His history of sexual misconduct. His rhetorical love affair with social media platform Twitter. His reputation for being infantile and temperamental. His affinity for dictatorial leaders. Even his willful disregard for the threat of certain aerosols like chemical weapons or pollutants or, well, coronaviruses. Most prominent, though, is President Trump himself toward the bottom of the frame, falling in a seated position with a petulant look on his face. In his immediate vicinity is an assemblage of warlike imagery: two nuclear symbols, a bomb with a lit fuse (emblazoned with the face of North Korean Supreme Leader Kim Jong-un), and—just below his rear end—an imperial crown topped with a gold "T." In the words of President Bush's Secretary of Defense, the War on Terror began with an acknowledgment of known unknowns, and pursuant to them things like the Patriot Act, domestic spying, and enemy torture. In the Trump era, the rabbit hole is a pathway to similarly blurred distinctions between reality and artifice, and a much more pervasive attitude that everything is contrariwise. Countless commentators and critics have remarked on President Trump's war on truth. Trump's Wonderland is a den for warring logics tout court whereby the War on Terror, threats of World War III, and homegrown political combat are political motifs.

Though distinctive, Presidents Bush and Trump share the perpetuation of warfare as a principle for dealing with known and unknown hazards. Democracy is supposed to do away with the fallacy of good tyrannies after bad. It is supposed to encourage collective self-awareness. Telnaes's caricatures of Bush and Trump offer a view of the madness in turning from one self-anointed clod (who doubles as a prodigal son with delusions of grandeur and a penchant to pawn himself off as a down-to-earth man of the people) to another (who poses as a populist that rises and falls on the patina of his commercial cum political brand). One is a foolish cowboy. The other is a con man. One is a political insider fulfilling his pilgrim's progress. The other is a political outsider known for stoking fires and settling scores. One is a compassionate conservative who once had no interest in exporting American values or building nations overseas, and then became a warmonger. The other is an antiwar campaigner who built his career on fighting words and, eventually, became a hawkish dove threatening adversaries with fire and fury. President Obama, especially with his drone strikes and shadow warfare, certainly let slip the dogs of war. But from the tenure of Bush II to the travesties of Trump's America, terror wars blend into daily contretemps, and presidential leadership bleeds into warism as the only means.

Soon after the terror attacks on September 11, 2001, questions were raised as to whether or not Americanism would be defined by a revitalized democracy or given over to a new generation of warfare. It took only nine days for President Bush in a speech to Congress to declare war on terror. Operation Enduring Freedom was announced less than a week later. By October, troops were on the ground in Afghanistan. Ongoing military actions were pegged as part of a crusade. One of the consequences of the ensuing War on Terror was a misguided discourse of intelligence, indeed of what Douglas Kellner calls "Bushspeak,"[20] that led a president and his cabinet to pull weapons of mass destruction (WMDs) out of political hats in the interest of rallying the nation around a false-flag event. Another consequence is that war, then as now, amplified a nationalistic sense of Us and Them, and a rhetorical basis for classifying enemies at home. The first casualty of the War on Terror was not truth. It was American democracy, which was set forth as *jus ad bellum*.

This makes sense. According to the July 2004 *Final Report of The National Commission on Terrorist Attacks Upon the United States* (colloquially known as the *9/11 Commission Report*), a generalized diminution of public debate about cultural differences, foreign relations, and public opinions fueled "cartoonish stereotypes" and "coarse expressions" of national character that actually fortified rather than enfeebled a popular "caricature [of] U.S. values and policies" in the aftermath of 9/11.[21] This caricature portrays democracy as something to be protected, not preserved through praxis. This caricature also constitutes a "cultural approach" to armed conflict that fosters "a total, restful attitude towards war itself."[22] A democracy like this is one for strong leaders—or strongmen—over and above resilient citizens. It is for powerful state agencies. It is for largely unchecked war powers. Accordingly, the War on Terror establishes not only that a world needs to be kept safe *for* democracy but also that democratic peoples need to be protected *from* themselves. A World War I–era notion that both Uncle Sam and suspicious fellow citizens are watching over YOU is hereby traded in for diffuse threats of un-Americanism, making abrogations of civil liberties, human rights, the writ of habeas corpus, and so on but some of the calling cards for a democratic empire in the Age of Terror.

This totalization of conflict reinforces what Telnaes herself mocks as the thrill of war over and above the ostensive torpor of democracy. Oftentimes such totalizations are manifest in verbal and visual ideographs, which in wartimes betray the treachery of Americanism in the loaded signifiers that encapsulate it. Flags are among the most totalizing of nationalistic images.[23] While they are talismans of dissent, they arouse moments in history wherein people pulled together for common cause. Hence an image of first responders raising an American flag in the rubble of the Twin Towers exudes the patriotic sentiment of the flag raising at Iwo Jima. Hence, too, H. G. Wells once quipped that flags have little import for peaceful activities. In the post-9/11 context, flags signify war readiness as an esprit de corps around shared beliefs, shared ideals, and shared traumas. A few years after the Gulf War, social psychologist Michael Billig described the American flag as "a *topos* beyond argument," part of a humdrum habit of constricting the public imagination of everyday political dealings by trading democratic practices for nationalistic abstractions.[24] Billig identified this topos in the broader phenomenon of "banal nationalism," which combines everyday representations of nationhood with a flagging sense of American national selfhood. A national flag communicates "the sacred character of the nation."[25] Yet, as Lauren Berlant suggests, the image and idea of national selfhood "is more latent and unconscious than it is in [generic citizens'] incidental, occasional relation to national symbols, spaces, narratives, and rituals."[26] President Bush reinstituted the Nixonian practice of wearing an American flag lapel pin. He signed the Freedom to Display the American Flag Act of 2005 into law in 2006. He infamously waved a flag at the 2008 Summer Olympics in Beijing. President Trump has taken his public affinity for the American flag even further with his penchant for literally embracing the Star-Spangled Banner. He hugged and kissed the flag after his speech at the Conservative Political Action Conference (CPAC) in 2020. The War on Terror makes the specter of terrorism itself banal.[27] Warism folds fantastical spectacles into everyday politics. It likewise normalizes freedom-loving rhetorics and forfeitures of political freedoms in the fog of presidential war powers.

Directly related to flag symbolism is the rhetorical act of flag-waving as a core characteristic of Americanism. By and large, scholars and commentators agree that the mainstream press was generally unwilling to question federal policymaking in the early years of the War on Terror. It is not uncommon for antiwar sentiments to be dubbed either unpatriotic or un-American. Immediately after 9/11, they were almost blasphemous. As late as February 2006, nearly three years into the Iraq War and five years after the Twin Towers collapsed, the Fourth Estate seemed to be the fourth branch of government. This journalistic adjustment parallels a rise of "militainment" in the commercial marketing of warfare, and the use of rhetorical as well as martial force as a policy imperative that underwrites warmongering in pictures of American national character.[28] Terrorism reinforces these logics as a mode of image warfare.[29] Media representations have constituted verbal-visual fields of battle, organizing principles of intelligibility for both violence against "evil" enemy combatants and violent depictions of otherness in public culture. As such, they have imposed a politics of embattlement onto an ethic of civic engagement. They have bolstered the national security apparatus. They have buttressed a military-industrial-*media* complex. And they have helped to establish Forever War as a backdrop for combat mentalities in cultural fronts at home.

All of this matters in light of what Telnaes in 2004 dubbed in an interview with Harry Katz the diffuse "flag waving" that followed 9/11, and with it the heightened need for a responsive and even acerbic comicality to fend it off.[30] Proclamations for the "death of irony" followed swiftly on the heels of the terror attacks. Embedded in these declarations was a generalized public opinion that humor fails as an interpretive framework for the darkest of days. Furthermore, in the post-9/11 milieu, there has been a decline of editorial cartooning.[31] The editorial cartoon is no longer an obvious comic outlet for grappling with the National Self in a looking glass clouded by the fog of war. As Chris Lamb notes, 9/11 scarred the sensibilities of so many people that "one editorial cartoonist's satire became another's sedition; one cartoonist's criticism of the Bush administration became someone else's anti-Americanism."[32] Yet post-9/11 humor has reshaped perceptions of and perspectives on the War on Terror.[33] Telnaes stands out so much because she has long nurtured the sort of critical urgency required of editorial cartooning as a democratic art, and thus as a way of facing ourselves. She did not balk at the rhetorical force of humor as a means of working through the repercussions of 9/11. She provoked it. In June 2019, Telnaes portrayed editorial cartooning as "democracy's canary in a coal mine."[34] It is the vulnerable rhetorical creature nonetheless announcing the horridness of its milieus even as, at times, it is busy dropping dead.

One cartoon in particular gets at this problematic of keeping up collective self-criticism in the face of utter self-defense. In it, Telnaes outs the machismo motivating journalism that did more to let slip the dogs of war than to rein them in. The cartoon features a male news reporter in silhouette with a massive microphone for an erection, aptly labeled "U.S. War Coverage" (fig. 26). Apart from the eroticism embedded in this caricature, the portrayal captures a "sovereign masculinity" in both the drive to chronicle warfare and the desire to promote the "manhood of the nation."[35] Additionally, as is discussed in more detail below, there is an underlying insinuation that men are justifiably the aggressors, waging war to liberate women (its foreign victims, for instance), to protect female citizens at home (by proclaiming what is and is not for their own good), and to carve a warpath around gender and other types of sociopolitical equity. Both war and peace are mocked as male privileges. These mockeries extend from the peculiar connotation that the reporter actually appears as Uncle Sam in profile (recollecting James Montgomery Flagg's oddly seductive "I Want YOU" poster) to the "gendered sprouting of American flags" that occurred immediately after 9/11.[36] Like Flagg, Telnaes takes on some of the most latent iconographies and ideographs of US American culture with a tongue-in-cheek mixture of patriotic zeal and palpable shame. Henri Bergson once claimed that humor emerges most vigorously from rigidity, or from those characteristics of a Self that make it rigid *against itself* and thereby make it rigid against Others. The news media here reveal the democratic impotence of warmongering journalists, and an idea that public opinion need only be a phantom of the body politic so long as citizens fall in line. Televisual news is the conduit for a nationalistic pact in waging war. A free press is no longer the custodian of "the people." With the protuberance of a phallic microphone, caricature humors a sense of reflexivity as *self*-reflexivity, however hard it might be on a citizenry to accept.

So it is that the president comes back into focus as the icon of a democratic culture gone down the rabbit hole of war. Presidentialism, historically, has entailed some embodiment of national pride, specifically around "an open society, consent of the governed, enumerated powers, Federalist 10, pluralism, due process, transparency . . . the whole democratic roil."[37] As of the turn of the twenty-first century, presidentialism has become a dangerous rhetorical and material touchstone for "the spirit of faction" that the Founders feared might undermine "the values of political freedom

FIG. 26 Ann Telnaes, U.S. war coverage, April 1, 2003. Used with permission of Ann Telnaes and The Cartoonist Group. All rights reserved.

and equal consideration" endemic to Americanism,[38] particularly when democracy is either threatened or considered a threat to national security—or when presidentialism takes on the attributes of showmanship. Telnaes's caricatures give presidentialism the mock royal treatment, cataloging the characteristics of a Leader of the Free World turned some kind of cross between the Pied Piper and the Village Idiot and then again a Petty Tyrant. Following Telnaes, both President Bush and President Trump embody the worst of US American national character in that they leverage homegrown animosities to represent democracy as part and parcel of war culture. Both presidents, for Telnaes, typify Idiot America. Both also typify the Ugly American, but in a manner that makes presidential appeals into "monarchist claims of executive power."[39] The president is a scion for nationalistic attitudes and culture war dispositions, and for what Benjamin Franklin once called "the hazards and mischiefs of war." A central caricature in Telnaes's canary-in-the-coal-mine cartoon exhibits a jester lifting up the robe of a king to picture the role of satire and ridicule in relocating the place of power in democratic politics. Fantastical imagery and fairy-tale iconography and, occasionally, mixed metaphors make up Telnaes's view of what it means to go down the rabbit hole of the War on Terror, again and again. It means making democracy the collateral damage of US war culture. However, Telnaes does not simply portray wartime national character as a comic travesty. She reveals a democratic people led astray. She lays bare the byproducts of cultural torment. She portrays American national character in the wake of 9/11 as a comedy of despotism.

Comic Travesty, or the Comedy of Despotism

In "Bayard vs. Lionheart," an article published in the *Evening Sun* in July 1920, agitational American journalist H. L. Mencken wrote of the strange consequence of democracy made perfect. "As democracy is perfected," wrote Mencken, "the office of president represents, more and more closely, the inner soul of the people. On some great and glorious day the plain folks of the land will reach their heart's desire at last and the White House will be adorned by a downright moron." This premonition precedes the sort of idiocy that animates the core themes of his *Notes on Democracy* (1926). Such idiocy, in Mencken's words, was variously embodied by Dunderheads, Cads, Trimmers, Cowards, and Frauds—or, what Charles P. Pierce more recently cast as the sum total of Idiot America (the wellspring of the War on Terror). And it bespeaks a corruption of the body politic by candidates corrupted by the very people who, idiotically, choose to elevate them.

Both President Bush and President Trump loom large here. So does a notion of idiocy that goes beyond mere stupidity. The ancient Greek term, *idiotes*, yields an idea of the idiot as a foolish person. However, it is also rooted in judgments about the relationship between people and the political community in which they claim to be a part. An *idiotes* is a person who is not simply a "private" citizen uninterested in public affairs but rather a *selfish* and *self-interested* person who does more to bolster a certain egoism than to work toward any common good. President Bush was regularly pegged as a common man whose so-called Bushisms laid bare his status as a commoner cum noble villain, motivated by a sense of familial redemption. President Trump, too, has been classified as a political interloper and faux populist with a penchant to appear stupid as a chief executive despite his media savvy. Both presidents, in other words, are widely regarded as clumsy politicians who mortify the American populace with their idiocy.

Most troublesome in the combination of these two presidents is the folly in their political—and cultural—warfare. President Bush framed the War on Terror as a crusade, and then expanded that campaign into matters of homegrown politics around civil liberties, equal rights, and more. President Trump began his "looking-glass war" with the contention that Americanism is dead (long live Americanism),[40] and capped it off with an inaugural speech that described US culture in terms of "carnage." In the backdrop is a "Secret War on Terror,"[41] countervailed by public brinksmanship, bluster, and saber rattling that has prompted concerns about the potential for World War III precipitated by conflicts with a range of adversaries including

Iran, North Korea, and Syria. Indeed, even though his proclaimed foreign policy is predicated upon putting America first and nurturing global politics on second thought, President Trump typifies a post-9/11 war footing as a generalized politics of *bellum omnium contra omnes*.

To parlay Mencken's take, a perfect democracy ends up going to war on one hand and to war *with itself* on the other. Mencken was a critic of war, of fanatics, and of fascistic tub-thumpers, or people who voice their support for someone or something with imperiousness and bluster. He lived through the eras of the First and Second World Wars and argued intensely for a commitment to democratic principles over and above what might be seen as "the endless bloody, dirty, graceless wars fought by sociopaths and fools."[42] Mencken was cynical about the presidency. He foresaw John Adams's image of a democratic people succumbing to its own vanity, pride, and selfishness, never mind its latent fraudulence, violence, and cruelty. As Jeffrey K. Tulis notes in his formative study of the rhetorical presidency, the personification of presidentialism—if unchecked—devolves into a pathology of democratic politics. Presidents create an image of "the people" as the consolidation of American national character in the presidency. They create what Walter Fisher calls "rhetorical fictions" of democracy in action.[43] This is why the president is such a powerful heuristic for studying character alongside the eloquence and utility of presidential speechifying. The image, after all, can ultimately overwhelm the ideal, especially when what Tulis calls "crisis politics" becomes the norm—or when, following Alexander Hamilton's early warning, the unction of appeals to democratic signifiers embolden a president to begin as a demagogic rhetor and end as a tyrant.

Despotism is the hobgoblin of democracy, particularly in times of (endless) war. An unlikely thinker emerges from this outlook: Karl Marx. The war footing of American democracy, and its exemplification in the post-9/11 rhetorical presidency, has made democratic praxis obscene. The allure of obscenity—which is to say crassness, vulgarity, and atrocity—makes a mockery of the constructive conflict necessary for democracy to function. Additionally, "the very fascination with the obscenity we are allowed to observe prevents us from *knowing what it is that we see*."[44] Obscenity, when normalized, seems less obscene. Similarly, a democracy that is diminished by abuses of executive power seems normal when justified by states of ostensible exception. There is good reason to believe that war is a tragic basis for democracy. Marx's point about tragedy and comedy is instructive here. The antistrophos of tragedy is not comedy; it is farce. A farce is a comic travesty.

FIG. 27 Ann Telnaes, Americans of the decadence, August 9, 1997. Used with permission of Ann Telnaes and The Cartoonist Group. All rights reserved.

Comic travesty, in Marx's terms, is riddled with caricatures of "world-historic facts," and riven by self-deceptions, Old Guards, and lost Orders. A farce is a comic travesty because it revives the outmoded pretenses and pretexts of other times, converting them into crudities, absurdities, omnishambles, and laughingstocks. The word "travesty" comes from the Latinate *travestir*, which means to disguise. A comic travesty exposes the smallness of false greatness. It exposes the folly, madness, and vice behind, in this case, imperial presidents. It excites humor in portrayals of idiocy and begs the question of how ridiculous it might be that something so seemingly far-fetched (i.e., a tyrannical US president) might be so close to fruition. Put simply, farce amplifies what Marx called the "comedy of despotism."[45] The comedy of despotism beckons a comic democracy to locate a moral center in humor that challenges the degeneration of democratic mentalities. In the Age of Terror, comicality comes out of an unwitting contempt for democracy that follows the folly of war. Marx perceived in the idea of despotism a rise in monarchical attitudes that render "man," or one might say "the people," despicable. Despotism makes the ship of state into a Ship of Fools, piloted by the biggest fool of all, disguising "national shame" beneath the veneer of "glorious robes."[46] Marx, of course, was writing in the shadow of the German Confederation. But his underlying point lets loose a means of figuring out the farcical nature of national character in hollow patriotism, false liberalism, and buffoonish (presidential) kingliness.

Despotism is a travesty of democracy. Alexis de Tocqueville saw the threat of tyranny in populist degradations, and more specifically in the enervation of democratic principles and practices by a body politic that ends up taking individual freedoms for granted. He imagined vicious leaders who would prey on the weakness of the American public. He envisaged a citizens' brigade constituted by unwitting servants of tyrannical institutions and corporate entities and governmental actors. He admonished his readers of the drift from a majoritarian tyranny to a tyranny of executive power. This is the specter of democracy in America. In the Jacksonian Age, it could have been read as borderline tragic. It is farcical in the post-9/11 era. In Telnaes's work, it is an ipso facto comedy of despotism, made up of so many comic travesties of wartime presidentialism. It is *the* way to see, and thus to humor, US American national character.

The Bush Liege of a Nation

Four years before 9/11, Telnaes was documenting the descent of American democracy into imperial self-indulgence and degeneracy. In August 1997, for instance, she published a cartoon that portrayed overconsumption as a new national pastime (fig. 27). The image is a caricature of Thomas Couture's nineteenth-century painting, *Romans of the Decadence*, which displays "a group of debauched revelers, exhausted and disillusioned or still drinking and dancing."[47] In Telnaes's rendition, three plump men and a pair of bulky women recline and dine in a triclinium, variously munching on fast food (indicated by Big Gulps, bags of chips, and McDonald's paraphernalia) in the company of three televisions, one of which rests on an Ionic column. On the body of a man in the center is the word "Americans." The man sprawled out before him is the only individual who is obviously attending to a screen. All the others consume with eyes closed, in self-satisfaction.

This is an important foundational image for Telnaes's wartime cartoons. The Roman imagery and iconography establishes a sense of a protectionist state that suits citizens as long as they are content with themselves. It also prefigures a collective consciousness of war that would allow a populace to become consumed by the War on Terror and at the same time enmeshed in a war culture that largely upholds democracy in name only. In Couture's original image, a couple of foreigners look upon the scene with disgust. Telnaes provides a similar lens for comic judgment with her grotesque mockery of national character as a feast of fools, and a picture of civic engagement that flagged long before 9/11 inspired a nation to rally 'round the flag.

The true colors of American national character vis-à-vis the president in particular came to light in the shadows of the 2003 invasion of Iraq. In July of that year, Telnaes depicted President Bush calling the combat tune to a throng of trifling Americans, all waving flags and grinning with nationalistic abandon. The two-panel image appeared toward the end of May. Bush is a fatuous pied piper, wearing tight pants, a long cape, and a feathered hat, prancing along while whistling out the melodies of a warmonger. The myth of the pied piper establishes Bush as a commander in chief controlling intelligence by espousing the cultural purchase of war, with the American Way as his implicit tune. This caricature aligns the folly of a president with the foolishness of the citizenry. It does not insinuate a deliberative body politic led by a measured chief executive. The American people are complacent, petulant, and puerile. The utter fidelity to a spirit of the patriotic times combined with brazen recourse to fantastical truths recollects Dr. Seuss's infamous World War II–era turn to the monstrous and horrid as resources for expressing how atrocious situations very often turn into the norm. Like Dr. Seuss, Telnaes folds tragic realities into comic fantasies in order to display snafus themselves as the standards of judgment applied to matters of democratic ways of being in times of war.

Even more pronounced, though, is the image of a democratic populace led astray. By July 2003, news outlets began reporting on rampant civil rights violations, specifically with regard to Muslims and Arabs coming under federal investigation. Widespread surveillance practices operated without political oversight and with the presumption of some civic good in the hypervisible (and hypervigilant) militarization of public spaces. During this time Telnaes began to draw the flag upside-down (an ensign for distress), and to align the exploits of President Bush with the behind-the-scenes legerdemain of Vice President Cheney. Most compelling for Telnaes's situation of US American national character in the comic looking glass is her mockery of President Bush as a hapless clod calling the war tune on one hand and as a crowned head doubling as a down-to-earth cowboy on the other. Right alongside this portrayal is Vice President Cheney as a hawkish power-grabber and Devil to the president's right hand. The CIA gave Cheney the alias Edgar Bergen, a reference to the famed ventriloquist. The president, then, was Charlie McCarthy; he was a puppet. Cheney is a

FIG. 28 Ann Telnaes, "You can see these guys wrapped in the flag on TV," October 23, 2003. Used with permission of Ann Telnaes and The Cartoonist Group. All rights reserved.

prime stooge in many of Telnaes's wartime caricatures.⁴⁸ After all, the Bush Doctrine was largely the Cheney Doctrine in that it made policies out of the pretense that a 1 percent chance of truth in intelligence reports about foreign terrorism or domestic wrongdoing was consequential enough for punitive measures against citizens and enemies alike. One consequence was a diffusion of war measures. Maybe an even more critical one was the disintegration of civil liberties.

A cartoon from October 2003 puts this disintegration on display (fig. 28). In it, President Bush holds court with other top officials in his administration. Together with the president and vice president, Secretary of Defense Rumsfeld and Attorney General John Ashcroft make up something of an American gang of four. Each is bedecked in cultural garb that, when merged into a nationalistic uniform with the flag as its unifying element, travesties the very confusion in their association. The gang stands in a line facing forward. On the left is Rumsfeld, with his recognizably little glasses and familiarly furrowed brow. He is dressed up in a lorica hamata and equipped with a feathered helmet, parma, sword, tunic, and loincloth so as to resemble an ancient Roman soldier. He is also wearing a flag for a paludamentum. In ancient Roman culture, the cloak was an imperial symbol. Here it suggests that the defense secretariat has supreme authority in war matters. Next in line is Cheney, who is clad in a thoub, or Arab robe, and affecting an empty stare with piercing white eyes. On top of his head is a keffiyeh made of a flag, the stars of which fall from his crown to his right shoulder while the stripes drape over his arms. Putting Cheney in "enemy" dress completes the circle of friend-enemy relationality, not to mention his (and President Bush's) connivances with Saudi Arabia, by mocking the deep surfaces of his public expressions of purpose. In the buildup to the 2003 invasion of Iraq, Cheney was known for faux diplomatic refrains and an unwillingness to admit that liberation was a front for occupation. As the *L.A. Times* reported, his talk of "nation-building and using Iraq as the cornerstone for creating democracy in the Arab/Muslim world" was a charade for what the *New Yorker* a month earlier had described as "War in the Ruins of Diplomacy."[49] Dressed in drag, Cheney reveals his motive to convert worst-case scenarios about, say, WMDs into "good" reasons for armed conflict. The caricature also discloses the madness in his shape-shifting politics of war.

Heading up the ruins, and signifying the drift into despotism, is President-as-Emperor Bush. The president grasps his right shoulder with his left hand while standing at perplexed attention and staring ahead with tiny black dots for eyes, upraised and bushy eyebrows, a long face beneath a pointed nose, and oversized ears that protrude from the side of his head to intimate his role as the "Dumbo" turned dummy. On top of this is the trope of an emperor with no clothes. An American flag is draped around his body like a toga praetexta and he is essentially insulated from the cabinet. To his left stands Ashcroft, a sour look on his face, sharp eyebrows bent downward over angry white eyes, and a staunch demeanor mirroring that of both Rumsfeld and Cheney. Ashcroft, too, is dressed to kill, with a robe over a shirt and tie and an American flag wrapped like a turban on his head. Like Cheney, Ashcroft regularly spouted provocations about the treasonous nature of any form of identification with the enemy. In a cartoon from October 2001, Telnaes parodies the "I Want YOU" poster with a caricature of Ashcroft in place of Uncle Sam and the declarative "I Want YOUR Civil Liberties." Like the original World War I poster, Telnaes's cartoon calls attention to wartime characterizations of civic duty. Ashcroft infamously threatened democratic freedoms in the name of national security and appealed to what could be called a newfangled Covenant of Nation, as evinced by Telnaes's conversion of the attorney general into a New England Puritan complete with a doublet and a wide-brimmed hat. Ashcroft stages a conversion of bad conscience into a bad uncle, and then into a tormenting big brother. This cartoon is not a caricature of an olden guilt trip to support the troops, or even to join in the war efforts; instead, it is a command for serving the nation by keeping it in check. It should be little surprise that Privacy International, a watchdog coalition for human and civil rights, named Ashcroft the 2002 "Worst Government Official" at its fourth annual "Big Brother Awards" ceremony in the United States. That same year, the American Civil Liberties Union reported on Ashcroft's "assault on civil liberties" and his penchant for undermining the authority of the federal judiciary, ordering covert military tribunals, and undermining "reproductive choice, religious liberty, freedom of speech, criminal defendants' rights, and equal opportunity."[50] With this image, war is less about some higher calling of hysterical jihadists than the homegrown hysteria of those elected to the highest US political offices.

Even more significant than the quasi-criminal lineup of US leaders is what appears on the second panel of this two-panel spread. "You can see these guys wrapped in the flag on TV," reads a caption below the gang of four. In the accompanying panel is a flag-draped coffin, with a follow-up caption informing us ". . . But you can't see this guy." The Bush administration banned news coverage and photography of caskets returning from battle through Dover Air Force Base. Inasmuch as Telnaes ties this policy to her thematic of a demise in democratic principles, it is easy to imagine (through the figure of the invisible soldier) the sociopolitical casualties that were carried over with the war dead as collateral damage. It is also easy to imagine the Wonderland of an American homeland kept in the dark about the human costs of keeping the world safe for—and from—democracy. What is more, this cartoon encapsulates the culmination of an early basis of the War on Terror in fearful fantasies about un-Americanism.

Just as there are resonances of Flagg and Dr. Seuss in Telnaes's caricatures of Self and Other, so are there resonances with Cold War era cartoons of Ollie Harrington, especially along the colored lines of race and ethnicity. The portrayals of President Bush and key members of his cabinet contain crudely characteristic imagery of US Americanism that does as much to reappropriate cultural attire for political purposes as to dredge up the racism and ethnocentrism so inveterate in some of the cultural politics behind Founding Principles. As Telnaes put it in an interview in 2007, these polluted wellsprings seep into the present day with tangents to war culture and to culture wars that include issues of "gun violence, environmental destruction, family planning, racism, the separation of church and state, [and] civil liberties."[51] One can add to this the idea that Telnaes's caricatures trouble the cultural politics of Americanism itself by showing matters of militarism, race, ethnicity, and more as the aggregated "other" of a "predominantly white aesthetic and cultural discourses."[52] Herein dwells what Tocqueville infamously dubbed a sort of "soft despotism," or a generalized and institutionalized and degraded anxiety about difference.

Telnaes's take on the War on Terror magnifies the comedy of despotism in a crisis of national character. Soon after 9/11, hundreds of hate crimes cropped up in what seemed like a coordinated backlash against anyone deemed to be guilty by association. One result was that Arabs became Muslims who became Sikhs who became South Asians and so on, with few to no mainstream attempts to distinguish racial, ethnic, geographic, or nationalistic characteristics. Within two weeks of the terrorist attack, mistaken identifications were seen as *the* collateral damage of cultural warfare in the War on Terror. Telnaes responded with caricatures of a particularly cruel aspect of American national character that spilled over from war policy into civic vigilantism: revenge killing. Revenge killing is the name given to a murder carried out in the name of retributive justice against those who have perpetrated a fatal act. Numerous Sikhs fell victim to violent crime after 9/11. Most notable was Balbir Singh Sodhi, who was shot dead at his gas station in Phoenix, Arizona, on September 15, 2001. His killer, Frank Roque, reportedly vowed to take out "towel-heads." First, he gunned down Sodhi. Then he fired errant shots at a Lebanese clerk in a Mobil station before shooting at the home of an Afghan family. Incidentally, Roque once owned the home. Later, when he was arrested, Roque was heard shouting, "I stand for America all the way!" A simple assumption is that Roque proclaimed his allegiance to the United States and staked a claim in his own sense of national selfhood by enacting a vigilante version of the dictum, "United We Stand." A more troubling interpretation is that Roque *stands in* for the sort of war mentality that underwrites national character in the face of armed conflict, meaning that we collectively permit cultural warfare as the exchange of an eye for an eye while representing complicity in war even (or especially) when it is conducted in support of shared values.

Telnaes's cartoon "Guide to identifying people by their headgear" was published on September 26, 2001 (fig. 29). It features four headshots that appear in a line not unlike that of the Bush administration officials. Each head (none of which has eyes or a mouth) is situated above a racial tag. On the left is a man with a turban and a full beard. The caption beneath him reads, "SIKH." To his immediate right is a woman wearing a hijab.

FIG. 29 Ann Telnaes, "Guide to identifying people by their headgear," September 26, 2001. Used with permission of Ann Telnaes and The Cartoonist Group. All rights reserved.

Underneath her is the word "MUSLIM." To the right of the Muslim woman is a "JEW," designated by a man with a kippah. Finally, to the far right is the laughably squelched head of a man whose face is squished by the weight of his hat, the base of which rests on the bridge of his nose. Below him is the word "RACIST." The hat on his head is a conical headpiece inscribed with the word "DUNCE." The dunce cap resembles the iconic pointed hat typical of Ku Klux Klan regalia. The cartoon establishes an important relationship between the four figures and the presumed ways people can be identified. First, the caricature mocks a predisposition toward mistaken and/or mistaking identities (or, worse, folding certain racial, ethnic, or religious markers into a grand stereotype). Second, it laughs at the notion that one might actually need a cheat sheet in order to sort out who is who. Third, and finally, Telnaes portrays the grim truth that prejudices are often sustained by (willed) ignorance, and so much so that the spirit behind certain tenets of a racialized view of the world can be so easily, and stupidly, conflated with systems of religious or spiritual belief.

The caricature is, first and foremost, a comic travesty of Sodhi's murder. But it displays a deeper travesty of the sort of democratic-cum-despotic thinking that allows for idiotic errors in civic judgment. Consider what is missed. Sikh men are required by the laws of Guruship to wear a dastar. A hijab (literally a "screen" or "curtain") is called in the Qur'an a public partition and is referenced in some interpretations of Islamic law to be a commandment for discretion. Many Jewish men adopt a yarmulke in accordance with halachic orthodoxies. And the dunce cap as a symbol of madness and folly dates back to the thirteenth-century philosopher John Duns Scotus, whose Scotist "Dunsmen" were well respected until the sixteenth century, when humanists denounced their hair-splitting ideas as foolish pretensions. As for Roque's arrogance and unintelligence, the larger proclivity to confound identity categories and apply prejudices to political perspectives on "other" people could be chalked up to the misguided travails that often accompany public trauma. They can also be reduced down to the accoutrements of a US Americanism that typifies ill humor as much as it embodies cruel attitudes and activities that are all too *in* character.

This is how caricature "connects the tableau of cruelty with that of stupidity,"[53] situating the freedom to be uninformed and the right to relinquish responsibilities to civil society as wartime liberties. Telnaes's image exposes the habits of mind that establish those allegiances and antagonisms needed to sustain a warring nation, and a nation at war with itself. Caricature entails a simple and immediate ascertainment of a point. Even more, though, it is about the cultivation of a capacity to pause, reconsider, and rehabituate. When Telnaes reduces longstanding problems of pride and prejudice to a seemingly artless confusion about which piece of clothing goes with which heritage (as if to suggest that Roque would have been more in the right if he had just known the difference, since at least then he would have gone after the "right" target), she actually provokes the "imperialist delusions" of an "entrenched war system" that encourages "jingoism (stirred up by the media)."[54] A crucial problematic here is that civil liberties become sites of struggle that are at once defined as public goods and derided as burdens to war efforts.

Nowhere, then, is Telnaes's concern with the despotic corruption of democratic character more pronounced than in conceptions of "others" as "foils for images of the national self."[55] The "War on Women" coincides with the War on Terror. Women have been at the center of tensions in American war culture since terror*ized* and terror*ist* bodies have come to exemplify a national security state that is "thoroughly masculine, paranoid, quarrelsome, secretive, greedy, aggressive and violent."[56] The War on Terror began with appeals to chauvinistic nationalism. The US-led campaign against terrorism has largely made the plight of both American and Islamic women worse.[57] Masculine moral orders have established a Westernized front for patriarchal (never mind imperial) modes of national character that rely on the colonial imperatives of an oddly global feminism, or a feminism appropriated by mostly white male power brokers who presume to know what oppressed female bodies politic really need or want. Telnaes's wartime cartoons are comic pictures of the War on Terror as a backdrop for the Imperial Presidency. But they are also indices of cultural matters that are meant not only to address "female" issues but also to provide a "woman's take" on public affairs.[58] In the lead-up to the invasion of Iraq in 2003, the US president is the dunce in this comic redux.

Following Telnaes, though, the paradoxes and perversions of a *global* war on women began well before 9/11. In September 1996, Telnaes looked at women under the Taliban regime before they were made into symbols of US magnanimity. One cartoon in particular displays a pair of woman's eyes encased by black paint. Protruding from the right of the frame is an arm labeled "Afghan Radicals" and a hand that grips a paint roller, covering over the woman's body like a burqa. In the first instance, the image captures the documented civil (and human) rights abuses that many women faced under the Taliban regime and its militant interpretations of Shari'a law.[59] Radicalism was widely agreed to be a source of oppression and inspired US manifestos for liberation. Telnaes provides an image of gendered blackout, with a traditional piece of Muslim attire serving as the symbol for the public disappearance of women. She does little to resist a trope of "white men saving brown women" and its use as a justification for war. "It is," says Shahnaz Khan, "the burqa-clad woman as disembodied spectacle that appears to capture our imagination. It is her image that reinforces stereotypes about Muslims."[60] Telnaes imagines this "spectacle" as a men's issue, suggesting that it is *radicals* who characterize the female body as a threat to some Islamic bodies politic just as it is would-be liberators at home who promote both white-washing cultural politics and machoistic militarism as gendered practices of subjugation. This comic reimagination is even more apparent in Telnaes's provocation to see the world through the female eyes of the oppressed "other"—an impossibility if the contextual surrounds are blacked out.

This is where Telnaes's wartime cartoons magnify her critique of US American national character through the lens of the "wartime

Everywoman,"[61] with at least two implications. First, women are central to war as cultural production. This is the case in presumptions that a burqa can only signify oppression. It relates as well to how easily surface features prefigure American soldiers as righteous guardians of "their" women (a drill that belies problems of sexual harassment and assault of women in the military, not to mention domestic violence that befalls women of military as well as civilian families). Too often, extremist activities overshadow more banal infringements on women's rights. Second, allusions to oppressed "others" cover up a specifically American image of womanhood. The prominence of the female gaze insinuates the standpoints of women themselves, which is why onlookers might also be encouraged to turn away from a particularly masculine vantage by turning the focus back upon the National Self. This caricature makes a mockery of the ordinary burdens of nationalistic pride and patriarchy. While female citizens in the United States were not impacted in the same ways as those in the Middle East and North Africa, for instance, they were caught up in the same gender politics that led many US officials to marginalize women even as they brought them to the fore.[62] A major consequence here is that the rhetorical force against women in the United States mirrors, distortively, the violent force carried out in the name of women abroad. Both rely upon male-driven discretions over rights of choice and control over bodies. If wars on women indicate what Zillah Eisenstein calls an "imperial democracy," then President Bush is the prime mover for the culture wars of a post-9/11 American empire. This image of warfare as the basis of culture wars (and not, as usual, vice versa) persists in Telnaes's cartoons for many of the early years following 9/11. Women of war actually end up being folded into the broader problems of civil liberties and flag symbolism. Telnaes made a constant point of mocking the failures of military operations to secure "democratic" liberations abroad at the same time as she was lampooning the homegrown war on women's rights as a contradiction in American principles. Moreover, she maintained the overlap of imperialist predilections with executive idiocy in the image of President Bush as a foolish leader. And so it goes into the presidency of Donald J. Trump.

Trumped-Up War

A piece of satire from The Borowitz Report on September 19, 2017, reported that Kim Jong-un called US president Trump a "Honky Cat." The remark, according to Andy Borowitz, came in response to President Trump's speech to the United Nations, wherein he called the North Korean dictator a reckless and suicidal "Rocket Man." In Borowitz's account of what he deemed a mode of rhetorical warfare, Trump responded in kind, urging that any "Elton John–based attack" would "be seen as an act of war," to which Kim retorted, "The bitch is back," before dubbing Trump a "Yellow-Wigged Toad."[63] Such an exchange would seem ridiculous if two days prior Kim had not branded Trump a "dotard" and a "frightened dog" in an international dispatch. Or if less than one month later Trump had not announced National Character Counts Week, driven by his definition of character as the sum of habits made visible "in the way we treat others and ourselves."[64] Or if days before that members of Congress, commentators, and critics alike were not making projections about World War III, impelled by the president's ham-fisted foreign policy and penchant for playing with domestic cultural politics in ways that satirists might struggle to dream up.

National character is an index of cultural time and temperament. Honky Cats and Rocket Men fill out a humorous, yet no less horrid, picture of a contemporaneous war culture wherein the president is the insult comic in chief.[65] There is a longstanding argument about President Trump making a career of being a genuine caricature of himself. But there is good reason to see caricatures of him for the alternative view of grotesqueries that he is so ready to indulge. In September 2017, Telnaes published a cartoon that featured the president screaming from a large dumpster. In it, he is the prevailing symbol of political trash accompanied by the dirty remnants of an American flag, the tatters of the Constitution, a sullied Presidential Seal, a broken balance from the Scales of Justice, and the torch of Lady Liberty—and a swarm of flies. The president cries out for respect. The squalor around him belies his habit of embodying effrontery, and tossing the trappings of Americanism onto the garbage heap of history. The term "Trumpster Fire" has become a boilerplate for many people who are critical of the Trump administration. The comic looking glass reveals a dumpster. It reveals a national character in the ill humor of the president.

If Telnaes's wartime artwork constitutes a triangulation of "character, words, and actions,"[66] then her oeuvre of Trump caricatures exemplifies American national character as a comic travesty. President Bush was a "war president." He embraced the moniker. "I'm a war president," he told TV journalist Tim Russert in February 2004. "I make decisions . . . with war on my mind."[67] In March 2020, as the dire impacts of the coronavirus pandemic were becoming more and more apparent, President Trump adopted the moniker "wartime president" and made references to the "invisible enemy" of COVID-19 part of his press conference refrain. But even before his refusal to take responsibility for failures in federal responses to the disease and its transmission, his pushback against public health professionals, his peddling of misinformation about supposedly miraculous remedies like doses of hydroxychloroquine and injections of disinfectants into the lungs, and his racialized approach to regional stay-at-home policies and economic recovery measures, President Trump had been dubbed "a war president of a different sort: a culture war president."[68] The specter of armed conflict creeps around his man-at-arms presidency. In the Age of Coronavirus, it is manifest in abhorrent and evasive remarks about the "Chinese Virus." It appears in tweets that call for the liberation of states wherein some members of the president's political base protested social distancing measures and economic restrictions. It comes out in his castigations of reporters who question his handling of the coronavirus in the early months of spread in 2020, as in April when he called one journalist a disgrace and her network an epitome of "fake news." A couple years earlier, a film entitled *Trump @War* (2018), produced by Steve Bannon, captures the flippancy, the foolhardiness, and really the danger of these sentiments. Its premise is that Trump became president of a nation in quasi–civil war. It foregrounds anti-Trump protestors lashing out alongside bloodied Trump supporters. It features Trump proclaiming that so-called Trumpsters are "fighting a war" for their national culture. What is more, it highlights the social media handle "@war" as the icon, the key signifier, indeed the username of the chief executive leading the charge of cultural warfare. A global pandemic is simply another conduit for nationalistic hysteria along so many color lines and political sides and class divides. For Telnaes, President Trump is a portrait of the post-9/11 drift from warmongery into MAGA era war mockery.

The Trump presidency, or what some call the capstone of a "Trump Revolution," is based on a notion that the world is unsafe and embroiled in a war of all against all such that democracy need only apply when it seems profitable or politically expedient. Trump's candidacy promised the rueful toppling of the American political establishment, especially as it radiates through the presidency. Part and parcel of this rout was an America First agenda that exploited many of the markers of post-9/11 war culture: the institutionalization, and cultural inculcation, of a combat stance; the accentuation of enemies without and within; the aggravation of mass outrage; the use of national security as a pretense for executive authority; the provocation of distrust for the free press; the popularization of terms like treason and shame as labels for social and political rivalry; and more. Commensurate with these markers is what many critics and commentators have since called Trump's more generalized war on American democracy. On one level, this war stokes fears of a turn to tyranny in the manner of an it-can't-happen-here slippery slope. On another level, it bespeaks a Trumpian notion that status quo Americanism is a cottage industry of nationalistic carnage, with olden (even old timey) "traditions" being traded in for the new world order of nonsensical "snowflakes" who are incapable of managing the politics of offense. Regardless, there is in Trump's presidentialism a powerful resurrection of what Marx might have seen as the selective histories of "dead generations," replete with powerful conjurations of Drained Swamps and white Americanism and Love of Country, all in service of a nostalgia that looks to a better future for "the forgotten." The tensions herein typify what Bergson claimed to be the substance of humor in the tensions between the "living" and the "dead." They also make sense of President Trump's warism and his revelry in conflict as a modus operandi.

Telnaes's caricatures connect the comedy of despotism to the kingly comportment of President Trump. They are rooted in her take on his transmogrification of endless war into *everywhere* war. Central to this take is a sense that Trump's presidency is not so much the follow-on from choices made by a democratic electorate ready to proceed down a rabbit hole as the consequences of a body politic that has dug its own hole, then fallen into it. As one commentator put it in February 2012, kingly ambitions clothed in the brazen falsehoods and alternative facts of a naked emperor are the hallmarks of the "Trump Farce."[69] Trump has been likened to Andrew Jackson, to Richard Nixon, and to Ronald Reagan, with various references to everything from cronyism to corruption to celebrity. Telnaes lines this all up with the realities of power. An animated cartoon from June 2019, for instance, portrays President Trump standing in profile, his pouty lips protruding from his pudgy face, his large body hunched over while he bounces a large round bomb on the palm of his left hand. The word "WAR" is stamped on the explosive. The fuse is lit. From the side, Trump appears to be wearing a baggy Mao suit with a notoriously long red tie dangling to the ground. The suit could surely be seen as regular business attire, except that Trump had recently been exchanging letters with North Korean leader Kim Jong-un and publicly threatening Iran with "obliteration" in advance of leaning in to dictators at the 2019 G20 Osaka summit and then visiting the DPRK's Supreme Leader in the demilitarized zone just days before the Fourth of July. Telnaes's caricature shows Trump for his willingness to excite chaos and adopt the temperament of a tyrant with a constituency of one. Additionally, it ridicules the overweening rhetoricity of Trump's war games.

By the end of 2019 and nearly three years into his term, President Trump was warring on countless fronts. He was carrying out trade wars. He was battling the fallout from the Report on the Investigation into Russian Interference in the 2016 Presidential Election (colloquially known as the Mueller Report) and thus the aura of impeachment around the "Mueller War," which some of his supporters said could spawn a second Great Rebellion. On December 18, he was impeached by the House of Representatives for abuse of power and obstruction of Congress. There remains talk of a "new cold war" with Russia and a burgeoning cold war with China in the wake of the coronavirus pandemic. He began his presidency with the threat of a Third World War and nuclear winter. Detractors continue to accuse the president of conducting a war on constitutional norms and trampling American principles of life and liberty, equality, and justice. Trump's political warfare was made even more flagitious following his loss to Joe Biden in the 2020 presidential election, after which he contested the results and tried his level worst to get them overturned. On the battlefront of Trumpism is an intense brand of identity politics that situates gender, racialism, geographic affiliations, religious liberties, and more at the center of claims to national character. The coronavirus presented an opportunity for the president to call a different tune. If anything, it has made a broken record of President Trump's rhetorical presidency, betraying just how much his principles of governing and his electoral politics resound with a bluster of someone intent on amplifying "certain groups, particularly people who are white and Christians, as allies," and recasting "others, often those who are nonwhite, as enemies."[70] Declarations that Trump is "Not My President" and that his presidency is "Not Normal" are still as common as his own appeals to "Make America Great Again." So, too, are assertions that his most ardent supporters are the idiot disciples of a false prophet, especially as the president's dealings with the coronavirus have fomented new levels (or new lows) of propaganda, Twitter trolling, and attacks on the media.[71] The point is that a war mentality, from foreign policy to stateside politicking to crisis management, impels President Trump's ugly embodiment of US Americanism.

For Telnaes, comic travesty is the best response. This begins with attention to President Trump's perversion of the Dionysiac hero. President Trump is a "comic character" insofar as he is "invisible to himself while remaining visible to all the world."[72] This is not to say that he is not self-aware. Quite the contrary, the president has an earned reputation for narcissism and spiritual bankruptcy. It is to say, however, that President Trump cannot see beyond his own egotism. He exudes what Bergson would deem the comic *in* character, or the idiocy that comes from the idiotic type who is self-involved without being self-aware. Dionysius was a comic hero because he mocked this sort of ostentation and denuded the nakedness of vice in the cult of personality. In Telnaes's caricatures, the comic in character becomes the comic in *national* character. The American people are—in a rhetorical, imagistic sense—the very person in the Office of the President. Telnaes sees President Trump as a comic travesty because he desecrates The People, degrades Founding Principles, and deforms the consent of the governed. He *is* the arrogance, pomposity, and deluded grandeur of "The Ugly American." In fact, he is something of an Oppugnant American—egotistic at base, but also hostile, antagonistic, belligerent, and celebratory of the competing imperialisms that gave the originary stereotype purchase in the first place.

First and foremost is Telnaes's struggle with President Trump's cavalier attitude toward actual war with foreign adversaries. Literal effects came early in his presidency, such as when he ordered a missile strike on the Shayrat Airbase in Syria following a suspected chemical attack in Khan Shaykhun in April 2017. The day of the strike, Telnaes published a caricature of the president in profile holding up an oversized magnifying glass in one hand while gazing through squinted eyes at the other. The scourge of vanity meets the heavy hand of power in this image, magnifying President Trump's overt alignment of egomania with militarism. This expands upon what Telnaes elsewhere branded the spirit of 2017, with a notably disgruntled Uncle Sam parading with the president while flying an upside-down American flag. Additionally, it stands out in a context of diffuse war rhetoric. In September 2017, at a speech before the United Nations General Assembly, the president infamously threatened North Korea with total destruction and slighted Kim Jong-un as a suicidal "Rocket Man." Soon thereafter, as mentioned above, Kim Jong-un called President Trump a foolish "rogue," a "frightened dog," a "dotard," and a "gangster fond of playing with fire." In the summer of 2019, the two leaders seemed to make some amends, but there is little that can mitigate an American president threatening a foreign adversary with "fire and fury" as Trump did just a month before this exchange of insults. There is little, too, that can alter President Trump's alignment of the so-called "Forgotten War" on the Korean peninsula with his doctrine for putting America First. It is in this light that the Brookings Institution called the 2019 summit in Hanoi a spectacle of "the

FIG. 30 Ann Telnaes, pissing contest, January 3, 2018. Used with permission of Ann Telnaes and The Cartoonist Group. All rights reserved.

good, the bad, and the ugly."[73] One wonders which is the graver caricature here, the tragedy of Trump's presidentialism or Telnaes's comic travesty.

Glaringly, Trump's rhetorical war games define the American national character in terms of standoffs between "Great" Men. In a cartoon from January 2018, Telnaes positions both Trump and Kim as dogs poised to piss on a fire hydrant emblazoned with a nuclear symbol (fig. 30). The two men lift a leg as they stare each other down. The obscenity in this visual display of a pissing contest conveys just how much President Trump converts a Great Men theory of leadership into an expression of territorial markings, fights for upper hands, and ploys for pack orders. His ostensive heroics are laughable. They amount to the derring-do of a wrongheaded president who is more interested in dog-whistle politics than diplomacy. They provoke what commentators came to call an "axis of idiocy." Furthermore, they insinuate the real-life barbs between the leaders about who has the bigger nuclear button. Another cartoon reinforces the point, with the two presidential caricatures squaring off in an arm wrestling match. Hunched over either end of a tiny table, Trump and Kim lean in to one another with quivering little hands just about to meet above two equally little flags for their countries. The men matter more than the nations they lead. Theirs is a battle of egos—not so much a battle of wits on the world stage as a battle of twits, eager to bolster their own brands in a show of conspicuous, nationalistic male aggression.

These belletristic displays are even more pronounced when considered alongside Telnaes's caricature of President Trump as a commander in tweet. A core modality of Trumpian rhetoric is Twitter warfare. Telnaes has depicted the president as an angry baby, a disgruntled housewife in a terrycloth bathrobe, a man with a birdbrain (seen as the Twitter logo in flight from his empty head), and more, all to encapsulate the president's penchant for conducting Twitter wars. Famed journalist Bob Woodward went so far as to suggest that President Trump could start an actual war with a single tweet.[74] Twitter is a space wherein, via presidential rhetoric, an image of national character can be constituted. As Brian L. Ott and Greg Dickinson have demonstrated, the "Twitter Presidency" of Trump is fueled by and inflammatory for off-hand policymaking and hostile cultural politics, which have "undermined our national character" and "eroded the principles, norms, and institutions of American democracy."[75] In October 2017, Trump tweeted a reiteration of his "Little Rocket Man" insult. Simply, from summits to tweets, President Trump has redefined what it means for the figurehead of American national character to go nuclear.

Perhaps most concerning in his rhetorical war games, though, is their foundation in what some have labeled "dictator envy." During an impromptu news conference on the White House lawn in June 2018, President Trump reflected on the North Korean dictator's prestige. More specifically, he shared his observation that, when Kim speaks, his people stand at attention. "I want my people to do the same," said Trump. A few months earlier, Telnaes published an animated caricature of President Trump marching with "a good goose step," wearing the military garb of the KPA, or the Korean People's Army, complete with KKK hoods for patches on his sleeves and a golden "T" for a belt buckle (fig. 31). The caricature came out soon after the president ordered the Pentagon to hold a military parade. Such martial pageantry is common in dictatorships, particularly in Pyongyang. President Trump, however, averred that his want of a parade was inspired by the one he saw along the Champs-Élysées on Bastille Day the previous July. Telnaes made a comic travesty of the president's desire to militarize the pomp and circumstance of his political power. What eventually became his "Salute to America" on July 4, 2019, was widely seen as a tribute to himself, and to the imagined triumphs of Trump Nation. Idiots here are those who

FIG. 31 Ann Telnaes, the Donald loves a good goose step, from an animation, February 7, 2018. Used with permission of Ann Telnaes and The Cartoonist Group. All rights reserved.

trade in popular sovereignty and self-government for the frills of supreme leadership.

Presidential idiocy is what makes Telnaes's compendium of an American president qua petty tyrant qua idiot king a weighty articulation of democracy's demise under an imperialistic leader. In September 2007, toward the end of President Bush's second term, historian Joanna Bourke remarked on the problem of a chief executive unilaterally waging war in the name of democracy. It leads to "tyranny in disguise."[76] In many ways, the War on Terror has enabled once rogue dictatorships to overlap with the democratic empire. Following Telnaes, the problem is less that Trump's war footing betrays some hidden despotism and more that the president's tyrannical proclivities are on full, even obscene, display.

Published in June 2018 as a cartoon essay of sorts, "The Lyin' King" is a comic travesty of President Trump's ascendency, from his campaign for "absolute monarch" to his tenure as megalomaniacal and imperial president. It opens with an animated caricature of the president dressed as royalty, sitting on a throne, and staring forward as a red carpet rolls out in front of him. Here is "His Royal Grumpiness." Next is the abovementioned caricature of candidate Trump as the Queen of Hearts, which is followed by Telnaes's first real visual commentary on President Trump's faux kingship.

The caricature is from November 2016, right after he was elected. It features the president-elect in side profile, seen from the waist up wearing an iconic red MAGA hat fitted out with a tiny crown and a gold "T." At the time, numerous writers and thinkers across the political spectrum were speculating on the ripeness for tyranny in America and the possibility that Trump's inauguration would be more like a coronation. The crownish MAGA hat stands out in this caricature not so much because it reinforces Telnaes's historical use of headgear as a means of exposing both idiocy and indignation but rather because it locates the rhetorical force of the guise. Trump's red hat represents an entire cultural aesthetic for a cult of personality. It is a talisman for the cultural warfare that set Trump off on his presidential warpath, and thus a signifier for the populist hopes for a strong leader who gained power in spite of his resemblance to the strongman. The red hat, as one commentator puts it, is "a pop culture curio" that doubles as "a political weapon—as logo, shield, personal dogma, and insignia of contempt."[77] In other words, it is a marker of the return to a "new" US Americanism.

Following Telnaes, in the makeup of King Trump is the anger and avowed victimage of an American culture that sees a way to founding principles in the strange appeal of a wannabe despot. The thing is that many Trump supporters do not see in the president a peculiar temptation to tyranny (or they do and that is the point) and similarly see brusque comicality where others see cruelty. Telnaes sees things differently. For her, there is good reason to look upon the kinglike disposition of a US president as a reflection of national character, however distorted, and thereby as a potential byproduct of failures in the democratic experiment. Hence she emphasizes the tyrannical creep in Trump's leadership. One example has to do with President Trump's ire at the news media. An animated cartoon from February 2017, just a month into his presidency, shows the president again in a regal robe. Facing viewers with the robe wrapped around his body, President Trump promptly becomes the Emperor With No Clothes, throwing open his mantle to lay bare a plump, naked body (fig. 32). But he is not entirely naked. In denuding himself, the president reveals a black box for a fig leaf covering his genitals, with the words "FAKE NEWS" inscribed on it. The perversion here is President Trump's longstanding appeal to freedom *from* the press. From his candidacy through his time in office, he used the epithet "fake news" to undermine any reproach of him, his words, or his actions (another caricature in *The Lyin' King* shows Emperor Trump signing a proclamation against criticism). Like the slogan "Make America Great Again," the phrase "fake news" is an emblem of a culture war mentality. It sums up Trump's media feud, and with it a historical tactic of tyrants to demand the praise and adoration of those who might otherwise evaluate him on the grounds of public service. The free press in America stands for freedom from tyranny. In Telnaes's caricature, President Trump reveals a prime way that he clothes his power, as well as his idiocy. An Emperor With No Clothes is patently unfit for his leadership position. He is both self-indulgent and self-deluded. The "fake news" fig leaf shows the president for his ignorance (or debauchery) of the very cornerstones of civil liberty that empowered his rise to high political office, and with it his arrogance in defiling the Fourth Estate.

President Trump is a man who imagines himself a lord over and above the people. He is also a man who lavishes himself with a largesse that only swells over time. These notions are touchstones for Telnaes's enhancement of his mock kingliness. As his presidential tenure carried on, so did his robe go from red to purple. It got longer and more decadent. His crown, too, became purple and more pronounced on his head. Telnaes increasingly latched onto the president's habit of spewing out talking points like decrees and using the just-a-joke defense for racialized comments, demands for loyalty oaths, and suggestions of a lifetime presidential term. In a caricature from February 2018, captioned "The megalomania of Donald Trump," the president appears in the backdrop while his royal mantle stretches forward into the foreground. The purple robe is hemmed with dollar signs. Covering the garment itself is a selection of direct quotations from the president. "I have absolute right to do what I want to do with the Justice Department." "The fake news media . . . is the enemy of the people." "One of the things I'm going to do if I win . . . is I'm going to open up our libel laws." And more. At the bottom edge of the robe are remarks made about Democrats who did not stand up and applaud during his State of the Union Address. "Un-American." "Treasonous." For love of country, Trump proclaimed. For love of kingship. His megalomania, in caricature, is mania: passion, rage, fury, madness. Trump has all the makings of a Madcap King.

Consequently, although the compendium is titled "The Lyin' King," the culmination in an image of "The Imperial President" suggests that a better title might be "The Loutish King" (fig. 33). Trump is not just a bad president but also a bad actor, who makes the presidential office into a bad object. He is the embodiment of egoistic impulses that have destructive effects on democracy. Telnaes's emphasis on physiognomy reinforces the sort of "comical distortion" in caricature that "unmasks inner character."[78] But her caricature expands even further outward into comic travesty

FIG. 32 Ann Telnaes, Emperor Trump has no clothes, February 16, 2017. Used with permission of Ann Telnaes and The Cartoonist Group. All rights reserved.

insofar as the American president constitutes a nationalistic type, which has implications for images of the collective being represented by the individual. The president is supposed to be a guardian of freedoms and civil liberties. He is supposed to hold the power of the people in public trust. In Telnaes's caricatures is an image of the president as their usurper, discernible in her series of what journalist Jack Shafer might identify as "American Emperor Moments."[79] Trump, as the imperial president, is a man above the law. Heavy is the crown on his head, but the burden is on the American people. Trump, after all, locates political power in *himself*, not in the presidential *office*.

The president therefore appears as a potentate. His power madness is pronounced in imbrications of militarism and politics, especially in the context of bluster with foreign adversaries (and allies) and behavior at home that devolves from touts of military might through anti-immigration border policies to brazen racism. Trump embodies Americanism as warfare over a sense of Self. His culture-war style is "angrier, more tribal, and more fundamental than ever before," and so frightfully indicative of an "American *Kulturkampf*."[80] For Telnaes, Trump incarnates the Age of Terror as an Age of American Tyranny, and with it an unsettling mix of shameless power grabbing and sheer idiocy. Part of this has to do with the vileness Telnaes captured a month before his election with a caricature of then candidate Trump as "Despicable Don," gazing at himself in a hand mirror (with his eyes closed, no less) intoning, "Mirror, mirror on

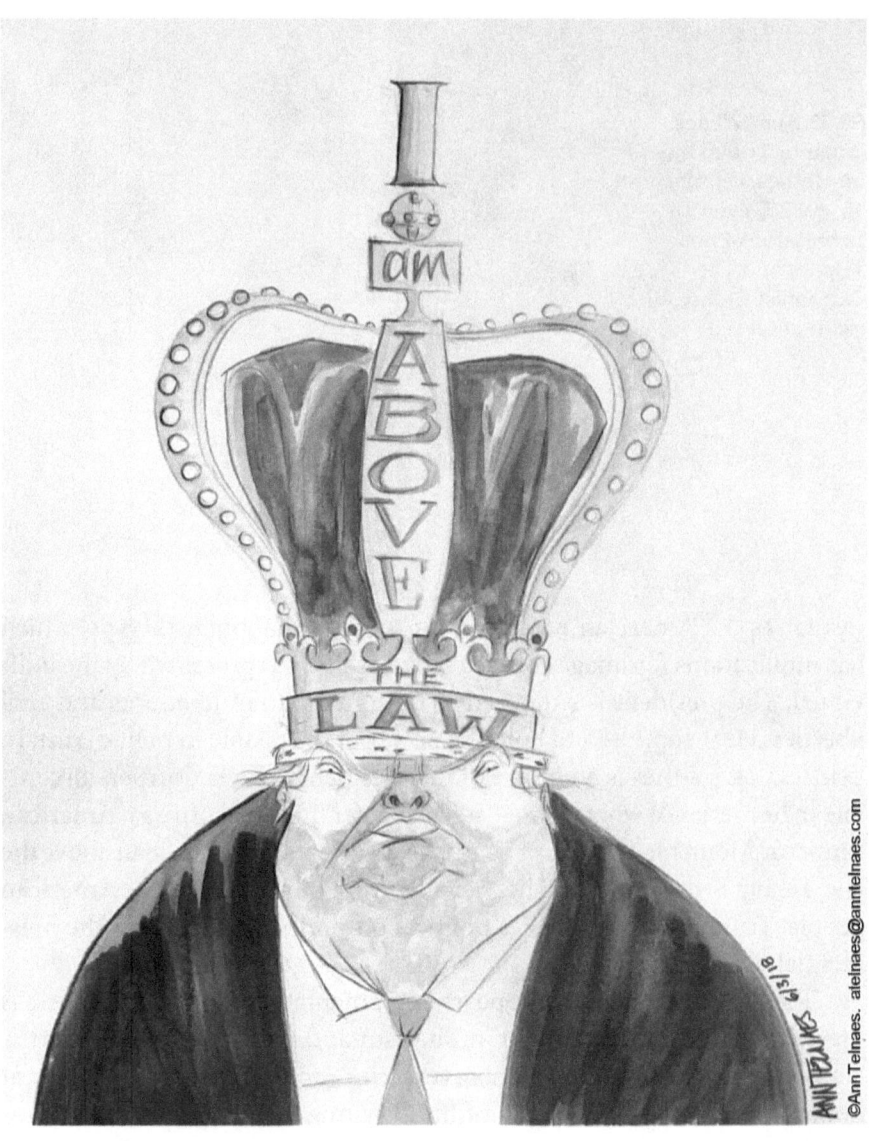

FIG. 33 Ann Telnaes, the imperial president, June 3, 2018. Used with permission of Ann Telnaes and The Cartoonist Group. All rights reserved.

the wall... Who's the most despicable one of all?" There is humor here in what James Baldwin might have seen in the president as a comic foil for the "tyranny of the mirror."[81] Trump's looking glass will tell the truth, hand to mouth and wall to wall. There is also humor in the aura of those who don political power. Two years later, Telnaes dangled Trump in a swing on a hanging tree of fear and hate and projected with the image so many historical matters of multiracial democracy, domestic terror, white supremacy, lynchings, rapes, the dark essence of an Invisible Empire made plain, and lately the reign of Trumpism. His mouth is gaping. The tree branches betray his temperament. Anti-immigration. Misogyny. Anti-Semitism. Racism. Bowdlerization. Beside the trunk is Senate Majority Leader Mitch McConnell, holding a watering can, nourishing the tree. Here is a picture of democracy in cloaks and mirrors, with an Idiot Tyrant in full swing.

How short the distance from president to pinhead.

A Caricature of Hindsight, or the Hindsight of Caricature, in 2020

With all due regard for the comic spirit, hindsight will surely be 2020.

The beginning of the year was taken up by a Senate trial that ultimately acquitted President Trump of the charges brought forth in his impeachment by the House of Representatives. In late January, Telnaes had the president gazing (eyes closed) into a hand mirror once again, thinking about the "Big Stuff." He had three thoughts. "Winning." "My brand." "Me." This reflection, of course, turned out to be a projection, as Telnaes suggested with a caricature of King Trump after the Senate trial. King Trump appears bedecked in his purple regalia, a crown topped with a golden "ME" on his head, and a generally triumphant appearance. His defense lawyer, Pat Cipollone, stands beside him announcing that his only job was to "convince you that this self-serving conman and wannabe despot is actually a democracy-loving guy whose only motive is doing what's good for the national interest." Self-interest is nationalistic in President Trump's despotic power politics. The Cartoonist Group declared as much with a tweet of Telnaes's caricature along with hashtags like #ShamTrial, #Democracy becoming #Monarchy, and #KingDonald. There is little need to affect much of a comic stretch to imagine the partisan, party-politicking executors of American democracy clad in dunce caps.

At the time of this writing, the COVID-19 pandemic carries on. There is much anxiety about ongoing transmission of the virus. There are questions about herd immunity and vaccinations. The global economy is shaky, and social norms amount to calculated risks in the Age of Coronavirus. Distance and time are the watchwords of the day. Public comportment is defined by private lives and privations. Facemasks are fodder for cultural politics. Yet President Trump has urged the US American populace to forget the horrors of the pandemic—from the failures in federal responses around testing and treatment to the very real human suffering that has taken place—and get back to business as usual. In particular, the president has approached the so-called reopening of the country with the guile of a chief executive bent on building up a wartime economy. This does not just entail an activation of the Defense Production Act. In entails Trump's insistence on rebuffing the recommendations of public health experts and calling for people to get back to work. And he is doing all of this while declaring his total authority. So it is appropriate that President Trump was called out by an array of commentators and critics for his petty, despotic, and transactional schemings. It is fitting, too, that questions have once again emerged about the authoritarian stupidities inherent to the so-called Trumpocracy. In short, the Trump Show goes on, and so much so that some opinion makers have called on the media to "drop the curtain on the Trump Follies" by removing his access to captive audiences.[82]

Caricatures of the president as King Trump remain a show of rhetorical force in this context. His self-dealings and denials have goaded Telnaes in particular to augment her comic attitude to the "Me Presidency." Trump's presidentialism is not soft despotism, for Telnaes. It is stupid despotism. It is selfish. It situates the coronavirus as a threat to what decriers across the political spectrum have come to call the Trump Show. What is more, the tyrannical tendencies are stroppy and warlike insofar as they feed into a militaristic disposition that President Trump has so long embraced. Countless world leaders refer to the coronavirus as an "enemy." President Trump has declared war against it and even proclaimed himself a "wartime president," which Telnaes mocked in late March with a caricature of him standing at an enormous podium emblazoned with the words "THE WAR TIME PRESIDENT." The podium is flanked by one small statue of a general on horseback and another that looks like a child mounted on a rearing pony. The comicality here comes from an image of Trump as an inflated commander in chief with no regard for people on the front lines, every interest in his own pomp and circumstance, and an utterly outsized sense of political authority.

Yet there is even more to be gleaned from the enduring notion that a US president is an emblem of national character. On one hand is the obvious continuation of warism as the cornerstone of a democratic nation bent on perpetuating warfare (cultural and otherwise) in a venal espirit de corps. The Trump administration emboldened this attitude when it forced states to rely on the market and compete for medical resources when the federal government relinquished its own responsibility to facilitate support. War *with* a viral disease is war with one another in this perverse political game of survival of the fittest. On the other hand, then, there is the potentially more inveterate matter of warring principles. President Trump has scarcely ceased to call the coronavirus an *invisible* enemy. He also refuses to stop giving it quite vulgar visibility with incessant references to either a *foreign* or a *Chinese* virus, dredging up the very discourses of racial tension and ethnic stereotype that plague images of US Americanism. Material realities meet up with these rhetorical machinations when one considers that communities of color have fared the worst in the fight against COVID-19, and not least because of ongoing nationalistic struggles over racist policies, classist cultural politics, unequal access to health care, and stratified financial insecurities.

It is therefore significant that Telnaes took to portraying President Trump not just as a vector for misinformation and mismanagement but also as a pathogen unto himself. An animated cartoon in late February 2020 displayed the president puffing his cheeks and then exhaling large green renderings of coronavirus droplets. The tagline that accompanied the cartoon was "spreading misinformation." On April 2, Telnaes put out a comic picture of President Trump reading from *Coronavirus Tales*, a mock playbook for carrying out a propaganda war in order to push back on reports of his failures to adequately prepare the nation for the pandemic and to shape the narrative of the aftermath. The president's hulking body is hunched over. His face is orange. He is scowling. Beside him is a large placard that reinforces the contents of his book, revealing text that misrepresents the federal response and puts the public at risk with an obvious commitment to instinct, gut feelings over scientific truth, and an overwhelming interest in reputation management. Also implied in the cartoon is that those who enable Trump's corrupt presidentialism, those who are blighted by his brinksmanship, those who are downstream of an image of US Americanism that makes cultural *dis*-ease out of an all too real disease—all are afflicted by the contamination of rhetorical cultures. President Trump, after all, tells his Coronavirus Tale as if it was a Canterbury Tale, full of political warfare, self-love, and the guiltless laughter of an agelast.

An even more compelling characterization by Telnaes takes the anamorphic quality of this view of the president and turns it into a portrayal of him *as* the virus. An exemplar actually comes from her sketchbook. On April 4, Telnaes unveiled "The Coronavirus President." The outline of his face and his shoulder-up profile is indeed sketchy. But the comic judgment appears all over President Trump's face. His infamous orange complexion is now a countenance that is pocked with tiny depictions of the coronavirus. Montesquieu once described despotism with metaphors of sickness, and saw the despot as a terroristic, sick man full of laziness, ignorance, maliciousness, and caprice. For Telnaes, despotism in the image of a US president can be captured as a sickness in the comedy of democracy. In a Deleuzian sense, presidential sickness and the health of a democratic body politic combine to represent an inflection point for humor in particular as an apt response to a sorry state of affairs, especially when public health is on the line in its most metaphorical and material senses. À la Deleuze, there are presidencies and diseases, but there are also presidential diseases. Telnaes's caricatures of President Trump as a vector, and then again as a viral affliction transmitting the sicknesses he should be suppressing in the body politic, make his very presidentialism a matter of susceptibility over immunity. More broadly, her caricatures showcase what it means to make the presidency comprehensible *as the people* with a comic view of wrongs that help us right the image of ourselves relative to the conduct of our chief executive.

Telnaes has drawn numerous caricatures of President Trump as a would-be king, with everything from bags of money to boxes of ballots stuffed in his crown. A sense of humor is helpful in confrontations with this imagery even during the worst of political horror shows. It helps to bear comic witness to stark realities that impose themselves upon a way of living that is only seen clearly when it is thrown out of whack. Herein lies a clear-eyed way of seeing through a comic looking glass. Herein, too, is the conceit of caricature: the comic image in the distorted mirror is an image of the critical issue itself, the moment of judgment, the *hypokrisis* (that is, the pretense or the deceit) that revels in a revelation of unseemly, unspeakable truths that lie below the surface—in this case, the crisis of national character in the presidential façade. To mistake the farce for a tragedy in this context is to miss the point of anamorphic possibilities in the kind of humor that caricature represents.

Conclusion: Scenes of Idiocy and Traducement

In his famous statement on national liberty, Thomas Paine wrote of emerging democracies in the face of flagrant despotism, and of despotic governments that thrive on scenes of iniquity and oppression. Flagrancy is part of what animates the comedy of despotism in Telnaes's caricatures, along with scenes of idiocy and traducement.

Humorist Groucho Marx established some grounds for a conditional conclusion somewhat better than these sallies. Do not be fooled, Marx admonished, by those who look like idiots and talk like idiots. They might actually *be* idiots. The same could be said of a presidential crusader on a fool's errand. Of a wannabe king who pronounces kingliness in the name of democracy. Of petty tyrants who occupy an Oval Office with the trappings and loaded talk of tyranny. Of presidents who make national character *the* weapon of war in defense of US Americanism.

The Age of Terror is not the first moment in history when there arose some public concern around the idea that wartimes might make democratic freedoms cede their ground to the push of American Empire. Nor is it the first cultural milieu to witness the rise of imperialist sentiments, especially in the hearts and minds of heads of state, and with them the unbearable lightness of caricature as a means of bringing some sense of humor to dark matters. On Independence Day in 2019, online comics publication *The Nib* posted two old caricatures of American national character. One is from a cover of *Life*, published in June 1898. It was drawn by Francis Gilbert Attwood. The cartoon scene is framed at the top by a bearded, godlike elder with wings, playing the violin. Two cherubs dance across from him. Along the bounded side are comical illustrations that bespeak Americanism via its drama, politics, literature, and society. In the center of the cartoon is a caricature of Uncle Sam equipped with a rifle and a sword strapped to his body. He is blindfolded. To add the potential for scattered injury to the conspicuousness of his impaired vision, he is armed with a gun, which he points into the open space that lies before a cliff he is walking off. A breeze appears to lift the top hat from his head. Beneath him is a caption: "HURRAH FOR IMPERIALISM!" Near the toes of the dancing cherubs is an eaglet hatching from an egg. The words *Americanus Sum* describe the eaglet. To Be American. Tellingly, for society, there is an illustration that appears to feature Alice taking lessons from the White Rabbit.

At the turn of the twentieth century, Attwood's cartoon encapsulates the farce in a democratic society the cultural politics of which betray *Americanus Bellum*. It was published just before the end of the Spanish-American War. The United States had just established itself as an imperial power. In the same month that Attwood's cartoon appeared, the American Anti-Imperialist League was codified. Mark Twain was a member. He was among the voices who called President William McKinley an imperialist and a conqueror (not a redeemer) heralding the American Century. Nearly twenty years into the twenty-first century, Attwood's attitude haunts what Telnaes takes up as the comic travesty of the New American Empire.

It is instructive that *The Nib* coupled its recollection of historical caricatures with its so-called "Empire Issue." In it, Telnaes contributed a cartoon made up of the statuary ruins and scattered refuse of an American Republic devolved into a Romanesque tyranny. Foremost in the image is a statue of President Trump dressed as a mock Caesar and poised on a broken pedestal, his figure set among the familial and political icons of a "Trumpian Empire" gone bust. In a cartoon from just over a decade and a half before, on the last Independence Day before 9/11, Telnaes published a cartoon that seems to prefigure the comic spiritedness of a post-9/11 American structure of nationalistic feeling: tyranny is dead, long live tyranny. President Bush is seen flying the Betsy Ross flag in lockstep with Vice President Cheney and a GOP elephant calling the tune. In this iteration of kingly presidentialism, a crowned vice president is beating the oil drum of war. The president himself is a nominal leader, a foolish cipher, a cowboyish dandy. What stands out in Telnaes's approach to both Bush and Trump is a conception of idiocy, implying that wartime presidents can be an index of the folly that might lead a democratic people to give away the political store. By the end of his tenure, President Bush was being lambasted for his "Absurdist Imperialism," with its mixture of political, cultural, and military theaters of war, and the "horrific farce" it propagated upon the American populace.[83] Trump has gone even more madcap, transforming himself from a celebrity businessman to a political popinjay. For Telnaes, President Trump is a wolf intent on clothing himself in imperial power and imagining the people as his sheep.

The Age of Terror has given way to the Age of Coronavirus. This milieu has brought about a new nadir of presidential politics. In another cartoon published by *The Nib* on April 22, 2020, this low point is seen for its trickle-down effect on Trumpsters in particular. *Sic semper tyrannis*. It is a Latin phrase that dates back to the age of Julius Caesar and his assassination at the hands of Brutus. It means "Thus always to tyrants." Cartoonist Jen Sorensen's cartoon, entitled "Sic Semper Tyrann-Us," makes fun of Trumpsters putting more trust in an authoritarian, plutocratic, self-interested president than government officials committed to the public interest. It laughs at the idea that there is a principle of freedom at play in a president proclaiming "total authority" over states and the well-being of their citizens. Real freedom, in Sorensen's caricature of President Trump, is predicated on a right to live and let others die. The depths of President Trump's preference for despotic leadership hereby bring to the surface a sense that war footings are defining features of US culture. Caricature appears as a constructively comic way of seeing aggregated Selves in and through individuated Others. Many cartoonists have mocked President Trump's tendencies toward tyranny. Telnaes has created a cartoon stock to laugh the comedy of despotism out of court. Indeed, her Trumpian hoard is a veritable rabbit hole of caricatures. Down it, Trump is a king, but he is also a choleric infant, a mob boss, Pinocchio, a man infested with rats, a closet Ku Klux Klan patron, a literal Red Herring for the Republican Party agenda, chief executive of a dumpster fire, Death slaying the Statue of Liberty, a Twitter bird, a bullhorn for xenophobia, a "Fake News Boy," a rotten apple core, and the Devil Incarnate. He is the embodiment of a political official lavishing praise upon himself. In this way, he embodies the worst angels of Americanism. He is the comic travesty of an American war president. He is a national caricature.

A nationalistic sentiment that President Bush expressed in a speech on August 4, 2005, prefigures Trump *in praesidens*, which is that the War on Terror is "more than just a military war on terror," just as the War on Coronavirus is more than just a fight for public health.[84] It is a cultural war. It is the unstated assumption of democracy's Double, blending "the familiar and the unfamiliar by placing within the familiar an amorphous sense of otherness, strangeness, and potential danger."[85] Caricature is a catalyst of rhetorical morphology. In Telnaes's oeuvre, it enables a full-circle glimpse at the crooked traverse from Uncle Sam's World War I–era seductions via James Montgomery Flagg and the Creel Committee of President Woodrow Wilson to twenty-first-century perversions in pledges of nationalistic allegiance, perhaps best encapsulated by a caricature of President Trump sullying the American flag with his soiled hands (fig. 34). The caricature was done after Trump's appearance and speech at the 2019 Conservative Political Action Conference (CPAC), which was something of a fantastical scene from *Absurdistan* and literalization of metaphors for Black Hand societies, full of self-indulgence and sardonicism, fear and loathing, unification and death, deceits and extortions.[86] In kind, it was also a tipping point in the comic travesty of a sentiment from President Bush's second inaugural address, which warned of the sort of hatred and resentment and pretension that innervates tyranny. This is not a chapter on the history of freedom. It is about comic takes on an end-of-history drift into vile despotism propelled by a president who sees in the power of "the people" an opportunity to dirty up a symbolic wellspring of the American democratic experiment.

Nevertheless, Telnaes reaffirms caricature as a rhetorical art of visualizing "other possibilities."[87] Her cartoon politics show forth some of the ways

FIG. 34 Ann Telnaes, Trump's appearance at CPAC, March 3, 2019. Used with permission of Ann Telnaes and The Cartoonist Group. All rights reserved.

that a president's warring attitude takes attention away from the ongoing armed conflicts that underwrite America's war culture, and how it converts a generalized aversion to war among those in the American body politic to a diffuse fetish for picking fights. Simply, Telnaes's wartime caricatures visualize what Bacevich articulates in a play on the revolutionary idiom attributed to Marie Antoinette: "Let them eat Trump."[88] In her caricatures are means of imagining rhetorical regicide. They offer a comic looking glass for the feast of nationalism in the famine of American democratic politics. Even more, the caricatures seem to constitute the cake that Alice ate, yet left over for a body politic overwhelmed by the outsized influence of presidentialism and conditioned "into the way of expecting nothing but out-of-the-way things to happen."[89] Telnaes sees in this conditional influence an unhealthy diet of out-and-out idiocy. She sees the creeping tyranny in a US war culture that makes a democracy of useful idiots. And she sees, via the comedy of despotism in caricature, the possibilities of trading in cake for crow.

Conclusion
Warring Caricatures

Caricature relies on comic iterations. Its pretense relies on some visual deployment of periphrasis. It is excessive and overloaded. Caricature is burdened. There is, of course, humor in tautology. The humor in caricatures of national character very often comes from portrayals of the symbolic legs a body politic stands on, and with which it walks the walk. Caricature then takes its own legs out from under it, makes its leading characters stand on their heads, and shows objects of ridicule where they stand (usually on unstable ground, with unsure footing). This is why caricatures, while profoundly shaped by and settled in historical moments, stand the test of time. It is also why caricatures are burdensome. In the comic looking glass, they reveal what Lewis Carroll might now see as the verbal and visual jabberwocky of histories that repeat themselves—or at least rhyme. They remake the worst of lesser angels, and they make them stand out, in all their beastliness. They goad us to understand ourselves as we are in accordance with who we were, and yet, as we can be, anew. In the distorted reflections of wartime crises in national character, these peculiarities insinuate but some of the differences that caricature makes.

But then there are caricatures that are made in the name of making or unmaking war. That war is war—in actual armed conflict as well as in contemporary democratic praxis—typifies what some have called the "ethical failure" of Americanism.[1] Warring positions and nationalistic pronouncements of pro-war patriotism, antiwar pacifism, or combat agnosticism betray a palpable sense in which dialectical pairs like war and peace, rhetoric and violence, or democracy and tyranny are no longer appropriate (if they ever were). In fact, in caricatures from James Montgomery Flagg's Uncle Sam through Ann Telnaes's King Trump, one can see how such couplings might poison the well of war culture if and when they suggest either that opposites attract or that one mutually excludes the other. Caricature, as such, is an art of rhetorical war with a potent historical relationship to the problem of how collective selfhood is embodied, imaged, imagined, and idealized. In its comic travesties of national character in particular, caricature holds the ostensively contrary undertakings of war and democracy together in the same, disturbingly sensical space. Throughout this book, there has been an underlying view of cultural warfare at play in particular wartimes, and a sense that this sort of embattlement is relatively extraordinary, even exceptional, in the conduct of the American democratic experiment. In this conclusion, I pursue the idea that caricatures place a unique burden on national character when they illustrate how and why war footings, never mind pursuits of armed conflict and otherwise warring dispositions, allow for a view of ordinary warism as a distorted reflection of US democracy.

In the year after the United States made its formal commitment to enter the Good War, Kenneth Burke observed that "several kinds of war, all going on simultaneously," were confusing the "actuality" with the "purpose" of democracy.[2] Interestingly, Burke pointed to Edward Steichen's "Whitmanesque" photographic portrayal of national identity, *Road to Victory: A Procession of Photography of the Nation at War*, which Ralph Steiner described in the daily newspaper, *PM*, as an "assault [on] vision."[3] Burke turned to Steichen's exhibit for its encapsulation of American exceptionalism in what really had nothing to do with war at all: endless fields of grain, the Mississippi waterways, the Red Man, farmworkers, cattle herds, home dwellers, power dams, and so on. Of course, as the bulletin of the Museum of Modern Art admits, these are images before "the man behind the gun." As a species of war propaganda that doubled as a portrait of national selfhood, the exhibit was designed "to enable every American to see himself as a vital and indispensable element of victory" through pictures of the Japanese attack on Pearl Harbor, US production of warships, companies of American troops, and "birds of death" in flight.[4] Challenging what he called the emergent "collective-sacrificial-military nexus of motives," Burke appealed to the triumph of a democratic culture over conquests in war.[5] In other words, he drew a distinction between ways of life at home and military excursions abroad, contending that a body politic unwilling to lower its rhetorical weapons in sociopolitical spheres would eventually be unable to remove itself from "roads to victory" that placed viewing subjects amid visions of war in addition to wars of words and images.

Burke's observation is unnervingly prescient today. War has become—or, has long been—a cultural way of life. Not in the sense that ordinary citizens participate in its conduct, but rather that war sustains the very ordinariness of violent rhetoric, political vitriol, and actual violence that characterizes so many views of contemporary national culture in the United States. One entailment has to do with American militarism, and with it, so many ongoing armed conflicts within the War on Terror. Another is that war increasingly seems to be at once the groundwork and the *telos* of democracy insofar as democratic principles, however disparately they are interpreted, are to be protected at all costs (through the barrel of a gun, if necessary). Yet another entails banal democratic praxis in the United States as a sort of "everyday war," waged *un*democratically over matters of "class, race, religion, ethnicity, and gender," and driven by "underlying forces that produce the conditions of violence, ideological fundamentalism, militarism, and massive political and economic inequalities."[6] The notion of *Wilkommenskultur*, or a culture of welcoming, is hardly a condition of democratic possibility in the Trump Era. Political cohabitation is not about the "we" of a National Self. We are warring factions of Us and Them.

It is hard to have a sense of humor here. One might quickly recall Flagg's iconic Uncle Sam on the cover of *Leslie's Weekly* in December 1917, not pointing his finger but rather pointing a handgun. Or Ollie Harrington's notion that bombs are always already the bread and butter of US Americanism, hovering like a specter over its next generation. Or, more recently, Telnaes's mockery of President Donald Trump clutching a pistol (literally, a smoking gun) and bragging about shooting someone on 5th Avenue in New York City. Each instance seems to present a caricature of democratic freedom imbricated with a travesty of war culture as the defining feature of US national character. It is easy to feel that, when war comes to the door, democracy flies out the window. In the shadow of what many refer to as a cartoon presidency, spearheaded by a self-proclaimed wartime president who is infatuated with fighting words, there is reason to wonder whether or not caricature is the best index of who we are as a nation. Yet caricature, in a comic guise, can be like the warped glass of a windowpane, showing forth the very layers and distortions through which we imagine one another and ourselves. It can also reveal openings for alternative views of the world, its everyday people, and its leading characters (be they "the people" or their presiding political officers). Caricatures provide moments of observation, spectatorship, and witness in visual humor, wherein conflicts over national character can be restaged in the form of comic travesty.

The amplification of a conflicted space is important given the even greater need for comic struggle in the face of so many cruel intentions. I am not suggesting that comedy simply begets democracy, or vice versa. Some of the prides, prejudices, and pillories that are the very stuff of humor (and comic attitudes more broadly) mirror the warlike postures that compel violence to this day. Rather, I am suggesting that caricature makes it possible to see, take up, and take on different perspectives of both Self and Other, especially as they fill out the same imaginary space, and especially since they render images and ideas of national character as the very ridiculous objects worth reconsidering that they are. Herein lie the anamorphic qualities of the comic. Or, to borrow from Homi Bhabha, the possibility to glean characterological differences from some cultural *différance*, which reminds us that war can be a powerful means of cooperation even as it is a dangerous means of sustaining communities.[7] How telling that, in light of a looking-glass approach to things, James P. McDaniel and Bruce Gronbeck once noted that democracy lives and dies by its embodiments of civic judgment, and by extension, its collective attitudes about the Self's relation to the Other. To boot, it too often thrives on "dangerous moments" that lead, say, to the domestic terrorism of gun violence and mass shootings, and just as troublingly to the neoliberal responses to a climate crisis and then again a pandemic, constituting a tail to the kite of more global, more macroscopic war.[8]

The caricatures showcased in this book make it difficult not to challenge the conventional wisdom that the will to fight and die is an ordinary feature of democratic survival. This sentiment is at the center of Flagg's use of Uncle Sam as the embodiment of an Americanism that has become a grotesque illusion of democratic idealism. As I detail in chapter 1, Flagg's caricature advertises the chauvinistic overtones of a collective "YOU" that turns national obeisance into responsibility for civic duty. Resounding in these overtones are deep legacies of cultural warfare in American democracy, traditions of using democracy itself as a pretext for war, and habits of using warism as a foil for rhetorical judgments about mettle, guilt, and shame. National iconography is something of a rhetorical rabbit hole in this regard, but also a way into the hysterical (that is, frenetic, feverish, manic, and also hilarious) influence of cultural politics on historical realities.

Following Flagg, the temptation to fight is often greater than the prospect of losing some political ground or other because communication fails. There is a temptation as well to forget that war *for* democracy is a test of national character, particularly along lines of gender, race, and ethnicity, and particularly at home. To see Uncle Sam is to see him as a comic crucible for portrayals of US national character-cum-tensions around who an American can and cannot be. It is also to see him pointing his finger with a wry smile on his face. Like the Cheshire Cat, the body is gone, but that smile remains.

The military fervor in Flagg's orientation to Americanism filters into the nit and grit of Dr. Seuss's pro-war posture, which converted pro-war coercion into a playful carnival of warism that functioned as a stomping ground for civic education. Indeed, if the first chapter saw caricature as a rhetorical resource for utilizing the realism of distorted imagery to betray a fantastical representation of civic responsibility and a rather grotesque picture of a disconcertingly mannish seduction in the very idea of war, chapter 2 realized its potential to evince some of the fantasies embedded in expressions of good and bad citizenship. Dr. Seuss imagined the democratic citizen as largely an extraordinary creation of war. But he was wary of weaklings. Hence his pattern of mocking the very ethic of a democratic nation that might encourage people to stuff their heads in the sand rather than fight off threats to an American way of life. Recall here that Benjamin Franklin ruminated on the prospect of a turkey symbolizing the United States better than an eagle. Under the welkin of World War II, Dr. Seuss preferred the ostrich, and he used it to imagine his countrymen as ill birds fouling their own nest. He also imagined fetid enemies acting more like vermin than humans, and a swath of "bugs" sickening a people that seemed to have no political immune system for battling "Hitler-itis" and "Fascist Fever." Caricature was an antidote to deprived cultural politics. Dr. Seuss's humor was sometimes out of humor and off color, but it was utterly democratic in its comic travesties of "free" birds in their little nests, who refuse to see that foreign conflicts are somehow separate from either Democracy's Arsenal or homegrown forms of warfare.

In the work of Dr. Seuss as well as Flagg, one can see how caricatures are rhetorical expressions that emerge out of, and filter back into, lived experiences. Their caricatures are as reflective of public sentimentality as they are projective of something like sentimentalism for the prospect of an America lost. Caricature helped Flagg and Dr. Seuss to distill judgments about civic responsibility as it was magnified by the cultural transformations that take place in times of war. Within these distillations are the concomitant burdens of deep-seated institutions and cultural practices made up of everything from racial, gender, and ethnic prejudices to historical abstractions, like democratic freedom. This is why Ollie Harrington stands out as a caricature artist who took the comicality of national character a step further by showing children as the inheritors of democracy in war culture and democracy *as* war. For Harrington, war no worse than democracy can serve as the catalyst for revelations about the peculiarities of "black-and-white" relations. A crucial aspect of Harrington's oeuvre had to do with his travesty of the progression from so many "great" wars to the dream of a "great" society. The plight of Black children in the United States was enough to suggest that war could no more redeem the principles of democracy than it could manage longstanding crises of racialism. In fact, the menace of racial division betrayed a truly American heritage, encapsulating the ordinariness of warring positions in everyday life while exposing a US culture of war less for its overseas entanglements than its problems of cultural impoverishment at home. Although this detail was not dwelled upon in chapter 3, the dining table stands out as a central image in Harrington's caricatures, and an emblem of racial hierarchy, class division, and finally a nation bent on eating particular portions of its young. This emblem looms large in the caricature of a general in full dress uniform scarfing down a decadent spread of food while two "damn starvin' brats" wait in the lurch for scraps. It figures prominently, too, in a perturbing cartoon that sees two gaunt Black children reaching for bread and milk atop a large table that has ballistic missiles for legs. Given that these mockeries of military excess were folded into matters of civil rights, Harrington provided a strong sense in which Black children were themselves caricatures of national character at the same time as they were weapons of war. The comic looking glass reveals a window on the consequences of "lost innocence" and the threat of the American democratic experiment becoming a "lost cause."

In the historical march of American warfare, there is in these caricatures a parallel story of US democracy in which wartimes pronounce the ridiculousness of color lines, the foolish paternalism of a nation-state, and the laughably untenable nature of patriarchal, ethnocentric, and racialized social or political privileges that are simply taken for granted. In steps Telnaes. Her caricatures exemplify the sorry revival of an olden ethic of warfare as the old vainglory of the United States. Before turning to these caricatures as particularly apt reference points, though, a quick detour is needed. When Antonio Gramsci wrote of war and politics in "War is

War," he did so in 1921, during the rise of Benito Mussolini's Kingdom of Italy. "War is war," he wrote, "and he who embarks on that adventure must feel the force of the beast that he has awoken."[9] In Gramsci's view, war is a footing for political struggle just as politics form the foundations for war. What is more, any *res publica* must be reinforced by the people and the things they hold dear. The Spirit of 1776, in an American argot, captures this sentiment. It betokens a revolutionary zeitgeist. When Telnaes takes this precept (as she does in numerous cartoons) and uses it to mock the spirit of post-9/11 war culture, she brings to bear a comic travesty of US democracy in some of the most sacred spaces presently occupied by those who are warring for cultural and political position. The looking glass becomes a windowpane in her comic images of presidentialism.

From President Bush to President Trump, images and ideas of American national character have largely taken shape in discourses of battlegrounds, enemies, victories, deaths, defeats, and more. These discourses are driven by the late modern sense that an imperial president can preside over a democratic nation. A persistent War on Terror has infused cultural politics. In the Bush era, actual war was justified by speculations and specious claims about both internal and external threats. Such bogus rhetoric, which traversed the Downing Street memo to Islamophobia and a generalized War on Women, enabled extraconstitutional assertions of executive privilege to make the president more an embodiment of "the people" than its custodian. President Trump picked up this mantle, combining the rhetorical horseplay of a clown with the accoutrements of a con man to further militarize American national character. President Trump's tenure has been defined by a time of war, with the War on Terror remaining a rabbit hole that has one way in and seemingly no ways out. It has also been circumscribed by a coronavirus pandemic. With both of these existentialities as backdrops, Trump's presidency is one of a newfangled culture war based on "alternative facts," "fake news," wild conspiracy theories, inflammatory foreign relations, racist and misogynistic grandiloquence, and—to top it all off—repeated "jokes" made by Trump himself that he has unilateral power. Countless presidents have been characterized as "at war." The Trump era has been one of diffuse war footings, urged on by an egoistic president with the political attitude of a dictator and the brash inclination to construct a Wonderland of American war culture. As one writer put it, in the course of reflecting on the cultural hegemony at stake in Trump's America, the gist is this: "Under Trumpism, no defense of the *volk* is a betrayal, even if it undermines the republic, and no attack on the *volk*'s hegemony can be legitimate, even if it is a defense of democracy."[10] Warfare in Trumpism is War on Democracy.

Telnaes's caricatures are crucial in this milieu. She takes seriously the idea that President Trump actually *does* have kingly predilections. Her caricatures are not alarmist. They are not akin to something like the ubiquity of Nazi comparisons and Hitler tropes that grew up and out of the Cold War and even saw a new birth of ignominy during Barack Obama's presidency. Instead, they are comic reflections on the extent to which a president embodies a populist spirit—indeed, its predominant or at least prevailing national character. Telnaes's caricatures have become increasingly vital as editorial cartooning has come under some threat in the United States. There are fewer staff jobs among news outlets. More worryingly, there have been public firings of prominent artists for the politics in their caricatures, most notably when they are patently anti-Trump. President Trump has over and again railed against free speech and rallied support for stricter libel laws and insulted journalists who challenge his policymaking or his judgment. Telnaes's caricatures do more than just humor the idea that post-9/11 warism can (and has) threatened American democracy by giving comic image to the "wrath of tyrants."[11] By shifting attention from the tyranny of the Other to the tyranny of the Self, her caricatures bring what Herblock once called the "special prod" of editorial cartooning full circle from Flagg to situate US national character itself in the comic looking glass.[12]

At least one funny thing in all of this is that the very images of national character that enable us to recognize ourselves are oftentimes the same images that embolden us to reimagine monstrosities. Sometimes through comic imagery of people and things already deemed monstrous outside of the transmogrifications of visual humor. Sometimes through comic imagery that makes Otherness of Selfhood. Sometimes through comic imagery that projects outward, puts the characteristics of personages and principles before the looking glass, and thereby reflects common senses and taken-for-granted images and ideas back at us as if constituting some disturbing, distorted, deformed, even dangerous presence. For a recent example, Telnaes posted a sketch on Twitter following one in a series of baffling press briefings on the federal response to COVID-19 in mid-April 2020. Telnaes portrays the president as an orange reptilian beast working "its horrible, horrible spell." The humor in caricature is monstrous. Ancient Roman satirist Horace once described poiesis as so many *disiecti membra*, or literally the dissected members or dismembered pieces that make up new works of art. Art, in other words, is artful inasmuch as it exposes its own artistry. Good rhetoric reveals as much as it conceals. The rhetorical work of humor lies in its cutups and comic flourishes. There is humor in disjunctures, in disunions, and in disseverances that are shown forth for the lambast and the laugh, even those that subject what might be horrific to incongruities that stress comicality over terror. President Trump as a reptile, in both senses of the word, makes sense here. But think, too, of Beowulf joking about the dismemberment of Grendel. Think of the "monstrous craws" and "character flaws" that exemplify James Gillray's entire oeuvre.[13] Or recall Franklin's MAGNA Britannia. Its central rhetorical feature is a dismembered woman, standing in as a country torn asunder and left to die with severed limbs. Writing as Silence Dogood, Franklin had earlier mocked the fashion of hoop petticoats by comparing them to an army fortification refigured for personal use. These things are "monstrous topsy-turvy Mortar-Pieces," looking more like "Engines of War" than "Ornaments of the Fair Sex."[14] Caricature might be so defined. Its humor is topsy-turvy, driven by an artful disruption of the order of things. Yet its dismemberments reveal the rhetorical artistry of images and ideas when they are put back together as comic monstrosities—as caricatures. MAGNA Britannia is a nationalistic claim to sums over parts. It is monstrous in its visualization of colonial dependency on imperial power, but it is perfectly revelatory in its conversion of a legislative conundrum into a laughing matter in the rhetorical force of democratic argument over the force of arms. To play on Franklin's own political logic of the colonies reduc'd, caricature turns damaging reductions into constructive amplifications.

Maybe the weightiest implication of wartime caricatures of national character is their view of warfare in the United States as more endemic to the so-called American experiment than it is exceptional. This goes both for moments of armed conflict and for everyday efforts to persuade public audiences into one position or another. Caricatures are prime movers for dispositional matters as well as in images of public conduct. President Trump, at present, is fighting wars on multiple fronts. On terror. On truth. On American traditions. On coronavirus. He is battling Congress with delusions of grandeur around constitutional rights and war powers. He is carrying out "shadow wars" (on climate science, for example). He is making spectacles of trade wars with foreign adversaries and allies. He is fanning the flames of all-too-familiar race wars. He is firing those in various governmental agencies who speak truth to power. He is sustaining his public distrust of science, and thereby turning the "madness" of his megalomania into what one commentator called a "national tragicomedy" in light of Trump's boasts about his own "medical perceptiveness" relative to the wisdom of public health officials.[15] At each step along the way, Telnaes has characterized this ill-will orientation and *ressentiment*-laden mode of articulating US Americanism. The monstrous disproportions in her caricatures use ugliness as a comic foil for recharacterizing an American president as an exemplar of an entire people out of humor in the world. Caricature is to ugliness as humor is to perceptual undoings. The most cherished of nationalistic belief systems are monstrosities when seen through caricatures of national character that fabricate humor in and from distorted images of collective being. Sometimes these images appear as the prima facie comportments of a singular person or principle, like Trump or Trumpism. These fabrications urge us to face ourselves for our darkest cultural features and fantasies, most forcefully when a progenitive Ugly Americanism forecloses attitudinal frames and rhetorical cultures that accommodate ways of seeing outside of warism.

In sum, just as caricature can be a distillation of cultural mindsets and manners, so can it visualize a comic way of seeing the consequences of rhetorical activity as militaristic activity. From Flagg to Telnaes, the caricatures in this book picture what might befall a nation based on characteristic examples of Americanism. A national character is a means of understanding collective being (socially, politically, economically, and more) according to the everyday interactions of leading political figures, regular people, and the ordinary deployment of nationalistic images and ideas in public culture. It is also a mechanism for imagining some of the wretched ways that foundational principles of freedom, equality, and even peace get colored by notions of *un*-Americanism. Consider what Sophie Gilbert recently called the "complicated relevance" of some of Dr. Seuss's wartime caricatures.[16] Building on his advertising campaigns for the poison Flit, Dr. Seuss pictured things like isolationist impulses and rampant Nazism as cultural toxins that are strikingly similar to, say, homegrown racial prejudice. The result was a series of caricatures that aligned practices of "gassing" citizens by either spoiling their capacities to think (and therefore act) properly or purifying their corrupted perspectives. This series and others complemented Dr. Seuss's attendant views of war machinery, as well as the depictions of cultural warfare at home that are similarly rampant in Flagg's exploitations of gendered nationalism, Harrington's mockeries of US race relations, and Telnaes's caricatures of American Tyranny as it is carried out at the whims of Useful Idiots. A more wide-ranging consideration, then, is that caricatures of national caricature trouble the norms of collective selfhood when combined with ideas about the types of wars that should or should not be waged—a consideration that is even more troubling inasmuch as it almost demands an amplification of the scrapes among homegrown *citizens* of war.

None of this is to mention the multitude of other "wars": the immigration war, partisan warfare, the "pander war" on vaccines, policy war at the Grammy Awards, the war on good government, the war on the young (and education), radio personality Alex Jones's absurd "infowars," persistent class warfare, Trump's war on facemasks, and so on ad absurdum. Then there are the war metaphors embedded in struggles with pandemic disease, which have been compared to the global War on Terror and all of its implications from national security through blanket surveillance of the potentially infected to "black sites" that are unbound from common views of human justice. Alongside, and part of, these "normal" rhetorical operations are the mass shootings so characteristic of the United States, the fatal police engagements with people of color (many of whom are said to be living in war zones), and too many other warlike realities so tied up with keeping the world safe for American democracy. "War *is* cultural," says Burke.[17] Culture is a front for war.

While it is fitting to take up issues of warfare in terms of things like combat trauma in public life, it is also important to approach the inconsistencies between what we tell ourselves about national character and how honest we are about American culture and its utter reliance on militarism. War culture pushes the bounds of military warfare into the realm of civic engagement as a politics of intimidation, browbeating, and displaced hostility, thereby facilitating an acculturation to communication failure as the de facto mode of warring for position. Similarly, warfare is a countersign to democracy. Ambrose Bierce once quipped that war is a "by-product of the arts of peace."[18] At home, social and political cultures have seen the devaluation of controversy such that "bloodless warfare" and "the facile tongue" render citizens at arms something more akin to snakes fastened to the ground.[19] This observation brings about the incommensurability of warring logics and principles of sociopolitical justice. When warfare is just the way it is, knowledge structures and standards of judgment are presumed in advance, moving rhetorical cultures out of the realm of humane possibilities and into the trap of defensiveness, anger, and resentment. It might be that a key risk of preemptive war footings emerges out of a disregard for other ways of seeing, thinking, or acting *from the outset*. In this sense, caricature shows how our frames of recognition are out of whack, and how they are, ipso facto, caricatures through and through.

Let me therefore suggest in closing that wartimes are particularly interesting moments for scrutinizing rhetorical modes of humor. One thing that stands out across the chapters in this book is that certain images and ideas endure from one historical milieu to the next, meaning that the prides and prejudices therein also move in and out of focus with the times. Additionally, when what we recognize as characteristic of our national selfhood seems to come under threat, we are burdened with recharacterizing warfare as well as the dispositions that merit its conduct. Outsiders looking in can provide alternative vantages, just as caricature artists can use an anamorphic orientation to step in and out of and beyond the fray. No surprise that cartoonists like Harrington and Telnaes are, in various senses, "outsiders." No surprise either that they—along with Flagg, Dr. Seuss, and numerous other artists who are beyond the scope of this book—evoke the hard work of reconsidering foundational principles and normative standards of rhetorical judgment. It is difficult to imagine the peacemaking ethos of democracy when violent rhetorics are as commonplace as military force in processing social issues, political snags, and cultural differences. It is also imperative to do just that, which is what the caricatures in this book do when they realize the ugly truth in the comic truth that things *are* as bad as they seem. Hence my interest in caricatures that account for distortions that are not artful shams or comic exaggerations per se but rather familiarly farcical articulations of virtues and vices, crude combinations of persons and principles, brutish icons of civic being, and grotesque portrayals of the dark and dirty realities that sustain social, political, and cultural relations. In wartimes, caricatures can demonstrate how the offshoot of war is a democratic culture of Zarathustra's "frothing fools" who are disgusted by the very idea of a democratic polis since they have grown "overwhelmed by the vulgarity of its inhabitants."[20] President Trump might just be "a caricatural prophet of doom" par excellence in this regard, "spewing overwrought damnations upon passers-by."[21] The trick is to see how the folly of war is part and parcel of the comedy of democracy, and then again to find ways away from a Wonderland of war fools.

It might therefore be useful to close with an outsider's perspective of Americanism. In 2017, Australian editorial cartoonist David Rowe pictured the truth and consequences of President Trump as a caricature—and Leviathan-like culmination—of American Empire. Rowe has compiled numerous cartoon characterizations of Americanism as utterly divided but

FIG. 35 David Rowe, "The Three-Ring Circus," November 2017. *Behind the Lines*. Museum of Australian Democracy. Used with permission.

also driven by a powerful sense of domestic warfare with establishment principles underwriting the global posturing of a warmonger. In many of Rowe's caricatures, Trump is cast as a monstrous emperor, which is to say the leading character of America as a foolish nation that is saddled by the folly of statecraft. In the words of Holly Williams, curator of the 2017 iteration of *Behind the Lines* (a yearly exhibition of the best cartoons on display at the Museum of Australian Democracy), the humor of Rowe's work derives from its "dark intensity" and conversion of "our uneasy feelings on the state of the world" into "visual form."[22] Rowe was the featured artist for *Behind the Lines 2017: The Three-Ring Circus*, the showpiece for which is a caricature of Trump as the ridiculous ringleader for a new world order (fig. 35). The gist here is that Trump is a wartime president who embodies the worst of American national character. He brings out the beast of war. He moves democracy away from the phantasmagoria of Wonderland and toward paraphilia. What is worse, he embodies the American national character

CONCLUSION   195

like the robber baron of the "beast-garden."²³ Caricature is a rhetorical beast of burden. It dwells like a laughing snake in the garden path. And it brings matters of national character back to the drawing board by bringing them back into focus in the comic looking glass.

Coda:
Caricature in End Times, or the Future of Caricature

Standing in the Rose Garden in June of 2017, President Trump made a solemn announcement: the United States would withdraw from the Paris Agreement. The global plan had been drafted and signed just over a year earlier in accordance with the United Nations Framework Convention on Climate Change. It was, and is, an international peace treaty of sorts, with the primary mission of reducing greenhouse gas emissions to sustain life as we know it. In the Rose Garden speech, President Trump proclaimed his undying commitment to put America First. He also lamented the risks of worldwide terror that continued to loom over the United States and its globalized economy. "It's a stupid and reckless decision," wrote environmental activist Bill McKibben soon after the president's announcement. "But it's not stupid and reckless in the normal way. Instead, it amounts to a thorough repudiation of two of the civilizing forces on our planet: diplomacy and science." McKibben goes on to call President Trump's withdrawal "our nation's dumbest act since launching the war in Iraq."[1] It was, in other words, an indication of the wrongheadedness in a logic to Make America Great Again, and the apparent comic futility of the notion that we might Make Peace, Not War.

The president's withdrawal from the Paris Agreement was something of a forerunner for things to come with regard to global commitments and public health pacts. For months before the United States became the epicenter of a coronavirus pandemic, President Trump ignored dire warnings from federal agencies as well as the World Health Organization (WHO). He disregarded reports presented to him in classified briefings. He discounted the counsel provided by intelligence officials who, a year earlier, lamented to *Time* that President Trump made policy decisions like he made political decisions: with information that supported positions he already held and thus required a grasp of nuance that went no further than "willful ignorance."[2] Hence, in large part, his administration's response to the novel coronavirus, COVID-19, has been almost unanimously deemed a failure, if not an idiotic and preventable one. As one reporter for the *Irish Times* put it, powerlessness "in the face of a natural disaster" is one thing, but it is "quite another to watch vast power being squandered in real time—willfully, malevolently, vindictively."[3] The president, in this reporter's estimation, is a monstrous imbrication of the Pleasure Principle and the Death Drive, showing forth "all the neuroses that haunt the American subconscious." His barefaced pride is abject. His brazen egotism is the culmination of a charmed life, and a creeping form of Republican Party politics that has evolved over decades into "a concoction of conspiracy theories, hatred of science, paranoia about the 'deep state' and religious providentialism (God will protect the good folks)."[4] President Trump is in his wrongful place.

As the saying goes, no one is an island. This, however, is precisely what President Trump pretends to be. Even further, he tends to comport himself as if he is the ruler of an island that is itself set apart from the world. There is a compelling definition of caricature, laid out in terms of individuals and populations, measures and weightings, norms and their exaggerations. It comes from David Perkins. Caricature, says Perkins, is an expression of an individual, population, or even idea that is patently out of whack relative to some scale or magnitude, symbolic or otherwise.[5] That is, caricature is by definition a portrayal of something out of humor, recognizable but distorted, unreal (even surreal) yet nonetheless realistic or true. Cartoonist David Rowe is once again helpful here, particularly with a caricature from July 2017 that features King Trump standing atop an iceberg in the shape of the United States. The United States is a frozen island surrounded by water that reflects like glass, with the Eiffel Tower appearing brightly in the backdrop. Trump is naked except for an imperial robe, a ridiculous crown, golden high heels, and a long red tie draped over his grotesque abdomen and covering his genitals. But he is not alone. Next to him, facing Paris, is a polar bear. "Excusez-moi," he says. One hand is clutching the knot of his tie where it meets his robe. The other hand is shoving the polar bear into the glassy water.

Rowe's caricature brings Perkins's definition to rhetorical life. It makes the president into an absurd image of the US national character, individuated and scaled down to the level of a misguided Gargantua. It shows him for his distortion of international norms. It reveals the vileness in his vanity. Inasmuch as caricature entails a complexity of rhetorical relationships that rely upon humorous resemblances to alter how we see ourselves (even, or especially, if in recognition of how we see others), it illustrates a comic abstraction of "the *realities of the human condition*."⁶ Rowe's caricature—and there are many more where this one came from—goads us to reexamine our sense of collective selfhood not in national or other terms of unity and division but rather in terms of what Joseph Meeker once dubbed "the comedy of survival," which "depends upon our ability to change ourselves rather than our environment."⁷ This makes it all the more crucial that "ugly caricatures" are seen for their capacity to *dis*individuate characteristics, to derive humor from *shared* defects, and to push the boundaries of any one individual's ethical failings so as to magnify the follies of an "individual culture."⁸ What might be called the caricature of survival makes it all the more crucial that attention is paid to caricatures that are anything but garden variety. It makes crucial, too, a resituation of the "comic way," or a renewal of human welfare in the face of a dehumanization so endemic to warfare. And it lays bare that other, all too essential aspect of *monstrosity* in caricature, from which the humor of the human condition emerges.

It is hard to imagine a more fitting time to face our own survival, and perhaps most fittingly with good humor and restorative comicality, than a time of pandemic disease. This is especially true when the imperious activities of humans and the imperial arrogance of world leaders not only facilitates but also foments damage to the natural world, never mind the cultural problematics that ail us. Numerous commentators have portrayed the coronavirus as a monster made of bad world leadership and runaway neoliberalism. The pandemic has become a freak show of sorts, with President Trump on center stage as a political aberration that nonetheless represents a longstanding "spectacle of racism, ultranationalism, anti-immigrant sentiment, and bigotry that has dominated the national zeitgeist."⁹ In this spectacle is the comic plague of a cultural politics that "celebrates capital over human needs, greed over compassion, exploitation over justice and fear over shared responsibilities."¹⁰ Rowe's caricatures are once again instructive—and monstrous! One from March 2020 pictures President Trump with his arms crossed across his chest, a stern look on his face, and an American flag for a bib covering his suit jacket. He is sitting at a table with the president of China, Xi Jinping. They are surrounded by other world leaders, all with worried looks on their faces. There is a globe in the center of the table. It is pocked with red marks to signify the spread of coronavirus. "The plum pudding has COVID-19," the caption reads. A handful of small plates with medical facemasks are situated in front of President Xi. A single small plate with a model airplane is set before President Trump, no doubt making fun of his trade wars with the Chinese government, his fetish for both tariffs and travel bans, and—in hindsight—his refusal to wear a mask. The entire cartoon is a remake of Gillray's famous etching from 1805, entitled "The Plumb-Pudding in Danger," which features Napoleon Bonaparte sitting with William Pitt carving out pieces of the world for France and England, respectively. In Rowe's rendition, the "state epicures" are as much emblems of economic and other forms of warfare as they are icons of failed states.

This theme of governmental folly is replete in Rowe's caricatures. Later in March, just before Easter, he depicted President Trump as a towering and demonic Easter Bunny standing in the charred, black rubble of the United States. The president has a gargantuan girth. He is holding a golden putter cane. A Twitter bird is his only article of clothing. It is wearing a medical facemask and covers his genitals. Most protuberant in the scene is the big basket in President Trump's hands. It is a basket of COVID-19. The eggs inside are viruses. That same month, journalist and news editor Susan B. Glasser characterized the president's conduct at the daily White House press briefings regarding the federal government's coronavirus response as a cipher for his leadership. With unapologetic whimsy and caprice reminiscent of Lewis Carroll's cultural glossology, Glasser referred to his daily dish-ups as "Trump O'Clock Follies," his moronic comportment and witless remarks as "monumental flimflammery," and his persona as "a cartoon caricature of a wartime President."[11] Glasser's characterizations came in response to President Trump's sense that reopening the United States on Easter, despite the spread of a deadly disease, would be a testament to good timing—not for public safety, but rather for his own showmanship in being something of a savior figure on a "beautiful" holiday. The United States did not reopen on Easter, and Trump blamed everyone from state governors to the Center for Disease Control and Prevention (CDC) to the Chinese.

One more caricature by Rowe is worth mentioning in this coda. It is from April 2020, and it was published after President Trump planned to halt funding to WHO as part of a broader push to place blame everywhere other than on his own administration. In this instance, his intent was to insulate himself by pitting leading global health experts against the administration's Coronavirus Task Force. The president appears as a comic image of grotesque kingliness. His milieu is a domestic space reeking of utter opulence, with gold-tasseled American flags for draperies. White silhouettes of the coronavirus appear where some stars should be on Old Glory, and President Trump looks more like a meretricious wannabe than a meritorious king. His body is familiarly gargantuan. He is wearing a recognizable crown with a caged Twitter bird in the *globus cruciger* and a dollar sign atop the orb where a cross should be. An imperial robe is draped over his shoulders, tied to his neck with a golden "T" medallion. He has tiny high heels on his feet, a putter for a cane, and a tattoo with the opening text from the Constitution (rendered in its original typography but not its original wording) on his bulging belly. "*Me*, the People." There is another amendment, "and Governors. . . ." On the day Rowe's cartoon was published, President Trump asserted his total authority to decide when individual states could reopen. All governors could hope for was his authorization. Such authority is specious at best, and it betrays the trappings, pomp, and circumstance of President Trump's faux kingship. Alongside him in Rowe's cartoon is a globe. The letters "WHO" are stamped on its surface, stretching from the United States to China. On one hand, this seems an outlandish piece of décor for someone so keen on putting America First. On the other, it makes all the sense in the world: it epitomizes President Trump's self-centeredness, and his notion that he is the only Who's Who that matters. He is One President who shuns not only the very idea of We, the People, but also the very concept of One World.

The US president (and, more broadly, US presidentialism) is a necessary stooge in all of this, specifically when it comes to portraying situations normal all screwed up. Consider that Telnaes has pictured Trump using a flattened world as toilet paper while announcing his plan to pull the United States out of the Paris Agreement. Crudely, the president is seen making a mockery of the urge to be decisive in the idiomatic suggestion to shit or get off the pot. An animated cartoon published by the Real News Network in January 2018 goes further with a depiction of King Trump commanding something akin to the Great Wave to back off while he sits on a throne gripping a golden T-topped scepter. In the wave are words and phrases like "Climate Chaos," "Monster Storms," "Floods," and more. There are editorial cartoons of Trump holding the world hostage with a handgun. Of the president eating the world as if it was the innards of a hamburger. Of Trump literally doing battle with a globe armed with a rifle in a reimagining of cartoonist David Low's infamous World War II–era cartoon, "Very well, alone." "Arm yourself," said Winston Churchill in late spring of 1940, "and be ye men of valour, and be in readiness for the conflict, for it is better for us to perish in battle than to look upon the outrage of our nation."[12] Taken today, these are words that could be applied to the pervasive sense of a world continuing to compete for resources, a changing climate, migrant populations, refugees, class divisions, race divides, gender inequities, and a generalized aura of war as populations scramble to save themselves. Of course, they could also be applied to an image of global cooperation that pushes back against the descent into some olden war of all against all.

There are some eerie resonances here of Perkins's view that humor is a dubious bedfellow of caricature precisely because of the ways it can provoke new, potentially vexing images of Otherness in comic imagery of the Self. Lurking in this mix of monstrosities and magnitudes is a medicalized sensibility about culture and character that has come along with the coronavirus pandemic and will undoubtedly persist long after the world goes back to "normal." These resonances relate to the very art of caricature as it was established in the sixteenth and seventeenth centuries. There was a specific term for that relation. It was *figura caricata*, or "charged figure," and it connoted the monstrosities of particular bodies as they typify the monstrosities that are actually in and of an entire body politic. It was a term meant to capture what it means to imagine the right and wrong ways of being together relative to caricature as a potential harbinger of critical judgments—or, better, critical *admonitions*—about the human condition.[13] Caricature, in other words, was seen as a rhetorical appurtenance for proper, or improper, ways of seeing *and* being. Similarly, monsters and monstrosities are more than reflections of malformations. They are more than distorted images of ourselves revealed in a comic looking glass. The word "monster" comes from the Old French *monstre*, but it also comes from the Latin *monere*, which means "warning." Caricatures are comic portrayals of monstrous characters and characteristics. They are, at times, monsterful unto themselves. But they are also very often warnings that are meant to make us see what might come of, say, human cruelties or deformed cultural principles. Caricature comes from monstrosities. It reminds us of people like the White Kings in Carroll's looking-glass world who find it difficult to see people *as* people. It is the rhetorical thing that, like Alice, brings the plum cake before the Lion and the Unicorn. Caricature is most surely of a kind with Alice, a "fabulous monster," carrying the weight of the comic (and not-so-comic) worlds we make as if they were looking-glass cakes. The mirror, or the medium of comic anamorphosis, is not the thing distorted; what is in the mirror—that is what is twisted, mangled, bent. A caricature of world leaders failing in their responses to a pandemic is not only a caricature of people. It is a caricature of the plum pudding, too.

It would not be inappropriate to proclaim at this point, "Hand 'round the caricatures, Monster!" After all, the future of caricature has a stake in showing forth the miscreations and the *aide-mémoires* in the Human

Comedy. Its rhetorical ecology is such that, at the end of the day, the human condition is the fundamental site of its comic abstractions—of kings and subjects, of citizens and soldiers, of Selves and Others, of Us and Them. Its wartime sense of humor, as has been captured throughout this book, makes it possible to grapple with what are undoubtedly the grotesqueries of peace as they square off with the vainglories of war. Caricature reminds us that no one is an island, and that no rhetorical force of nature can face off with the natural world. It laughs at the idea that a comic looking glass might be rose-colored, and the common sense that anyone can safely have a cake and eat it, too. What is more, caricature parlays the so-called comic way into a comic way of seeing and being that resembles a caricature of survival such that we can look upon the world for what matters in our charge to live together, differently. It would be folly, then, to look for caricature in the normal course of things.

Notes

INTRODUCTION

1. From Benjamin Franklin's address to the Massachusetts House of Representatives on July 7, 1773. Founders Online, National Archives, https://founders.archives.gov/documents/Franklin/01-20-02-0155.

2. Benjamin Franklin, letter to Jane Mecom, 1773, Founders Online, National Archives, https://founders.archives.gov/documents/Franklin/01-20-02-0246.

3. Benjamin Franklin, "Rules by Which a Great Empire May be Reduced to a Small One," Founders Online, National Archives, https://founders.archives.gov/documents/Franklin/01-20-02-0213.

4. See Mulford, *Benjamin Franklin and the Ends of Empire*.

5. See Perez, *Cuba in the American Imagination*. See also Neiberg, *Path to War*.

6. Schuck, "Immigration System Today," 5. See also John Hingham's notion of "resurgent nativism" in *Strangers in the Land*, and more recently what E. Johanna Hartelius and others characterize as the rhetoricity of nativism, identity, and otherness in *Rhetorics of U.S. Immigration*.

7. The gist here is that ethnicity overlaps with nationality in a manner that lets humor slip into shared assumptions and collective predispositions that drive cultural politics, especially in systems of dominance. For more on this overlap, see work on ethnic and racial humor by Mahadev L. Apte, Arthur Asa Berger, Christie Davies, James H. Dormon, John Lowe, Lawrence E. Mintz, Elliott Oring, Victor Raskin, and Henry B. Wonham.

8. See, for instance, Grant E. Hamilton's cartoon entitled "The Spanish Brute Adds Mutilation to Murder," which appeared in *Judge* in July 1898, and Victor Gillam's cartoon entitled "The White Man's Burden (Apologies to Rudyard Kipling)," which appeared in *Judge* in April 1899. An article in the literary journal *Bookman* about nineteenth-century caricature summarized a prevailing feeling in the years just after the Spanish-American War (not to mention a gloss on the rhetorical difference that caricature makes as a way of seeing). Remarking on Hamilton's caricature in particular, the authors write, "It shows a hideous ape-like monster representing Spain, one blood-dripping hand smearing the tombstones erected to the sailors of the *Maine* and the other clutching a reeking knife. All about him under the tropical trees are the bodies of his mutilated victims. The expression of the monster's countenance is *a lesson in national prejudice. It shows how far a well-balanced nation may go in moments*

of bitterness and anger." See Cooper and Maurice, "History of the Nineteenth Century in Caricature," 65.

9. McCartney, *Power and Progress*, 45.

10. Woodrow Wilson, December 1902, "The Ideals of America," *Atlantic*, Ideas Tour, https://www.theatlantic.com/ideastour/idealism/wilson-full.html.

11. Eco, *On Ugliness*.

12. Franklin, "His Examination Before the House of Commons." See also Lester C. Olson, "MAGNA Britannia," 100, 102.

13. Ceaser, "Origins and Character of American Exceptionalism." See also McDaniel, "Speaking Like a State."

14. Benjamin Franklin, letter to Mary Hewson, January 27, 1783, Founders Online, National Archives, https://founders.archives.gov/documents/Franklin/01-39-02-0028.

15. See, for instance, Chapman et al., *Comics and the World Wars*; Knopf, *Comic Art of War*; Kemnitz, "Cartoon as a Historical Source"; Banta, *Barbaric Intercourse*; Caswell, "Drawing Swords"; Coupe, "Observations on a Theory of Political Caricature"; DeSousa and Medhurst, "Political Cartoons and American Culture"; Dewey, *Art of Ill Will*; Heller and Anderson, *Savage Mirror*; Howes, "Imagining a Multiplicity"; Streicher, "On a Theory of Political Caricature"; Hess and Northrop, *American Political Cartoons*.

16. Specifically, see Chute, *Disaster Drawn*, and Scott, *Comics and Conflict*. For an early rendition of this kind of critical thinking, see Hecht's edited volume, *War in Cartoons*. See also Gilbert and Lucaites, "Bringing War Down to Earth."

17. Porterfield, "Efflorescence of Caricature."

18. Scott, *Baudelaire's "Le Spleen de Paris,"* 17.

19. Benjamin Franklin, letter to Sarah Bache, January 26, 1784, Founders Online, National Archives, https://founders.archives.gov/documents/Franklin/01-41-02-0327.

20. See "Rattlesnake as a Symbol." Franklin's essay was published in the *Pennsylvania Journal* under the pseudonym "An American Guesser" on December 27, 1775. Great Seal, https://greatseal.com/symbols/rattlesnake.html.

21. This was one of Franklin's well-known mottos. It was also part of Thomas Jefferson's personal seal. Information about the seal can be found under "Benjamin Franklin's Great Seal Design" at Great Seal, https://greatseal.com/committees/firstcomm/reverse.html.

22. See, for instance, Theiss-Morse, *Who Counts as an American?*, 5–6; Lieven, *America Right or Wrong*; Huntington, *Who Are We?*, 116; Miller, *Citizenship and National Identity*; Anderson, *Imagined Communities*; Laclau, "On Imagined Communities," 28.

23. "Terminological Chaos" is the title of the fourth chapter of Connor's book, *Ethnonationalism: The Quest for Understanding*.

24. Waldstreicher, *In the Midst of Perpetual Fetes*, 49.

25. Ibid., 56.

26. This line is from Franklin's response during his questioning at the House of Commons in 1766. See "Examination of Dr. Benjamin Franklin in the House of Commons," *Digital History*, http://www.digitalhistory.uh.edu/disp_textbook.cfm?smtID=3&psid=4119.

27. See Gilbert, "Obama the Grotesque."

28. Wonham, *Playing the Races*, 46. See also Barry, *Visual Intelligence*, 80.

29. Billig, *Banal Nationalism*.

30. Fischer, *Liberty and Freedom*, 228.

31. See Schmidt, *Folly of War*.

32. Bergson, "Laughter," 79.

33. Carrier, *Aesthetics of Comics*, 84. See also Kris and Gombrich, "Principles of Caricature." It is worth pointing out here that caricature disposes its viewers to considering comic objects of ridicule for their display of what Gombrich might call the *artificiali perspectiva*, or the artifice of perspective. Gombrich, an art historian from Austria who wrote in the fog of World War II, long argued that distortions in caricature goad us to rethink our relationship to what we imagine to be *un*distorted. Gombrich submits that this goes for the critic of caricature as well. Exaggerations provoke attention to particular features, or what Gombrich might call artifactual, if not artificial, aspects in "the evidence of images."

34. George Washington, Letter to David Humphreys, July 25, 1785, Founders Online, National Archives, https://founders.archives.gov/documents/Washington/04-03-02-0142.

35. Boyesen, "Plague of Jocularity," 529.

36. Anderson, *Imagined Communities*, 188.

37. Ibid., 69.

38. Fischer, *Liberty and Freedom*, 224.

39. Ibid., 232, 521.

40. Vonnegut, *Deadeye Dick*, 253.

41. Banta, *Barbaric Intercourse*. See also Hannoosh, *Baudelaire and Caricature*.

42. W. H., "Slick, Downing, Crockett, Etc.," 138–39.

43. Rourke, *American Humor*, 20.

44. Nickels, *Civil War Humor*, x, 12.

45. Berger, *Anatomy of Humor*, 36.

46. Hervey, *Holbein's "Ambassadors*," 1.

47. Lyotard and Thébaud, *Just Gaming*, 73. See also Lyotard, "Fiscourse Digure."

48. Holzer, "With Malice Toward Both," 113.

49. Heller and Anderson, *Savage Mirror*.

50. Koestler, *Act of Creation*, 70.

51. Cooley, *Human Nature and the Social Order*, 152.

52. Foucault, "Nietzsche, Genealogy, History," 161.

53. See "Eleventh Series of Nonsense" and "Twelfth Series of the Paradox" in particular in Deleuze, *Logic of Sense*.

54. Peirce, "Man's Glassy Essence."

55. See Rosenkranz, *Aesthetics of Ugliness*. For a take on this notion more directly related to my study, see also "America in a Mirror." Also note that caricature *as* ugliness is constitutive of Georg Wilhelm Friedrich Hegel's definition of it in *Philosophy of Fine Art*. See George Wilhelm Friedrich Hegel, *Philosophy of Fine Art*, Project Gutenberg, http://www.gutenberg.org/files/55334/55334-h/55334-h.htm.

56. See Shrum, *In the Looking Glass*.

57. See Zijderveld, *Reality in a Looking-Glass*. See also Zijderveld, "Trend Report."

58. *Magazine of Science, and School of Arts*, 66.

59. Boyle, "Anamorphic Image," 1.

60. Berlant, *Anatomy of National Fantasy*, 21.

61. See Lynch, *History of Caricature*.

62. For a compelling discussion of the distinction between, and distinct union of, caricature and cartoons, see Banta, *Barbaric Intercourse*, 52–61.

63. Burke, *Permanence and Change*, 112.
64. Ibid., 115.
65. Boskin, "History and Humor," 19.
66. See Gilbert, "Decolonizing Caricature."
67. Engelhardt, *End of Victory Culture*.
68. Deleuze, *Logic of Sense*, 139.
69. The comic disposition embodied by most editorial cartoonists, and even humorists more generally, inheres the outsider status. In other words, to better deal with or make fun of what is familiar among those who belong, those trafficking in rhetorics of humor very often act as if they are strangers in their own home.
70. Edelman, *From Art to Politics*, 12.
71. Apel, *War Culture and the Contest of Images*, 12.
72. Gombrich, *Art and Illusion*, 93.

CHAPTER 1

1. Chesterton, "Unanswered Challenge," 64.
2. Masson, "Our Beginnings," 340–43.
3. Ben Franklin actually wrote an article, "A Witch Trial at Mount Holly," which appeared in an October 1730 issue of the *Pennsylvania Gazette*. It was a hoax, ridiculing the notion that there are both male and female witches. In many ways, Franklin's piece reads like a script for a Monty Python episode, with Priests and Gallows and Scales of Justice, and also sailors jumping on the back of an Accused Man to try to sink him. There is a faction of so-called Thinking Spectators who realize that an Accused Woman bound in clothes and tossed into the water will surely drown, and so to be sure of her witchery they plan to test her buoyancy—but only when the weather is warmer and she could be naked. All in all, the article mocks the sublimity of origins.
4. Kammen, *People of Paradox*, xviii.
5. Legman, *Rationale of the Dirty Joke*, 217–35.
6. See DesRochers, *New Humor in the Progressive Era*.
7. Du Bois, "Returning Soldiers," 13.
8. Stahl, *Militainment, Inc*, 4.
9. Bernays, "Engineering of Consent," 115.
10. O'Leary, *To Die For*, 7.
11. Brydges, *Uncle Sam at Home*, 164.
12. Banta, *Barbaric Intercourse*, 126.
13. See Kennedy, *Over Here*.
14. See Aman, "Edward Harrigan's Realism of Race." See also Dormon, "Ethnic Cultures of the Mind."
15. See Mintz, "Humor and Ethnic Stereotypes."
16. See Winokur, *American Laughter*.
17. Basso, *Portraits of "The Whiteman,"* 44, 82.
18. This is how it was described by Horace Kallen, an antiwar, anti-empire professor of philosophy, writing in *The Nation* in 1915.
19. Woodrow Wilson, Third Annual Message to Congress, December 7, 1915, The American Presidency Project, https://www.presidency.ucsb.edu/documents/third-annual-message-19.
20. Zangwill, *Melting-Pot*, 96.
21. Quoted in Hall, *Max Beerbohm Caricatures*, 15.
22. Simply, I understand the "state" as a set of governmental organizations and institutions and the "nation" as a national community with common values, histories, traditions, ideals, and more.

23. For more on President Wilson's transcendentalism, see Stuckey, "'Domain of Public Conscience.'"
24. Creel, *How We Advertised America*, 397.
25. Bakhtin, *Rabelais and His World*, 122.
26. Capozzola, *Uncle Sam Wants you*, 17–18.
27. Warner, *Monuments and Maidens*, 12.
28. US Committee on Public Information, *Creel Report*, 40.
29. Capozzola, *Uncle Sam Wants you*, 7.
30. Morgan, *American Icon*, 64.
31. Hills, "Cultural Racism," 115.
32. Maurice and Cooper, *History of the Nineteenth Century in Caricature*, 118.
33. Maurice, "International Wit and Humor," 263, 264.
34. Fischer, *Liberty and Freedom*, 327.
35. DeGuzmán, *Spain's Long Shadow*, 100.
36. See Bartholomew, *Cartoons of the Spanish-American War*.
37. Lubin, *Grand Illusions*, 60.
38. Fuchs, "Images of Love and War," 275.
39. Even further, the image seems a reproduction of an earlier illustration by Flagg that later became a cover to *Judge*, circa 1908. It displays a tomboyish woman with a hat and similarly open arms over the caption "Yours Truly."
40. Mitchell, *What Do Pictures Want?*, 39.
41. Hinton, "'Uncle Sam' as a Business Man," 481.
42. O'Leary, *To Die For*, 230.
43. Creel, *How We Advertised America*, 226.
44. Fischer, *Liberty and Freedom*, 432.
45. Bernays, *Crystallizing Public Opinion*, 172.
46. Kennedy, *Over Here*, 51.
47. Creel, *How We Advertised America*, 5.
48. See Tholas-Disset and Ritzenhoff, *Humor, Entertainment, and Popular Culture*.
49. Zieger, *America's Great War*, 83.
50. Meyer, *James Montgomery Flagg*, 51, 53.
51. Ibid., 21.
52. Capozzola, *Uncle Sam Wants you*, 6.
53. Nussbaum, *Anger and Forgiveness*, 131.
54. Ahmed, *Cultural Politics of Emotion*, 101–10.
55. See Berlant, "Uncle Sam Needs a Wife."
56. Lubin, *Grand Illusions*, 68.
57. Creel, *How We Advertised America*, 226.
58. James, "Introduction," 4, 10.
59. Wanzo, *Content of Our Caricature*, 16.
60. Creel, *How We Advertised America*, 454.
61. Capozzola, *Uncle Sam Wants you*, 43, 135.
62. Sherwood, "Uncle Sam," 333.
63. Keene, "Images of Racial Pride," 209.
64. Ibid.
65. Du Bois, "Close Ranks." It is notable that critics among the Black press dubbed W. E. B. Du Bois a traitor. See Rudwick, "W. E. B. Du Bois." See also Smith, "*Crisis* in the Great War."
66. Du Bois, "African Roots of War."
67. Du Bois, "Awake, America."
68. Du Bois, "Superior Race."
69. Painter, *Standing at Armageddon*, 279.

70. Gallagher, *World Wars Through the Female Gaze*, 4.

71. Haytock, *At Home, at War*, xxii.

72. Capozzola, *Uncle Sam Wants you*, 95–103.

73. Summerfield, "Gender and War," 4.

74. Brown, *Enlisting Masculinity*, 84.

75. Meyer, *James Montgomery Flagg*, 21, 42.

76. Kitch, *Girl on the Magazine Cover*, 63.

77. Rourke, *American Humor*, 19.

78. Ballif, *Seduction, Sophistry*, 29.

79. Kitch, *Girl on the Magazine Cover*, 61.

80. Burke, *Rhetoric of Motives*, 115.

81. Ibid., 177.

82. Consolati, "Grotesque Bodies, Fragmented Selves," 44.

83. Irigaray, *This Sex Which Is Not One*, 130.

84. Trout, *On the Battlefield of Memory*, 11.

85. Beard, "Age of Caricature," 206–7.

86. Creel, *How We Advertised America*, 184, 242.

87. Lippman, *Public Opinion*, 96.

88. "Crucible: Life and Death 1918," The National WWI Museum and Memorial, April 3, 2018–March 10, 2019, https://www.theworldwar.org/explore/exhibitions/current-exhibitions/crucible-life-and-death-1918.

89. Lamb, *Drawn to Extremes*, 89.

90. Ong, *Fighting for Life*, 67.

CHAPTER 2

1. Burroughs, *Cat Inside*, 33.

2. Ibid., 61.

3. Cahn, "Wonderful World of Dr. Seuss."

4. Nel, "Was the Cat in the Hat Black?," 72.

5. Elick, *Talking Animals in Children's Fiction*, 30.

6. Wilmes, "Dr. Seuss' Forgotten Anti-War Book."

7. See some of the artworks from the so-called "Secret Art" and Archive in the online collections at The Art of Dr. Seuss Collection, available at http://www.drseussart.com/secretandarchive.

8. A number of Dr. Seuss's most famous characters were based on himself, including the Grinch.

9. Dr. Seuss's sensible weirdness is perhaps most notable in his famous children's stories, which are full of adult matters of war, peace, politics, and more. It is also noticeable in his largely uncelebrated taxidermy, as well as the pre–World War II advertising work that help make Dr. Seuss a household name with dinosaur bulldozers called "Dozerpods" and raging radio creatures called "Wild Tones" and germs as picketing Microbes-at-Arms, all of which came before characters like the Once-ler, Horton the Elephant, and Sam-I-Am. His wordplay and weird imagery work together to make up a rhetoric of expanding vocabularies and adopting nonsensical views in order to see that which might not otherwise be seen.

10. Just as Twain saw Man as the only animal capable of indecency, grotesquery, and so on, he also saw Man as the only animal capable of war. See Twain, *Letters From the Earth*, 179.

11. See Nel, "'Said a Bird.'" See also Nel, "Dr. Seuss vs. Adolf Hitler."

12. Morgan and Morgan, *Dr. Seuss and Mr. Geisel*, 103.

13. Wilmes, "Dr. Seuss' Forgotten Anti-War Book."

14. Connolly, *Identity, Difference*, 193.

15. Griffin, *Nature of Fascism*, 2.

16. Hazlitt, "Truth About 'Appeasement.'"

17. Franklin D. Roosevelt, "Address Accepting the Presidential Nomination at the Democratic National Convention in Chicago," American Presidency Project, July 2, 1932, http://www.presidency.ucsb.edu/ws/?pid=75174.

18. Luce, "American Century."

19. MacDonnell, *Insidious Foes*, 12.

20. Daly, "When the 99% Had a Paper."

21. Blum, *V Was for Victory*, 27. See also "Dr. Seuss and *PM*" in Minear, *Dr. Seuss Goes to War*.

22. Bodnar, *"Good War" in American Memory*, 18.

23. Denning, *Cultural Front*, xvii (emphasis added).

24. Jenkins, "'No Matter How Small,'" 195, 196.

25. Denning, *Cultural Front*, 44.

26. Minear, *Dr. Seuss Goes to War*, 121.

27. See Jones, *Becoming Dr. Seuss*, 140–52.

28. Nel, "Was the Cat in the Hat Black?," 71.

29. Cohen, *Seuss*, 224.

30. Nel, *Dr. Seuss*, 6.

31. Minear, *Dr. Seuss Goes to War*, 10.

32. Ibid., 266.

33. Burke, *Philosophy of Literary Form*, 219.

34. Ernst Gombrich marked animalisms some time ago as archetypal in caricature. But Aristotle even earlier developed a notion of "hylomorphism" around the idea of a combination of form and matter to interrogate how the rhetorical matters of bodies—and bodies politic—take shape. In some ways, though, the cultural knowledge that follows from this concept makes the concept that "like goes with like" something of a distortion of vitalism. In this case, caricatures put forth wild portrayals of national characteristics as at once rhetorical and living matters, and thereby reorder conceptions of collective selfhoods.

35. "The Manly Art of Self-Defense," The Art of Dr. Seuss Collection, https://www.drseussart.com/secretandarchive/manly-art-of-self-defense.

36. Marcoci, *Comic Abstraction*, 10.

37. W. G. Rogers, *Springfield Union*, May 11, 1933. Quoted in Morgan and Morgan, *Dr. Seuss and Mr. Geisel*, 305.

38. See Turley, "David Low and America."

39. Deleuze, *Logic of Sense*, 141.

40. See Minear, *Dr. Seuss Goes to War*, 23.

41. Lim, *Anti-Intellectual Presidency*, 173.

42. See Stuckey, *Good Neighbor*.

43. Kimball, *Juggler*, 14, 8.

44. Deleuze and Parnet, *Dialogues II*, 68.

45. See Russell, "'Speaking of Annihilation.'"

46. Shepard, *Thinking Animals*, 167.

47. Lockwood, *Six-Legged Soldiers*, 123.

48. Carson, *Silent Spring*, 21. See also Russell, *War and Nature*.

49. Steuter and Wills, *At War with Metaphor*, 122.

50. Said, "Arabs, Islam, and the Dogmas of the West," 105.

51. Ibid., 104.

52. Ma, *Deathly Embrace*, 4.

53. Varisco, *Reading Orientalism*, 29–39.

54. The insecticide trope resonates, too, with the trope of American waste in so many of Dr. Seuss's cartoons. In one from September 1941, for instance, Lindbergh appears atop an "Anti-Semite

Stink Wagon" driven by a Nazi. The wagon is a dump truck, and Lindbergh wears a mask while standing in a bulging rubbish heap, shoveling rotten fish bones and infected cats out onto America. The caption indicates that racist isolationists like Lindbergh were "Spreading the Lovely Goebbels Stuff" in their America First rhetoric. These so-called interventionists meant that *white* America was preeminent, a sentiment that prefigured Dr. Seuss's plea for mental insecticides that might root out racism, chauvinism, and bigotry. Hence Dr. Seuss drew them out of whack in their act of carrying out garbage *delivery*, not pick-up. As with his references to the spread of disease, these allusions to waste and effluvium carried over into caricatures of "Goebbels Gas," "disunity gas," an "Anti-Labor Stink Bomb," and more. Here again, the toxins of things like race hatred and unthinking nativism were likened to wartime talks of wage freezes, inflation, isolationism, and—simply—foolish American pride.

55. Seldes, *Facts and Fascism*, 236.
56. Olson, *Those Angry Days*, 230.
57. Fussell, *Wartime*, 120.
58. Zieger, *For Jobs and Freedom*, 124.
59. Kersten, *Labor's Home Front*, 70.
60. Fussell, *Wartime*, 26.
61. Nel, *Dr. Seuss*, 183.

CHAPTER 3

1. Adapted from Spaulding, *Art of Storytelling*, 50.
2. Inge, *Dark Laughter*, xi.
3. Ibid.
4. Ivy, "Mordant Satire," 523.
5. Hughes, introduction, n.p.
6. Dolinar, *Black Cultural Front*, 177.
7. Inge, *Dark Laughter*, xx.
8. Eldridge, *Chronicles*, 218. See also Kercher, *Revel with a Cause*, 284.
9. Wanzo, *Content of Our Caricature*, 4.
10. Stevens, "Reflections in a Dark Mirror," 242.
11. Wanzo, *Content of Our Caricature*, 31.
12. Ibid., 22.
13. Freud, *Wit and Its Relation to the Unconscious*, 293.
14. Ibid., 295.
15. I borrow this term from Henry Louis Gates Jr., which he uses in *Signifying Monkey* to characterize the "signifyin(g)" practices of Black culture.
16. See Dwight D. Eisenhower's so-called "Chance for Peace" speech, which he delivered to the American Society of Newspaper Editors on April 16, 1953.
17. Quoted in Horne, *End of Empires*, 206.
18. Borstelmann, *Cold War*, 46.
19. Prattis, "Role of the Negro Press," 279.
20. Ivy, "Mordant Satire," 523.
21. Kellogg, "Negro Pioneers," 272.
22. Dudziak, "Desegregation as a Cold War Imperative," 62.
23. Delgado and Stefancic, introduction. Note, too, how this predilection mirrors a problem with rhetorical inventions of foreign enemies in terms of madness, pathology, miscreation, and more.
24. Appy, "Introduction," 4. See also Borstelmann, *Cold War*, 83.
25. Chafe, *Unfinished Journey*, 32.
26. Hepburn, "Educating for Democracy," 153.
27. Parry-Giles, *Rhetorical Presidency*, 59.
28. See Westheider, *Fighting on Two Fronts*, 141–42.

29. Beasley, *You, the People*, 56.
30. Eldridge, *Chronicles*, 213.
31. Kercher, *Revel with a Cause*, 282.
32. Lamb, *Drawn to Extremes*, 104.
33. Von Eschen, "Who's the Real Ambassador?," 123.
34. Prattis, "Role of the Negro Press," 275, 278.
35. Thurston, "'Bombed in Spain,'" 152.
36. Vogel, introduction, 11.
37. Forss, *Black Print*, 9.
38. Quoted in Washburn, *African American Newspaper*, 3.
39. Simmons, *African American Press*, 46.
40. Washburn, *African American Newspaper*, 4.
41. Prattis, "Role of the Negro Press," 273. See also Huspeck, "Transgressive Rhetoric in Deliberative Democracy," 160, 162.
42. Whitfield, *Culture of the Cold War*, 4.
43. Kwon, *Other Cold War*, 42, 146.
44. Dolinar, *Black Cultural Front*, 194.
45. Ibid., 172.
46. Gaines, *American Africans in Ghana*, 138.
47. Gaines, "From Black Power to Civil Rights," 261, 268.
48. Harrington, *Why I Left America*, 68.
49. Kercher, *Revel with a Cause*, 282.
50. Ellison, "What These Children Are Like," 555.
51. Mintz, "Changing Face of Children's Culture," 39.
52. Levin, "Veins of Humor," 191.
53. Gates, *Signifying Monkey*, 121.
54. Badiou, *Black*, 67.
55. Fauset, "Gift of Laughter," 515.
56. Wanzo, *Content of Our Caricature*, 35.
57. Braithwaite, "Negro in Literature," 205.
58. Maxwell, *New Negro*, 117.
59. Gates and Jarrett, introduction, 3.
60. Ibid., 10.
61. Watkins, *On the Real Side*, 12.
62. Boskin, "African-American Humor," 157.
63. Ibid., 153.
64. Gillota, *Ethnic Humor*, 2–4, 15.
65. Carpio, *Laughing Fit to Kill*, 4.
66. Ibid., 17.
67. Quoted in Inge, *Dark Laughter*, xxvii–xxviii.
68. Ibid., xxxix.
69. Ibid.
70. Dudziak, "Desegregation," 191.
71. Peacock, *Innocent Weapons*, 7–8.
72. Bernstein, *Racial Innocence*, 35, 4–8.
73. Given the recurrence of Luther's name and likeness across a number of Harrington's cartoons, as well as the frequency with which he refers to Bootsie as his uncle, it is likely that Luther is Bootsie's nephew.
74. Gotham, *Race, Real Estate, and Uneven Development*, 108–9.
75. Weaver, *Rhetoric of Racist Humour*, 108.
76. Engelhardt, *End of Victory Culture*, 5.
77. Davenport, "Blowing Flames," 121.
78. Eskew, *But for Birmingham*, 271.
79. The Lumbee in Robeson County, North Carolina, were particular targets. See "Bad Medicine" from *Life* and "2 Klansmen Face Charges in Clash" from the *New York Times*.
80. Mead, "Genesis," 268, 269.
81. Cooper, *Voice from the South*, 157.
82. Ritterhouse, *Growing Up Jim Crow*, 236.
83. Kammen, *People of Paradox*.

84. Lyndon B. Johnson, "State of the Union Address, 1966," PBS, http://www.pbs.org/wgbh/americanexperience/features/primary-resources/lbj-union66.

85. King, "Last Steep Ascent."

86. Lyndon B. Johnson, "The President's Address at Johns Hopkins University: Peace Without Conquest," April 7, 1965, LBJ Presidential Library, http://www.lbjlibrary.org/exhibits/the-presidents-address-at-johns-hopkins-university-peace-without-conquest.

87. Quadagno, *Color of Welfare*, 19.

88. Boskin and Dorinson, "Ethnic Humor," 81–97.

89. Lyndon B. Johnson, "State of the Union Address, 1969," PBS, http://www.pbs.org/wgbh/americanexperience/features/primary-resources/lbj-union69.

90. Harrington, *Other America*, 204.

91. Wanzo, *Content of Our Caricature*, 147.

92. Quoted in Ruotsila, *British and American Anticommunism*, 192.

93. Gombrich and Kris, *Caricature*, 26.

94. Allen, *Talking to Strangers*, 125.

95. Brown, "'Bootsie' in Berlin," 364.

96. See "Reviewed Work," 308. In another telling, the Crow devastates his own silk-cotton tree, which would have been his livelihood and the source of his beautiful plumage. The outcome of muck and waste is the same.

97. Rattray, *Ashanti Proverbs*, 106.

CHAPTER 4

1. Bacevich, "Theology of American National Security."

2. Ibid.

3. Engelhardt, *End of Victory Culture*, 10, 330.

4. Rostow, *Toward Managed Peace*, 3.

5. See Bennett and Berenson, "'Our Big War.'" See also LeBlanc, "Trump Calls Coronavirus a 'Foreign Virus.'"

6. See Erlanger, "Coronavirus Inflicts Its Own Kind of Terror."

7. See Gilbert, "Obama the Grotesque."

8. These labels come variously from staff, former cabinet members, members of the news media, and foreign leaders. What is more, they fill out a generalized sense that President Trump's idiocy is tied to his relatively infantile approach to brand (or, anger) management and cultural politicking, which is captured in sobriquets like Baby Trump and toddler in chief.

9. This, of course, is notwithstanding wild protestations that President Obama was a would-be tyrant, dictator, or king, a reincarnation of Hitler, and the Joker of *The Dark Knight* in disguise.

10. Quoted in Carroll, *Alice's Adventures in Wonderland*, 288. The line originally appeared in an essay entitled "Alice on the Stage" by Charles Lutwidge Dodgson (Carroll's birth name) in *The Theatre* in April 1887.

11. Singh, "This Is What Ancient Greeks."

12. Costa and Rucker, "Trump Casts Himself as Pandemic Patron."

13. *Korematsu v. United States*, 323 U. S. 214, 22 (1944) (Jackson J. dissenting opinion).

14. Deleuze, *Logic of Sense*, 78.

15. See Giroux, *America at War with Itself*.

16. Zulaika, *Terrorism*, 208.

17. This collection is cataloged online by the Prints and Photographs Division of the Library of Congress and was

exhibited as *Humor's Edge* by the library in June 2004. See "Humor's Edge: Cartoons by Ann Telnaes," Library of Congress, http://www.loc.gov/exhibits/telnaes.

18. Klein, *Shock Doctrine*. See also "'Coronavirus Capitalism': Naomi Klein's Case for Transformative Change Amid Coronavirus Pandemic," *Democracy NOW!* March 19, 2020, https://www.democracynow.org/2020/3/19/naomi_klein_coronavirus_capitalism.

19. Tristram Hunt, "A Puritan on the Warpath," *Guardian*, September 1, 2002, https://www.theguardian.com/education/2002/sep/01/highereducation.usa.

20. Kellner, "Bushspeak and the Politics of Lying."

21. National Commission on Terrorist Attacks upon the United States, *9/11 Commission Report*, 375. See also, Kellner, "Media and the Crisis of Democracy."

22. Burke, *Philosophy of Literary Form*, 240.

23. See Marvin and Ingle, *Blood Sacrifice and the Nation*.

24. Billig, *Banal Nationalism*, 96.

25. Ibid., 39.

26. Berlant, *Anatomy of National Fantasy*, 4.

27. Katz, "Banal Terrorism."

28. See Stahl, *Militainment, Inc.* See also the edited volumes Allen and Zelizer, *Reporting War*, and Hauser and Grim, *Rhetorical Democracy*, as well as Spigel, "Entertainment Wars."

29. Mitchell, *Cloning Terror*, xii, 64.

30. Telnaes, *Humor's Edge*, 51.

31. Note that this is at least in part an economic phenomenon, with further implications around problems of corporate editorship and changes in the nature of the cartoon medium and its modes of delivery.

32. Lamb, *Drawn to Extremes*, 7.

33. See Gournelos and Greene, *Decade of Dark Humor*.

34. Ann Telnaes, "Democracy's Canary in a Coal Mine," Bertelsmann Foundation, May 7, 2019, https://www.bfna.org/research/democracys-canary-in-a-coal-mine.

35. Mann, *Sovereign Masculinity*, 11.

36. Cohn and Enloe, "Conversation with Cynthia Enlo," 1189–90.

37. Wallace, "Just Asking."

38. Shane, *Madison's Nightmare*, 8.

39. Schwarz and Huq, *Unchecked and Unbalanced*, 201.

40. Chopra, "Donald Trump and the Looking-Glass War."

41. Rosenthal and Schulman, "Trump's Secret War on Terror."

42. Crowther, *Infuriating American*, 58–59.

43. Fisher, "Rhetorical Fiction and the Presidency."

44. Žižek, *First as Tragedy*, 8.

45. Marx, "Exchange of Letters," 204.

46. Quoted in Gisbertz, "On Beauty and Its Challenges," 104. Importantly, Gisbertz articulates how Marx saw comedy as an insufficient rhetorical weapon against the folly of a despotic state, and so turned to farce as the more apt framework for bringing the sublimity of authoritarian politics back to reality.

47. "Thomas Couture: *Romans During the Decadence*," Musée d' Orsay, https://www.musee-orsay.fr/en/collections/works-in-focus/search/commentaire/commentaire_id/romans-during-the-decadence-2105.html.

48. See Telnaes's collection, *Dick* (2010).

49. See "Right Way in Iraq," and Hersh, "Stovepipe." See also "War in the Ruins of Diplomacy."

50. "Attorney General John Ashcroft's Assault."
51. Harrison, "Interview with Ann Telnaes," 233.
52. Hall, "New Ethnicities," 442.
53. Deleuze, *Difference and Repetition*, 365.
54. Boggs, *Imperial Delusions*, 128.
55. Cloud, "'To Veil the Threat of Terror,'" 290.
56. Jones, "War Against Women."
57. See Jones, *War Is Not Over*; Ahmed, *The Thistle and the Drone*; Selod, *Forever Suspect*.
58. Harrison, "Interview with Ann Telnaes," 235.
59. These interpretations include dress codes, curfews, restrictions on movement, and prohibitions from education and healthcare, as well as rapes, kidnappings, and connubial controls. See Dupree, "Afghan Women Under the Taliban."
60. Khan, "Between Here and There."
61. Kimble and Olson, "Visual Rhetoric Representing Rosie the Riveter," 551.
62. Salime, "War on Terrorism."
63. Borowitz, "In War of Elton John Lyrics."
64. "President Donald J. Trump Proclaims October 15 Through October 21, 2017, as National Character Counts Week," The White House, October 13, 2017, https://www.whitehouse.gov/the-press-office/2017/10/13/president-donald-j-trump-proclaims-october-15-through-october-21-2017-0.
65. Wolcott, "How Donald Trump."
66. Kennedy, "Ann Telnaes," 16.
67. Horton, "George W. Bush."
68. Scher, "Culture War President."
69. Koppelman, "Trump Farce."
70. Bacon, "Trump's Latest Attempt."
71. Coppins, "False Prophet."
72. Bergson, "Laughter," 71.
73. Pak, "The Good, the Bad, and the Ugly."
74. Perper, "Bob Woodward."
75. Ott and Dickinson, *Twitter Presidency*, ix.
76. Bourke, "Tyranny in Disguise."
77. Parham, "Depth of Field."
78. McLees, *Baudelaire's "Argot Plastique,"* 5.
79. Shafer, "Trump's American Emperor Moment."
80. Hartman, "Culture Wars Are Dead."
81. Baldwin, *Fire Next Time*, 95.
82. Cottle, "Drop the Curtain on the Trump Follies."
83. "Bush's Absurdist Imperialism."
84. Stevenson, "President Makes It Clear."
85. Szpunar, *Homegrown*, 21.
86. See Denevi, "Fear and Loathing."
87. Astor, "Post-9/11 Review."
88. Bacevich, "'Let Them Eat Trump.'"
89. Carroll, *Alice's Adventures in Wonderland*, 15.

CONCLUSION

1. Shorris, "National Character."
2. Burke, "War and Cultural Life," 404.
3. Quoted in Faram, *Faces of War*, 63.
4. "The Road to Victory, 1942," PhotoEphemera: Poking Through the Dustbin of Photographic History, March 22, 2009, http://photemera.blogspot.com/2009/03/road-to-victory-1942.html.
5. Burke, "War and Cultural Life," 404.
6. Giroux, *America at War with Itself*, 200.

7. Bhabha, "Commitment to Theory," 11, 15, 20. See also Bhabha, "Introduction."

8. McDaniel and Gronbeck, "Through the Looking Glass and Back," 22.

9. Gramsci, "War is War."

10. Serwer, "What Americans Do Now."

11. Heer, "Why the Paper of Record."

12. Herb Block, "The Cartoon," The Library of Congress, https://www.loc.gov/exhibits/herblocks-history/cartoon.html.

13. I borrow this language from an exhibition put on by the Library of Congress with support from the Caroline and Erwin Swann Memorial Fund for Caricature and Cartoon in 1998. Comic judgment, for Gillray, was part and parcel of visual mockery, and it dwelled in the uncomfortable spaces of social customs and contradictions as well as political habits and ignominies.

14. Franklin, "Dogood Papers," 20.

15. Bishara, "Pandemic as a War."

16. Gilbert, "Complicated Relevance."

17. Burke, *Philosophy of Literary Form*, 237.

18. Bierce, "War."

19. Bierce, "Controversy."

20. Appel, *Nietzsche Contra Democracy*, 68.

21. Ibid.

22. Clare Sibthorpe, "Australian Financial Review's David Rowe Takes out 2017 Political Cartoonist of the Year," *ABC*, November 23, 2017, https://www.abc.net.au/news/2017-11-24/david-rowe-takes-out-2017-political-cartoonist-of-the-year/9187830.

23. Meredith, "On the Idea of Comedy," 55.

CODA

1. McKibben, "Trump's Stupid and Reckless Climate Decision."

2. Durkee, "Trump Was Warned."

3. O'Toole, "Donald Trump."

4. Ibid.

5. See Perkins, "Definition of Caricature."

6. Perkins, "Definition of Caricature," 7.

7. Meeker, *Comedy of Survival*, 21.

8. Perkins, "Definition of Caricature," 3.

9. Giroux, "COVID-19 Pandemic."

10. Ibid.

11. Glasser, "Trump O'Clock Follies."

12. Winston Churchill, "Be Ye Men of Valour," speech, May 19, 1940, International Churchill Society, https://winstonchurchill.org/resources/speeches/1940-the-finest-hour/be-ye-men-of-valour.

13. Agamben, "Proper and the Improper."

Bibliography

Agamben, Giorgio. "The Proper and the Improper." In *Stanzas: Word and Phantasm in Western Culture*, 141–51. Translated by Ronald L. Martinez. Minneapolis: University of Minnesota Press, 1993.

Ahmed, Akbar. *The Thistle and the Drone: How America's War on Terror Became a Global War on Tribal Islam*. Washington, DC: Brookings Institution Press, 2013.

Ahmed, Maaheen. *Monstrous Imaginaries: The Legacy of Romanticism in Comics*. Jackson: University Press of Mississippi, 2020.

Ahmed, Sara. *The Cultural Politics of Emotion*. New York: Routledge, 2004.

Allen, Danielle S. *Talking to Strangers: Anxieties of Citizenship Since "Brown v. Board of Education."* Chicago: Chicago University Press, 2004.

Allen, Stuart, and Barbie Zelizer, eds. *Reporting War: Journalism in Wartime*. New York: Routledge, 2004.

Aman, Michael. "Edward Harrigan's Realism of Race." *Journal of American Drama and Theatre* 24 (2012): 5–30.

"America in a Mirror: Caricature as History." *Quarto* 1, no. 3 (1995): 1, 12.

Anderson, Benedict. *Imagined Communities*. 1983. Reprint, London: Verso, 2006.

Apel, Dora. *War Culture and the Contest of Images*. Brunswick: Rutgers University Press, 2012.

Appel, Fredrick. *Nietzsche Contra Democracy*. Ithaca: Cornell University Press, 1999.

Appy, Christian G. "Introduction: Struggling for the World." In *Cold War Constructions: The Political Culture of United States Imperialism, 1945–1966*, edited by Christian G. Appy, 1–8. Amherst: University of Massachusetts Press, 2000.

Apte, Mahadev L. *Humor and Laughter: An Anthropological Approach*. Ithaca: Cornell University Press, 1985.

Astor, Dave. "A Post-9/11 Review of Editorial Cartooning." *Editor and Publisher*, February 4, 2002. https://www.questia.com/magazine/1G1-82757332/a-post-9-11-review-of-editorial-cartooning.

"Attorney General John Ashcroft's Assault on Civil Liberties." American Civil Liberties Union, October 30, 2002. Updated September 2003. https://www.aclu.org/national-security/attorney-general-john-ashcrofts-assault-civil-liberties-updated-september-2003.

Bacevich, Andrew J. "'Let Them Eat Trump.'" *Nation*, February 5, 2019.

https://www.thenation.com/article/let-them-eat-trump.

———. "The Theology of American National Security." TomDispatch.com, June 18, 2015. http://www.tomdispatch.com/blog/176012/tomgram%3A_andrew_bacevich,_the_theology_of_american_national_security.

Bacon, Perry, Jr. "Trump's Latest Attempt to Limit Immigration Isn't Really About the Coronavirus." FiveThirtyEight, April 22, 2020. https://fivethirtyeight.com/features/trumps-latest-attempt-to-limit-immigration-isnt-really-about-the-coronavirus.

Badiou, Alain. *Black: The Brilliance of a Non-Color*. Malden: Polity Press, 2017.

"Bad Medicine for the Klan: North Carolina Indians Break Up Ku Kluxers' Anti-Indian Meeting." *Life* 44, no. 4 (January 27, 1958): 26–28.

Bakhtin, Mikhail. *Rabelais and His World*. Translated by Hélène Iswolsky. Bloomington: Indiana University Press, 1984.

Baldwin, James. *The Fire Next Time*. New York: Vintage Books, 1963.

Ballif, Michelle. *Seduction, Sophistry, and the Woman with the Rhetorical Figure*. Carbondale: Southern Illinois University Press, 2001.

Banta, Martha. *Barbaric Intercourse: Caricature and the Culture of Conduct, 1841–1936*. Chicago: University of Chicago Press, 2003.

———. *Imaging American Women: Idea and Ideals in Cultural History*. New York: Columbia University Press, 1987.

Barber, Benjamin R. *Fear's Empire: War, Terrorism, and Democracy*. New York: W. W. Norton, 2003.

Barry, Ann Marie Seward. *Visual Intelligence: Perception, Image, and Manipulation in Visual Communication*. Albany: State University of New York Press, 1997.

Bartholomew, Charles Lewis. *Cartoons of the Spanish-American War*. Minneapolis: Journal Printing Company, 1899.

Basso, Keith H. *Portraits of "The Whiteman": Linguistic Play and Cultural Symbols Among the Western Apache*. New York: Cambridge University Press, 1979.

Beard, Frank. "The Age of Caricature." *Chautauquan* 7, no. 4 (January 1887): 206–7.

Beasley, Vanessa B. *You, the People: American National Identity in Presidential Rhetoric*. College Station: Texas A&M University Press, 2011.

Bennett, Brian, and Tessa Berenson. "'Our Big War': As Coronavirus Spreads, Trump Refashions Himself as a Wartime President." *Time*, March 19, 2020. https://time.com/5806657/donald-trump-coronavirus-war-china.

Berger, Arthur Asa. *An Anatomy of Humor*. London: Routledge, 1993.

———. *The Genius of the Jewish Joke*. New Brunswick: Transaction, 2006.

Bergson, Henri. "Laughter: An Essay on the Meaning of the Comic." In *Comedy*, edited by Wylie Sypher, 59–190. Baltimore: Johns Hopkins University Press, 1980.

Berlant, Lauren. *The Anatomy of National Fantasy: Hawthorne, Utopia, and Everyday Life*. Chicago: University of Chicago Press, 1991.

———. "Uncle Sam Needs a Wife: Citizenship and Denegation." In *The Female Complaint: The Unfinished*

Business of Sentimentality in American Culture, 145–68. Durham: Duke University Press, 2008.

Bernays, Edward L. *Crystallizing Public Opinion*. New York: Liveright Publishing Corporation, 1961.

———. "The Engineering of Consent." *ANNALS of the American Academy of Political and Social Science* 250 (1947): 113–22.

Bernstein, Robin. *Racial Innocence: Performing American Childhood from Slavery to Civil Rights*. New York: New York University Press, 2011.

Bhabha, Homi K. "The Commitment to Theory." *New Formations* 5 (1988): 1–23.

———. "Introduction: Narrating the Nation." In *Nation and Narration*, edited by Homi K. Bhabha, 1–7. New York: Routledge, 1990.

Bierce, Ambrose. "Controversy." In *The Devil's Dictionary*. Project Gutenberg. https://www.gutenberg.org/files/972/972-h/972-h.htm.

———. "War." In *The Devil's Dictionary*. Project Gutenberg. https://www.gutenberg.org/files/972/972-h/972-h.htm.

Billig, Michael. *Banal Nationalism*. Thousand Oaks, CA: SAGE, 1995.

Bishara, Marwan. "The Pandemic as a War and Trump, the 'Medic-in-Chief.'" *Al Jazeera*, April 27, 2020. https://www.aljazeera.com/indepth/opinion/pandemic-war-trump-medic-chief-200427105106026.html.

Blum, John Morton. *V Was for Victory: Politics and American Culture During World War II*. San Diego: Harvest Book, 1976.

Bodnar, John. *The "Good War" in American Memory*. Baltimore: Johns Hopkins University Press, 2010.

———. *Remaking America: Public Memory, Commemoration, and Patriotism in the Twentieth Century*. Princeton: Princeton University Press, 1992.

Boggs, Carl. *Imperial Delusions: American Militarism and Endless War*. Lanham, MD: Rowman & Littlefield, 2005.

Borowitz, Andy. "In War of Elton John Lyrics, Kim Jong Un Calls Trump 'Honky Cat.'" *New Yorker*, September 19, 2017. https://www.newyorker.com/humor/borowitz-report/in-war-of-elton-john-lyrics-kim-jong-un-calls-trump-honky-cat.

Borstelmann, Thomas. *The Cold War and the Color Line: American Race Relations in the Global Arena*. Cambridge: Harvard University Press, 2003.

Boskin, Joseph. "African-American Humor: Resistance and Retaliation." In *The Humor Prism in 20th-Century America*, edited by Joseph Boskin, 145–58. Detroit: Wayne State University Press, 1997.

———. "History and Humor." In *The Humor Prism in 20th-Century America*, edited by Joseph Boskin, 17–27. Detroit: Wayne State University Press, 1997.

Boskin, Joseph, and Joseph Dorinson. "Ethnic Humor: Subversion and Survival." *American Quarterly* 37 (1985): 81–97.

Bourke, Joanna. "Tyranny in Disguise." *Guardian*, September 30, 2007. https://www.theguardian.com/commentisfree/2007/sep/30/tyrannyindisguise.

Boyd, Herb. "Ollie Harrington in memoriam." *Black Scholar* 26, no. 1 (1996): 74.

Boyesen, Hjalmar Hjorth. "The Plague of Jocularity." *North American Review* 161 (1895): 528–35.

Boyle, Jennifer Ellen. "The Anamorphic Image." In *Anamorphosis in Early Modern Literature: Mediation and Affect*, 1–14. Burlington: Ashgate, 2010.

Braithwaite, William Stanley. "The Negro in Literature." *Crisis* 28 (1925): 204–10.

Brown, Melissa T. *Enlisting Masculinity: The Construction of Gender in U.S. Military Recruiting Advertising During the All-Volunteer Force*. New York: Oxford University Press, 2012.

Brown, Stephanie. "'Bootsie' in Berlin: An Interview with Helma Harrington on Oliver Harrington's Life and Work in East Germany, 1961–1995." *African American Review* 44 (2011): 353–72.

Brunner, Edward. "'This Job Is a Solid Killer': Oliver Harrington's *Jive Gray* and the African American Adventure Strip." *Iowa Journal of Cultural Studies* 6 (2005): 36–57.

Bryant, Mark. *World War I in Cartoons*. London: Grub Street, 2014.

Brydges, Harold. *Uncle Sam at Home*. New York: Henry Holt, 1888.

Burke, Kenneth. *Permanence and Change: An Anatomy of Purpose*. Berkeley: University of California Press, 1965.

———. *The Philosophy of Literary Form: Studies in Symbolic Action*. Berkeley: University of California Press, 1967.

———. *A Rhetoric of Motives*. 1950. Reprint, Berkeley: University of California Press, 1969.

———. "War and Cultural Life." *American Journal of Sociology* 48 (1942): 404–10.

Burroughs, William S. *The Cat Inside*. New York: Penguin, 1992.

"Bush's Absurdist Imperialism." *Nation*, April 10, 2007. https://www.thenation.com/article/bushs-absurdist-imperialism.

Cahn, Robert. "The Wonderful World of Dr. Seuss." *Saturday Evening Post*, February 28, 2016. https://www.saturdayeveningpost.com/2016/02/wonderful-world-dr-seuss.

Calafell, Marie. *Monstrosity, Performance, and Race in Contemporary Culture*. New York: Peter Lang, 2015.

Capozzola, Christopher. *Uncle Sam Wants you: World War I and the Making of the Modern American Citizen*. New York: Oxford University Press, 2008.

Carpio, Glenda R. *Laughing Fit to Kill: Black Humor in the Fictions of Slavery*. New York: Oxford University Press, 2008.

Carrier, David. *The Aesthetics of Comics*. University Park: Pennsylvania State University Press, 2000.

Carroll, Lewis. *Alice's Adventures in Wonderland* and *Through the Looking-Glass*. New York: Simon & Schuster, 2010.

Carroll, Noël. "Ethnicity, Race, Monstrosity: The Rhetorics of Horror and Humor." In *Engaging the Moving Image*, 88–107. New Haven: Yale University Press, 2003.

———. "Horror and Humor." *Journal of Aesthetics and Art Criticism* 57 (1999): 145–60.

Carson, Rachel. *Silent Spring*. New York: Houghton Mifflin, 1962.

Caswell, Lucy Shelton. "Drawing Swords: War in American Editorial Cartoons." *American Journalism* 21, no. 2 (2004): 13–45.

Ceaser, James W. "The Origins and Character of American Exceptionalism." *American Political Thought: A Journal of Ideas, Institutions, and Culture* 1 (2012): 1–25.

Chafe, William H. *The Unfinished Journey: America Since World War II*. 5th ed. New York: Oxford University Press, 2003.

Chapman, Jane, Anna Hoyles, Andrew Kerr, and Adam Sherif. *Comics and the World Wars: A Cultural Record*. London: Palgrave Macmillan, 2015.

Chesterton, G. K. "The Unanswered Challenge." In *Eugenics and Other Evils*, 61–72. New York: Cassell and Company, 1922.

Chopra, Deepak. "Donald Trump and the Looking-Glass War." SFGate, October 9, 2018. https://www.sfgate.com/opinion/chopra/article/Donald-Trump-and-the-Looking-Glass-War-9284330.php.

Chute, Hillary L. *Disaster Drawn: Visual Witness, Comics, and Documentary Form*. Cambridge: Harvard University Press, 2016.

Cloud, Dana L. "'To Veil the Threat of Terror': Afghan Women and the <Clash of Civilizations> in the Imagery of the U.S. War on Terrorism." *Quarterly Journal of Speech* 90 (2004): 285–306.

Cohen, Charles D. *The Seuss, the Whole Seuss, and Nothing but the Seuss: A Visual Biography of Theodor Seuss Geisel*. New York: Random House, 2004.

Cohn, Carol, and Cynthia Enloe. "A Conversation with Cynthia Enloe: Feminists Look at Masculinity and the Men Who Wage War." *Signs: Journal of Women in Culture and Society* 28 (2003): 1187–107.

Combs, James E., and Dan Nimmo. *The Comedy of Democracy*. Westport: Praeger, 1996.

Connolly, William E. *Identity, Difference: Democratic Negotiation of Political Paradox*. Minneapolis: University of Minnesota Press, 1991.

Connor, Walker. "Terminological Chaos ('A Nation Is a Nation, Is a State, Is an Ethnic Group, Is a . . .')". In *Ethnonationalism: The Quest for Understanding*, 89–117. Princeton: Princeton University Press, 1994.

Consolati, Claudia. "Grotesque Bodies, Fragmented Selves: Lina Wertmüller's Women in *Love and Anarchy* (1973)." In *Italian Women Filmmakers and the Gendered Screen*, edited by Maristella Cantini, 33–52. New York: Palgrave MacMillan, 2013.

Cooley, Charles Horton. *Human Nature and the Social Order*. New York: Charles Scribner's Sons, 1902.

Cooper, Anna Julia. *A Voice from the South*. New York: Oxford University Press, 1988.

Cooper, Frederic Taber, and Arthur Bartlett Maurice. "The History of the Nineteenth Century in Caricature." In *The Bookman: An Illustrated Magazine of Literature and Life* 18 (September 1903–February 1904): 36–68.

Coppins, McKay. "False Prophet." *Atlantic*, April 15, 2020. https://

www.theatlantic.com/politics/archive/2020/04/trump-coronavirus-message/610009.

Costa, Robert, and Philip Rucker. "Trump Casts Himself as Pandemic Patron, Personalizing the Government's Spread of Cash and Supplies." *Washington Post*, April 10, 2020. https://www.washingtonpost.com/politics/trump-coronavirus-pandemic-patron-cares-act-supplies/2020/04/10/c961a192-7aad-11ea-b6ff-597f170df8f8_story.html.

Cottle, Michelle. "Drop the Curtain on the Trump Follies." *New York Times*, April 7, 2020. https://www.nytimes.com/2020/04/07/opinion/trump-coronavirus-press-conference.html.

Coupe, W. A. "Observations on a Theory of Political Caricature." *Comparative Studies in Society and History* 11, no. 1 (1969): 79–95.

Creel, George. *How We Advertised America: The First Telling of the Amazing Story of the Committee on Public Information That Carried the Gospel of Americanism to Every Corner of the Globe*. New York: Harper & Brothers, 1920.

Crowther, Hal. *An Infuriating American: The Incendiary Arts of H. L. Mencken*. Iowa City: University of Iowa Press, 2014.

Daly, Christopher B. "When the 99% Had a Paper." *Columbia Journalism Review*, January/February 25, 2012. http://www.cjr.org/essay/when_the_99_had_a_paper.php.

Davenport, Christian. "Blowing Flames into the Souls of Black Folk: Ollie Harrington and His Bombs from Berlin to Harlem." In *Black Comics: Politics of Race and Representation*, edited by Sheena C. Howard and Ronald L. Jackson II, 111–32. New York: Bloomsbury, 2013.

Davies, Christie. *Ethnic Humor Around the World: A Comparative Analysis*. Bloomington: Indiana University Press, 1997.

DeGuzmán, María. *Spain's Long Shadow: The Black Legend, Off-Whiteness, and Anglo-American Empire*. Minneapolis: University of Minneapolis Press, 2005.

Deleuze, Gilles. *Difference and Repetition*. Translated by Paul Patton. New York: Continuum, 2004.

———. *The Logic of Sense*. Translated by Mark Lester. New York: Columbia University Press, 1990.

Deleuze, Gilles, and Claire Parnet. *Dialogues II*. Translated by Hugh Tomlinson and Barbara Habberjam. New York: Columbia University Press, 1987.

Delgado, Richard, and Jean Stefancic. Introduction to *Critical Race Theory: The Cutting Edge*, xv–xix. 3rd ed. Philadelphia: Temple University Press, 2013.

Denevi, Timothy. "Fear and Loathing at CPAC 2019, or Why I Yelled at a Fascist and Regretted It." *Salon*, March 8, 2019. https://www.salon.com/2019/03/08/fear-and-loathing-at-cpac-2019-or-why-i-yelled-at-a-fascist-and-regretted-it.

Denning, Michael. *The Cultural Front*. London: Verso, 1997.

DeSousa, Michael A., and Martin J. Medhurst. "Political Cartoons and American Culture: Significant Symbols of Campaign 1980." *Studies in Visual Communication* 8 (1982): 84–97.

DesRochers, Rick. *The New Humor in the Progressive Era: Americanization and the Vaudeville Comedian.* New York: Palgrave Macmillan, 2014.

Dewey, Donald. *The Art of Ill Will: The Story of American Political Cartoons.* New York University Press, 2007.

Dolinar, Brian. *The Black Cultural Front: Black Writers and Artists of the Depression Generation.* Jackson: University of Mississippi Press, 2012.

"Donald in Wonderland." Intercepted Podcast, March 1, 2017. https://theintercept.com/2017/03/01/intercepted-podcast-donald-in-wonderland.

Dormon, James H. "Ethnic Cultures of the Mind: The Harrigan-Hart Mosaic." *American Studies* 33 (1992): 21–40.

———. "Ethnic Stereotyping in American Popular Culture: The Depiction of American Ethnics in the Cartoon Periodicals of the Gilded Age." *American Studies* 30 (1985): 489–507.

"Dr. Seuss Went to War: A Catalog of Political Cartoons." http://libraries.ucsd.edu/speccoll/dswenttowar.

Du Bois, W. E. B. "The African Roots of War." *Atlantic Monthly* (May 1915): 707–14.

———. "Awake, America," *Crisis* 14 (September 1917): 216.

———. "Close Ranks." *Crisis* 16 (July 1918): 111–14.

———. "Returning Soldiers," *Crisis* 18 (May 1919): 13.

———. "The Superior Race (An Essay)." *Smart Set: A Magazine of Cleverness* 70 (1923): 55–60.

Dudziak, Mary L. "Desegregation as a Cold War Imperative." *Stanford Law Review* 41 (1988): 61–120.

Dupree, Nancy Hatch. "Afghan Women Under the Taliban." In *Fundamentalism Reborn? Afghanistan and the Taliban*, edited by William Maley, 145–66. New York: New York University Press, 1998.

Durkee, Alison. "Trump Was Warned About the Coronavirus More Than a Dozen Times In Daily Intel Briefings." *Vanity Fair*, April 28, 2020. https://www.vanityfair.com/news/2020/04/trump-received-coronavirus-warnings-daily-intelligence-briefings-pdb.

Eco, Umberto, ed. *On Ugliness.* Translated by Alastair McEwen. New York: Rizzoli, 2011.

Edelman, Murray. *From Art to Politics: How Artistic Creations Shape Political Misconceptions.* Chicago: University of Chicago Press, 1995.

Ehrenreich, Nancy. "Disguising Empire: Racialized Masculinity and the Civilizing of Iraq." *Cleveland State Law Review* 52 (2005): 131–38. https://engagedscholarship.csuohio.edu/clevstlrev/vol52/iss1/9.

Eisenstein, Zillah. *Sexual Decoys: Gender, Race, and War in Imperial Democracy.* New York: Zed Books, 2007.

Eldridge, Lawrence Allen. *Chronicles of a Two-Front War: Civil Rights and Vietnam in the African American Press.* Columbia: University of Missouri Press, 2011.

Elick, Catherine. *Talking Animals in Children's Fiction: A Critical Study.* Jefferson: McFarland, 2015.

Ellison, Ralph. "What These Children Are Like." In *The Collected Essays of Ralph Ellison*, edited by John F.

Callahan, 542–51. New York: Random House, 2003.

"Empire On Our Minds." *Nib*, July 4, 2019. https://thenib.com/empire-on-our-minds.

Engelhardt, Tom. *The End of Victory Culture: Cold War America and the Disillusioning of a Generation*. Rev. and exp. ed. Amherst: University of Massachusetts Press, 2007.

Enloe, Cynthia H. *Bananas, Beaches, and Bases: Making Feminist Sense of International Politics*. 2nd ed. Berkeley: University of California Press, 2014.

Erlanger, Steven. "The Coronavirus Inflicts Its Own Kind of Terror." *New York Times*, April 6, 2020. https://www.nytimes.com/2020/04/06/world/europe/coronavirus-terrorism-threat-response.html.

Eskew, Glenn T. *But for Birmingham: The Local and National Movements in the Civil Rights Struggle*. Chapel Hill: University of North Carolina Press, 1997.

Faram, Mark D. *Faces of War: The Untold Story of Edward Steichen's WWII Photographers*. New York: Penguin, 2009.

Fauset, Jessie. "The Gift of Laughter." In *The New Negro: Readings on Race, Representation, and African American Culture, 1892–1938*, edited by Henry Louis Gates Jr. and Gene Andrew Jarrett, 515–18. Princeton: Princeton University Press, 2007.

Finnegan, Lisa. *No Questions Asked: News Coverage Since 9/11*. Westport: Praeger, 2007.

Fischer, David Hackett. *Liberty and Freedom: A Visual History of America's Founding Ideas*. New York: Oxford University Press, 2005.

Fisher, Walter R. "Rhetorical Fiction and the Presidency." *Quarterly Journal of Speech* 66, no. 2 (1980): 119–26.

Fletcher, Angus. *Comic Democracies: From Ancient Athens to the American Republic*. Baltimore: Johns Hopkins University Press, 2016.

Forss, Amy Helene. *Black Print with a White Carnation: Mildred Brown and the "Omaha Star" Newspaper, 1938–1989*. Lincoln: University of Nebraska Press, 2013.

Foucault, Michel. "Nietzsche, Genealogy, History." In *Language, Counter-Memory, Practice: Selected Essays and Interviews*, 139–64. Translated by Donald F. Bouchard and Sherry Simon. Ithaca: Cornell University Press, 1977.

Franklin, Benjamin. "The Dogood Papers." In *The Writings of Benjamin Franklin*, edited by Albert Henry Smith, 2–48. New York: The Macmillan Company, 1905.

Freud, Sigmund. *Wit and Its Relation to the Unconscious*. New York: Moffat, Yard, 1916.

Fuchs, Esther. "Images of Love and War in Contemporary Israeli Fiction: A Feminist Re-vision." In *Arms and the Woman: War, Gender, and Literary Representation*, edited by Helen M. Cooper, Adrienne Auslander Munich, and Susan Merrill Squier, 268–82. Chapel Hill: University of North Carolina Press, 1989.

Fussell, Paul. *Wartime: Understanding and Behavior in the Second World War*. New York: Oxford University Press, 1989.

Gaddis, John Lewis. *The United States and the Origins of the Cold War,*

1941–1947. New York: Columbia University Press, 2000.

Gaines, Kevin K. *American Africans in Ghana: Black Expatriates and the Civil Rights Era.* Chapel Hill: University of North Carolina Press, 2006.

———. "From Black Power to Civil Rights: Julian Mayfield and African American Expatriates in Nkrumah's Ghana, 1957–1966." In *Cold War Constructions: The Political Culture of United States Imperialism, 1945–1966,* edited by Christian G. Appy, 257–69. Amherst: University of Massachusetts Press, 2000.

Gallagher, Jean. *The World Wars Through the Female Gaze.* Carbondale: Southern Illinois University Press, 1998.

Gates, Henry Louis, Jr. *The Signifying Monkey: A Theory of African-American Literary Criticism.* New York: Oxford University Press, 1988.

Gates, Henry Louis, Jr. and Gene Andrew Jarrett. Introduction to *The New Negro: Readings on Race, Representation, and African American Culture, 1892–1938,* edited by Henry Louis Gates Jr. and Gene Andrew Jarrett, 1–20. Princeton: Princeton University Press, 2007.

Gilbert, Christopher J. "Bawdy Blows: VET Tv and the Comedy of Combat Masculinity." *Women's Studies in Communication* 42, no. 2 (2019): 181–201.

———. "Decolonizing Caricature: *Prosopographia* in the Comic Politics of Marty Two Bulls, Sr." in *Decolonizing Native American Rhetoric: Communicating Self-Determination,* edited by Casey Ryan Kelly and Jason Edward Black, 127–51. New York: Peter Lang, 2018.

———. "Obama the Grotesque: A Parade of Racial Horribles." *Rhetoric Review* 36, no. 4 (2017): 311–20.

Gilbert, Christopher J., and John Louis Lucaites. "Bringing War Down to Earth: The Dialectic of Pity and Compassion in *Doonsbury*'s View of Combat Trauma." *Quarterly Journal of Speech* 101, no. 2 (2015): 379–404.

Gilbert, Sophie. "The Complicated Relevance of Dr. Seuss's Political Cartoons." *Atlantic,* January 31, 2017. https://www.theatlantic.com/entertainment/archive/2017/01/dr-seuss-protest-icon/515031.

Gillota, David. *Ethnic Humor in Multiethnic America.* New Brunswick: Rutgers University Press, 2013.

Giroux, Henry A. *America at War with Itself.* San Francisco: City Lights, 2017.

———. "The COVID-19 Pandemic Is Exposing the Plague of Neoliberalism." Truthout, April 7, 2020. https://truthout.org/articles/the-covid-19-pandemic-is-exposing-the-plague-of-neoliberalism.

———. "War on Terror: The Militarizing of Public Space and Culture in the United States." *Third Text* 18 (2004): 211–21.

Gisbertz, Anna-Katharina. "On Beauty and Its Challenges: Friedrich Theodor Vischer and Karl Marx." In *Aesthetic Marx,* edited by Samir Gandesha and Johan F. Hartle, 97–110. New York: Bloomsbury Academic, 2017.

Glasser, Susan B. "The Trump O'Clock Follies." *New Yorker,* March 27, 2020. https://www.newyorker.com

/news/letter-from-trumps-washington/the-trump-oclock-follies.
Gombrich, E. H. *Art and Illusion: A Study in the Psychology of Pictorial Representation*. Princeton: Princeton University Press, 2000.
———. "The Evidence of Images." In *Interpretation: Theory and Practice*, edited by Charles S. Singleton, 51–56. Baltimore: Johns Hopkins University Press, 1969.
Gombrich, E. H., and Ernst Kris. *Caricature*. Harmondsworth, UK: Penguin, 1940.
Gotham, Kevin Fox. *Race, Real Estate, and Uneven Development: The Kansas City Experience, 1900–2010*. Albany: State University of New York Press, 2014.
Gournelos, Ted, and Viveca Greene, eds. *A Decade of Dark Humor: How Comedy, Irony, and Satire Shaped Post-9/11 America*. Jackson: University Press of Mississippi, 2011.
Gramsci, Antonio. "War Is War." *L'Ordine Nuovo* 31, 1921.
Griffin, Roger. *The Nature of Fascism*. New York: Routledge, 1993.
Hall, N. John. *Max Beerbohm Caricatures*. New Haven: Yale University Press, 1997.
Hall, Stuart. "New Ethnicities." In *Stuart Hall: Critical Dialogues in Cultural Studies*, edited by David Morley and Kuan-Hsing Chen, 442–51. New York: Routledge, 1996.
Hannoosh, Michèle. *Baudelaire and Caricature: From the Comic to an Art of Modernity*. University Park: Pennsylvania State University Press, 1992.
Harrington, Michael. *The Other America: Poverty in the United States*. New York: Simon & Schuster, 1997.
Harrington, Oliver W. *Why I Left America and Other Essays*. Jackson: University Press of Mississippi, 2010.
Harrison, Brigid C. "An Interview with Ann Telnaes." *PS: Political Science and Politics* 40, no. 2 (2007): 233–36.
Hartelius, E. Johanna, ed. *The Rhetorics of US Immigration: Identity, Community, Otherness*. University Park: Pennsylvania State University Press, 2015.
Hartman, Andrew. "Culture Wars Are Dead. Long Live the Culture Wars!" *Baffler*, no. 39 (May 2018). https://thebaffler.com/outbursts/culture-wars-are-dead-hartman.
Hauser, Gerard A., and Amy Grim, eds. *Rhetorical Democracy: Discursive Practices of Civic Engagement*. Mahwah, NJ: Lawrence Erlbaum Associates, 2004.
Haytock, Jennifer Anne. *At Home, at War: Domesticity and World War I in American Literature*. Columbus: Ohio State University Press, 2003.
Hazlitt, Henry. "Truth About 'Appeasement.'" *New York Times*, September 17, 1940.
Hecht, George J. "How the Cartoonists Can Help Win the War." *Cartoons Magazine* 13 (1918): 260–64.
———, ed. *The War in Cartoons: A History of the War in 100 Cartoons by 27 of the Most Prominent American Cartoonists*. New York: E. P. Dutton, 1919.
Heer, Jeet. "Why the Paper of Record Hates Cartoons." *Nation*, June 18, 2019. https://www.thenation.com/article/new-york-times-netanyahu-cartoon-bennet.
Heller, Steven, and Gail Anderson. *The Savage Mirror: The Art of*

Contemporary Caricature. New York: Watson-Guptill, 1992.

Hepburn, Mary A. "Educating for Democracy: The Years Following World War II." *Social Studies* 81, no. 4 (1990): 153–60.

Hersh, Seymour M. "The Stovepipe." *New Yorker*, October 27, 2003. http://www.newyorker.com/magazine/2003/10/27/the-stovepipe.

Hervey, Mary F. S. *Holbein's "Ambassadors": The Picture and the Men*. London: George Bell and Sons, 1900.

Hess, Stephen, and Sandy Northrop. *American Political Cartoons: The Evolution of a National Identity, 1754–2010*. New Brunswick: Transaction, 2010.

Hills, Patricia. "Cultural Racism: Resistance and Accommodation in the Civil War Art of Eastman Johnston and Thomas Nast." In *Seeing High and Low: Representing Social Conflict in American Visual Culture*, edited by Patricia Johnston, 102–23. Berkeley: University of California Press, 2006.

Hingham, John. *Strangers in the Land: Patterns of American Nativism, 1860–1925*. New Brunswick: Rutgers University Press, 1955.

Hinton, Colonel Richard J. "'Uncle Sam' as a Business Man." *Chautauquan: A Magazine for Self-Education* 32 (February 1901): 481–89.

Hollihan, Thomas A. "Propagandizing in the Interest of War: A Rhetorical Study of the Committee on Public Information." *Southern Speech Communication Journal* 49, no. 3 (1984): 241–57.

Holzer, Harold. "With Malice Toward Both: Abraham Lincoln and Jefferson Davis in Caricature." In *Wars Within a War: Controversy and Conflict over the American Civil War*, edited by Joan Waugh and Gary W. Gallagher, 109–36. Chapel Hill: University of North Carolina Press, 2009.

Horen, Gerd. *Radio Goes to War: The Cultural Politics of Propaganda During World War II*. Berkeley: University of California Press, 2002.

Horne, Gerald. *The End of Empires: African Americans and India*. Philadelphia: Temple University Press, 2008.

Horton, Scott. "George W. Bush, War President." Browsings: The Harper's Blog, May 28, 2010. https://harpers.org/blog/2010/05/george-w-bush-war-president.

Howes, Franny. "Imagining a Multiplicity of Visual Rhetorical Traditions: Comics Lessons from Rhetoric Histories." *ImageText* 5, no. 3 (2010). http://www.english.ufl.edu/imagetext/archives/v5_3/howes.

Hughes, Langston. Introduction to *Bootsie and Others: A Selection of Cartoons by Ollie Harrington*, n.p. New York: Dodd, Mead, 1958.

Huntington, Samuel P. *Who Are We? The Challenges to America's National Identity*. New York: Simon & Schuster, 2004.

Huspeck, Michael. "Transgressive Rhetoric in Deliberative Democracy: The Black Press." In *Critical Rhetorics of Race*, edited by Michael G. Lacy and Kent A. Ono, 159–76. New York: New York University Press, 2011.

Inge, M. Thomas. *Dark Laughter: The Satiric Art of Oliver W. Harrington*. Jackson: University of Mississippi Press, 1993.

Ingebretsen, Edward J. *At Stake: Monsters and the Rhetoric of Fear in Public Culture*. Chicago: University of Chicago Press, 2001.

Irigaray, Luce. *This Sex Which Is Not One*. Translated by Catherine Porter. Ithaca: Cornell University Press, 1985.

Ivy, James W. "Mordant Satire." *Crisis* 65, no. 8 (1958): 523.

James, Pearl. "Introduction: Reading World War I Posters." In *Picture This: World War I Posters and Visual Culture*, 1–36. Lincoln: University of Nebraska Press, 2009.

Jenkins, Henry. "'No Matter How Small': The Democratic Imagination of Dr. Seuss." In *Hop on Pop: The Politics and Pleasures of Popular Culture*, edited by Henry Jenkins, Tara McPherson, and Jane Shattuc, 187–208. Durham: Duke University Press, 2002.

Jones, Ann. "The War Against Women, at Home and Abroad." *Nation*, March 21, 2013. http://www.thenation.com/article/173463/war-against-women-home-and-abroad#.

———. *War Is Not Over When It's Over: Women and the Unseen Consequences of War*. New York: Metropolitan Books, 2010.

Jones, Brian Jay. *Becoming Dr. Seuss: Theodor Geisel and the Making of an American Imagination*. New York: Dutton, 2019.

Kallen, Horace M. "Democracy Versus the Melting-Pot: A Study of American Nationality." *Nation*, February 25, 1915, 190–94, 217–20.

Kammen, Michael. *People of Paradox: An Inquiry Concerning the Origins of American Civilization*. Ithaca: Cornell University Press, 1972.

Katz, Cindi. "Banal Terrorism: Spatial Fetishism and Everyday Insecurity." In *Violent Geographies: Fear, Terror, and Political Violence*, edited by Derek Gregory and Allan Pred, 349–61. New York: Routledge, 2007.

Keene, Jennifer D. "Images of Racial Pride: African American Propaganda Posters in the First World War." In *Picture This: World War I Posters and Visual Culture*, edited by Pearl James, 207–40. Lincoln: University of Nebraska Press, 2009.

Kellner, Douglas. "Bushspeak and the Politics of Lying: Presidential Rhetoric in the 'War on Terror.'" *Presidential Studies Quarterly* 37, no. 4 (2007): 622–45.

———. "The Media and the Crisis of Democracy in the Age of Bush-2." *Communication and Critical/Cultural Studies* 1, no. 1 (2004): 29–58.

———. "9/11, Spectacles of Terror, and Media Manipulation: A Critique of Jihadist and Bush Media Politics." *Critical Discourse Studies* 1, no. 1 (2004): 41–64.

Kellogg, Paul U. "The Negro Pioneers." In *The New Negro*, edited by Alain Locke, 271–77. New York: Touchstone, 1925.

Kemnitz, Thomas Milton. "The Cartoon as a Historical Source." *Journal of Interdisciplinary History* 4, no. 1 (1973): 81–93.

Kennedy, David M. *Over Here: The First World War and American Society*. New York: Oxford University Press, 1980.

Kennedy, Martha H. "Ann Telnaes, Cartoonist: Singular in Style and Substance." In *Humor's Edge:*

Cartoons by Ann Telnaes, 12–19. San Francisco: Pomegranate, 2004.

Kercher, Stephen E. *Revel with a Cause: Liberal Satire in Postwar America*. Chicago: University of Chicago Press, 2006.

Kersten, Andrew E. *Labor's Home Front: The American Federation of Labor During World War II*. New York University Press, 2006.

Khan, Shahnaz. "Between Here and There: Feminist Solidarity and Afghan Women." *Genders* 33 (2001). https://www.colorado.edu/gendersarchive1998-2013/2001/03/01/between-here-and-there-feminist-solidarity-and-afghan-women.

Kimball, Warren F. *The Juggler: Franklin Roosevelt as Wartime Statesman*. Princeton: Princeton University Press, 1991.

Kimble, James J., and Lester C. Olson. "Visual Rhetoric Representing Rosie the Riveter: Myth and Misconception in J. Howard Miller's 'We Can Do It!' Poster." *Rhetoric and Public Affairs* 9, no. 4 (2006): 533–69.

King, Martin Luther, Jr. "The Last Steep Ascent." *Nation*, March 14, 1966. http://www.thenation.com/article/157689/last-steep-ascent.

Kitch, Carolyn. *The Girl on the Magazine Cover: The Origins of Visual Stereotypes in American Mass Media*. Chapel Hill: University of North Carolina Press, 2001.

Klein, Naomi. *The Shock Doctrine: The Rise of Disaster Capitalism*. New York: Picador, 2007.

Knopf, Christina M. *The Comic Art of War: A Critical Study of Military Cartoons, 1805–2014, with a Guide to Artists*. Jefferson: McFarland, 2015.

Koestler, Arthur. *The Act of Creation*. London: Hutchinson, 1964.

Koppelman, Alex. "The Trump Farce." *New Yorker*, February 2, 2012. https://www.newyorker.com/news/news-desk/the-trump-farce.

Kris, Ernst, and Ernst Gombrich. "The Principles of Caricature." *British Journal of Medical Psychology* 17 (1938): 319–42.

Kwon, Heonik. *The Other Cold War*. New York: Columbia University Press, 2010.

Laclau, Ernesto. "On Imagined Communities." In *Grounds of Comparison: Around the Work of Benedict Anderson*, edited by Jonathan Culler and Pheng Cheah, 21–28. New York: Routledge, 2003.

Lamb, Chris. *Drawn to Extremes: The Use and Abuse of Editorial Cartoons*. New York: Columbia University Press, 2004.

———. "The Fixable Decline of Editorial Cartooning." *Nieman Reports*, December 15, 2004. https://niemanreports.org/articles/the-fixable-decline-of-editorial-cartooning.

Lasswell, Harold D. *Propaganda Technique in World War I*. Cambridge: MIT Press, 1971.

LeBlanc, Paul. "Trump Calls Coronavirus a 'Foreign Virus' in Oval Office Address." CNN, March 11, 2020. https://www.cnn.com/2020/03/11/politics/coronavirus-trump-foreign-virus/index.html.

Legman, G. *Rationale of the Dirty Joke: An Analysis of Sexual Humor*. New York: Simon & Schuster, 1968.

Levin, Harry. "Veins of Humor." In *Playboys and Killjoys: An Essay on the Theory and Practice of Comedy*,

175–91. New York: Oxford University Press, 1987.
Lewis, George. *Massive Resistance: The White Response to the Civil Rights Movement.* New York: Bloomsbury, 2006.
Lewis, Paul. *Cracking Up: American Humor in a Time of Conflict.* Chicago: University of Chicago Press, 2006.
Lieven, Anatol. *America Right or Wrong: An Anatomy of American Nationalism.* New York: Oxford University Press, 2004.
Lim, Elvin T. *The Anti-Intellectual Presidency: The Decline of Presidential Rhetoric from George Washington to George W. Bush.* New York: Oxford University Press, 2008.
Lippman, Walter. *Public Opinion.* New York: Harcourt, Brace, 1922.
Lockwood, Jeffrey A. *Six-Legged Soldiers: Using Insects as Weapons of War.* New York: Oxford University Press, 2009.
Lowe, John. "Theories of Ethnic Humor: How to Enter, Laughing." *American Quarterly* 38, no. 3 (1986): 439–60.
Lubin, David M. *Grand Illusions: American Art and the First World War.* New York: Oxford University Press, 2016.
Luce, Henry. "The American Century." *Life*, February 17, 1941.
Lustick, Ian S. *Trapped in the War on Terror.* Philadelphia: University of Pennsylvania Press, 2006.
Lynch, Bohun. *A History of Caricature.* London: Faber and Gwyer, 1926.
Lyotard, Jean-François. "Fiscourse Digure: The Utopia Behind the Scenes of the Phantasy." In *Discourse, Figure*, 327–54. Translated by Antony Hudek and Mary Lydon. Minneapolis: University of Minnesota Press, 2011.
Lyotard, Jean-François, and Jean-Loup Thébaud. *Just Gaming.* Translated by Wlad Godzich. Minneapolis: University of Minnesota Press, 1985.
Ma, Sheng-Mei. *The Deathly Embrace: Orientalism and Asian American Identity.* Minneapolis: University of Minnesota Press, 2000.
MacDonnell, Francis. *Insidious Foes: The Axis Fifth Column and the American Home Front.* New York: Oxford University Press, 1995.
The Magazine of Science, and School of Arts. Vol. 1. 3rd ed. London: W. Brittain, II, 1842.
Mann, Bonnie. *Sovereign Masculinity: Gender Lessons from the War on Terror.* New York: Oxford University Press, 2014.
Marcoci, Roxana. *Comic Abstraction: Image-Breaking, Image-Making.* New York: Museum of Modern Art, 2007.
Markovitz, Jonathan. *Legacies of Lynching: Racial Violence and Memory.* Minneapolis: University of Minnesota Press, 2004.
Marvin, Carolyn, and David W. Ingle. *Blood Sacrifice and the Nation: Totem Rituals and the American Flag.* New York: Cambridge University Press, 1999.
Marx, Karl. "An Exchange of Letters" [Marx to Ruge: On the Canal-Boat Going to D., March 1843]. In *Writings of Young Marx on Philosophy and Society*, edited by D. Easton and Kurt H. Guddat, 203–15. Garden City: Doubleday, 1967.
Masson, Tom. "Our Beginnings." *Life* 49 (January–March 1907): 340–43.

https://catalog.hathitrust.org/Record/000548237.

Maurice, Arthur Bartlett. "International Wit and Humor as Expressed in Caricature." In *The World's Wit and Humor*, edited by Lionel Strachey, 11:231–92. Rahway: Quinn & Boden, 1906.

Maurice, Arthur Bartlett, and Frederic Taber Cooper. *The History of the Nineteenth Century in Caricature*. New York: Dodd, Mead, 1904.

Maxwell, William J. *New Negro, Old Left: African-American Writing and Communism Between the Wars*. New York: Columbia University Press, 1999.

McCartney, Paul T. *Power and Progress: American National Identity, the War of 1898, and the Rise of American Imperialism*. Baton Rouge: Louisiana State University Press, 2006.

McDaniel, James Patrick. "Speaking Like a State: Listening to Benjamin Franklin in Times of Terror." *Communication and Critical / Cultural Studies* 2 (2005): 324–50.

McDaniel, James P., and Bruce E. Gronbeck. "Through the Looking Glass and Back: Democratic Theory, Rhetoric, and Barbiegate." In *The Prettier Doll: Rhetoric, Discourse, and Ordinary Democracy*, edited by Karen Tracy, James P. McDaniel, and Bruce E. Gronbeck, 22–42. Tuscaloosa: University of Alabama Press, 2007.

McKibben, Bill. "Trump's Stupid and Reckless Climate Decision." *New York Times*, June 1, 2017. https://www.nytimes.com/2017/06/01/opinion/trump-paris-climate-accord.html.

McLees, Ainslie Armstrong. *Baudelaire's "Argot Plastique": Poetic Caricature and Modernism*. Athens: University of Georgia Press, 1989.

Mead, George Herbert. "The Genesis of the Self and Social Control." *International Journal of Ethics* 35 (1925): 251–77.

Meeker, Joseph W. *The Comedy of Survival: Literary Ecology and a Play Ethic*. 3rd ed. Tucson: University of Arizona Press, 1997.

Mencken, H. L. "Bayard vs. Lionheart." *Evening Sun*, July 26, 1920. https://www.newspapers.com/clip/21831908/hl_mencken_article_26_jul_1920_the.

Meredith, George. "On the Idea of Comedy and of the Uses of the Comic Spirit." In *The Works of George Meredith*, 23:3–55. New York: Charles Scribner's Sons, 1910.

Meyer, Susan E. *James Montgomery Flagg: A Portrait of America*. New York: Watson-Guptill, 1974.

Miller, Bonnie M. *From Liberation to Conquest: The Visual and Popular Cultures of the Spanish-American War of 1898*. Amherst: University of Massachusetts Press, 2011.

Miller, David. *Citizenship and National Identity*. Cambridge, UK: Polity, 2002.

Minear, Richard H. *Dr. Seuss Goes to War: The World War II Editorial Cartoons of Theodor Seuss Geisel*. New York: The New Press, 1999.

Mintz, Lawrence E. "Humor and Ethnic Stereotypes in Vaudeville and Burlesque." *MELUS* 21, no. 4 (1996): 19–28.

Mintz, Steven. "The Changing Face of Children's Culture." In *Reinventing Childhood After World War II*, edited by Paula S. Fass and Michael

Grossberg, 38–50. Philadelphia: University of Pennsylvania Press, 2012.

Mitchell, W. J. T. *Cloning Terror: The War of Images, 9/11 to the Present*. Chicago: University of Chicago Press, 2011.

———. *What Do Pictures Want? The Lives and Loves of Images*. Chicago: University of Chicago Press, 2005.

Morgan, Judith, and Neil Morgan. *Dr. Seuss and Mr. Geisel: A Biography*. New York: De Capo Press, 1996.

Morgan, Winifred. *An American Icon: Brother Jonathan and American Identity*. Cranbury, NJ: Associated University Presses, 1988.

Mulford, Carla J. *Benjamin Franklin and the Ends of Empire*. New York: Oxford University Press, 2015.

National Commission on Terrorist Attacks upon the United States. *The 9/11 Commission Report: Final Report of the National Commission on Terrorist Attacks upon the United States*. Washington, DC: National Commission on Terrorist Attacks upon the United States, 2004.

Neiberg, Michael S. *The Path to War: How the First World War Created Modern America*. New York: Oxford University Press, 2016.

Nel, Philip. *Dr. Seuss: American Icon*. New York: Continuum, 2005.

———. "Dr. Seuss vs. Adolf Hitler: A Political Education." In *Dr. Seuss: American Icon*, 39–62. New York: Continuum, 2004.

———. "'Said a Bird in the Midst of a Blitz...': How World War II Created Dr. Seuss." *Mosaic: An Interdisciplinary Critical Journal* 34, no. 2 (2001): 65–85.

———. "Was the Cat in the Hat Black? Exploring Dr. Seuss's Racial Imagination." *Children's Literature* 42, no. 4 (2014): 71–98.

Nickels, Cameron C. *Civil War Humor*. Jackson: University Press of Mississippi, 2010.

Nussbaum, Martha C. *Anger and Forgiveness: Resentment, Generosity, Justice*. New York: Oxford University Press, 2016.

O'Leary, Cecilia. *To Die For: The Paradox of American Patriotism*. Princeton: Princeton University Press, 2000.

Olson, Lester C. "MAGNA Britannia: Her Colonies REDUC'D, 1765–66." In *Benjamin Franklin's Vision of American Community: A Study in Rhetorical Iconology*, 77–111. Columbia: University of South Carolina Press, 2004.

Olson, Lynne. *Those Angry Days: Roosevelt, Lindbergh, and America's Fight Over World War II, 1939–1941*. New York: Random House, 2013.

Ong, Walter J. *Fighting for Life: Contest, Sexuality, and Consciousness*. Ithaca: Cornell University Press, 1981.

Oring, Elliott. "Colonizing Humor." In *Engaging Humor*, 97–115. Urbana: University of Illinois Press, 2003.

O'Toole, Fintan. "Donald Trump Has Destroyed the Country He Promised to Make Great Again." *Irish Times*, April 25, 2020. https://www.irishtimes.com/opinion/fintan-o-toole-donald-trump-has-destroyed-the-country-he-promised-to-make-great-again-1.4235928.

Ott, Brian L., and Greg Dickinson. *The Twitter Presidency: Donald J. Trump and the Politics of White Rage*. New York: Routledge, 2019.

Painter, Nell Irvin. *Standing at Armageddon: The United States, 1877–1919*. New York: W. W. Norton, 1987.

Pak, Jung H. "The Good, the Bad, and the Ugly at the US–North Korea Summit in Hanoi." Brookings, March 4, 2019. https://www.brookings.edu/blog/order-from-chaos/2019/03/04/the-good-the-bad-and-the-ugly-at-the-us-north-korea-summit-in-hanoi.

Parenti, Christian. *The Soft Cage: Surveillance in America from Slavery to the War on Terror*. Cambridge: Basic Books, 2003.

Parham, Jason. "Depth of Field: The Metaphor of Trump and the MAGA Hat." *Wired*, June 20, 2019. https://www.wired.com/story/depth-of-field-trump-maga-hat.

Parry-Giles, Shawn J. *The Rhetorical Presidency, Propaganda, and the Cold War, 1945–1955*. Westport: Praeger, 2002.

Peacock, Margaret. *Innocent Weapons: The Soviet and American Politics of Childhood in the Cold War*. Chapel Hill: University of North Carolina Press, 2014.

Peirce, C. S. "Man's Glassy Essence." *Monist* 3 (October 1892): 1–22.

Perez, Louis A., Jr. *Cuba in the American Imagination: Metaphor and the Imperial Ethos*. Chapel Hill: University of North Carolina Press, 2008.

Perkins, David. "A Definition of Caricature and Caricature and Recognition." *Studies in the Anthropology of Visual Communication* 2, no. 1 (1975): 1–24.

Perper, Rosie. "Bob Woodward Said Trump Nearly Provoked North Korea into War with a Single Tweet." *Business Insider*, September 9, 2018. https://www.businessinsider.com/trump-north-korea-bob-woodward-2018-9.

Pierce, Charles P. *Idiot America: How Stupidity Became a Virtue in the Land of the Free*. New York: Random House, 2009.

Porterfield, Todd. "The Efflorescence of Caricature." In *The Efflorescence of Caricature, 1759–1838*, edited by Todd Porterfield, 1–11. New York: Routledge, 2011.

Prattis, P. L. "The Role of the Negro Press in Race Relations." *Phylon* 7 (1946): 273–83.

Quadagno, Jill. *The Color of Welfare: How Racism Undermined the War on Poverty*. New York: Oxford University Press, 1995.

Rai, Amit S. "Of Monsters: Biopower, Terrorism and Excess in Genealogies of Monstrosity." *Cultural Studies* 18, no. 4 (2004): 538–70.

Raskin, Victor. "Ethnic Humor." In *Semantic Mechanisms of Humor*, 180–221. Hingham: Kluwer Academic, 1985.

"Rattlesnake as a Symbol of America." *American Heritage* 39, no. 2 (March 1988), https://www.americanheritage.com/rattle-snake-symbol-america.

Rattray, Robert Sutherland. *Ashanti Proverbs (The Primitive Ethics of a Savage People)*. Oxford: Clarendon Press, 1916.

"Reviewed Work: Akan-Ashanti Folk-Tales by R. S. Rattray." *Journal of American Folklore* 44 (1931): 307–9.

"The Right Way in Iraq." *Los Angeles Times*, March 14, 2003. http://articles.latimes.com/2003/mar/14/opinion/ed-iraq14.

Ritterhouse, Jennifer. *Growing Up Jim Crow: How Black and White Southern Children Learned Race*. Chapel Hill: University of North Carolina Press, 2006.

"The Road to Victory, 1942." PhotoEphemera: Poking Through the Dustbin of Photographic History, March 22, 2009. http://photemera.blogspot.com/2009/03/road-to-victory-1942.html.

Rosenkranz, Karl. *Aesthetics of Ugliness: A Critical Edition*. Translated by Andrei Pop. London: Bloomsbury, 2015.

Rosenthal, Daniel J., and Loren DeJonge Schulman. "Trump's Secret War on Terror." *Atlantic*, August 10, 2018. https://www.theatlantic.com/international/archive/2018/08/trump-war-terror-drones/567218.

Rostow, Eugene V. *Toward Managed Peace: The National Security Interests of the United States, 1759 to the Present*. New Haven: Yale University Press, 1993.

Rourke, Constance. *American Humor: A Study of the National Character*. New York: New York Review of Books, 1931.

Rudwick, Elliott M. "W. E. B. Du Bois in the Role of Crisis Editor." *Journal of Negro History* 43 (1958): 214–40.

Ruotsila, Markku. *British and American Anticommunism Before the Cold War*. Portland, OR: Frank Cass, 2001.

Russell, Edmund P., III. "'Speaking of Annihilation': Mobilizing for War Against Human and Insect Enemies, 1914–1945." *Journal of American History* 82 (1996): 1505–29.

———. *War and Nature: Fighting Humans and Insects with Chemicals from World War I to Silent Spring*. New York: Cambridge University Press, 2001.

Said, Edward. "Arabs, Islam, and the Dogmas of the West." In *Orientalism: A Reader*, edited by Alexander Lyon Macfie, 104–5. New York University Press, 2000.

Salime, Zakia. "The War on Terrorism: Appropriation and Subversion by Moroccan Women." *Signs: Journal of Women and Culture in Society* 33, no. 1 (2007): 1–24.

Scher, Bill. "The Culture War President." *Politico*, September 27, 2017. https://www.politico.com/magazine/story/2017/09/27/trump-culture-war-215653.

Schmidt, Donald E. *The Folly of War: American Foreign Policy, 1898–2005*. New York: Algora, 2005.

Schuck, Peter H. "The Immigration System Today." In *Citizens, Strangers, and In-Betweens: Essays on Immigration and Citizenship*, 3–16. New York: Routledge, 1998.

Schwarz, Frederick A. O., Jr. and Aziz Z. Huq. *Unchecked and Unbalanced: Presidential Power in a Time of Terror*. New York: The New Press, 2008.

Scott, Cord A. *Comics and Conflict: Patriotism and Propaganda from WWII Through Operation Iraqi Freedom*. Annapolis: Naval Institute Press, 2014.

Scott, Maria C. *Baudelaire's "Le Spleen de Paris": Shifting Perspectives*. New York: Routledge, 2005.

Seldes, George. *Facts and Fascism*. New York: IN Fact, 1943.

Selod, Saher. *Forever Suspect: Racialized Surveillance of Muslim Americans in the War on Terror*. New

Brunswick: Rutgers University Press, 2018.

SenGupta, Gunja. *From Slavery to Poverty: The Racial Origins of Welfare in New York, 1840–1918.* New York: New York University Press, 2009.

Senna, Car. *The Black Press and the Struggle for Civil Rights.* London: Franklin Watts, 1993.

Serwer, Adam. "What Americans Do Now Will Define Us Forever." *Atlantic,* July 18, 2019. https://www.theatlantic.com/ideas/archive/2019/07/send-her-back-battle-will-define-us-forever/594307.

Shafer, Jack. "Trump's American Emperor Moment." *Politico,* June 5, 2019. https://www.politico.com/magazine/story/2019/06/05/trumps-american-emperor-moment-227049.

Shane, Peter M. *Madison's Nightmare: How Executive Power Threatens American Democracy.* Chicago: University of Chicago Press, 2009.

Shepard, Paul. *Thinking Animals: Animals and the Development of Human Intelligence.* Athens: University of Georgia Press, 1978.

Sherwood, Margaret. "Uncle Sam." *Atlantic Monthly* 121 (January–June 1918): 330–33.

Shorris, Earl. "The National Character." *Harper's Magazine,* June 2007. https://harpers.org/archive/2007/06/the-national-character.

Shrum, Rebecca K. *In the Looking Glass: Mirrors and Identity in Early America.* Baltimore: Johns Hopkins University Press, 2017.

Simmons, Charles A. *The African American Press: A History of News Coverage During National Crises, with Special Reference to Four Black Newspapers, 1827–1965.* Jefferson: McFarland, 1998.

Singh, Devin. "This Is What Ancient Greeks Would Have Called Donald Trump." *Time,* March 18, 2016. https://time.com/4261816/trump-ancient-greeks.

Smith, Shane A. "*The Crisis* in the Great War: W. E. B. Du Bois and His Perception of African-American Participation in World War I." *Historian* 70, no. 2 (2008): 239–62.

Spaulding, Amy E. *The Art of Storytelling: Telling Truths Through Telling Stories.* Lanham, MD: Scarecrow Press, 2011.

Spigel, Lynn. "Entertainment Wars: Television Culture After 9/11." *American Quarterly* 56, no. 2 (2004): 235–70.

Spivak, Gayatri Chakravorty. "Terror: A Speech After 9–11." *boundary 2* 31, no. 2 (2004): 81–111.

Stabile, Carol A., and Deepa Kumar. "Unveiling Imperialism: Media, Gender and the War on Afghanistan." *Media, Culture and Society* 27, no. 5 (2005): 765–82.

Stahl, Roger. *Militainment, Inc: War, Media, and Popular Culture.* New York: Routledge, 2009.

Steuter, Erin, and Deborah Wills. *At War with Metaphor: Media, Propaganda, and Racism in the War on Terror.* Lanham, MD: Lexington Books, 2008.

Stevens, John D. "Reflections in a Dark Mirror: Comic Strips in Black Newspapers." *Journal of Popular Culture* 10, no. 1 (1976): 239–44.

Stevenson, Richard W. "President Makes It Clear: Phrase Is 'War on Terror.'" *New York Times,* August 4, 2005. http://www.nytimes.com/2005/08/04/politics/04bush.html.

Streicher, Lawrence H. "On a Theory of Political Caricature." *Comparative Studies in Society and History* 9, no. 4 (1967): 427–45.

Stuckey, Mary E. *Defining Americans: The Presidency and National Identity*. Lawrence: University Press of Kansas, 2004.

———. "'The Domain of Public Conscience': Woodrow Wilson and the Establishment of a Transcendent Political Order." *Rhetoric and Public Affairs* 6, no. 1 (2003): 1–23.

———. *The Good Neighbor: Franklin D. Roosevelt and the Rhetoric of American Power*. East Lansing: Michigan State University Press, 2013.

Summerfield, Penny. "Gender and War in the Twentieth Century." In *The American Experience in World War II*, edited by Walter Hixson, 3–13. New York: Routledge, 2003.

Szpunar, Piotr M. *Homegrown: Identity and Difference in the American War on Terror*. New York: New York University Press, 2018.

Telnaes, Ann. *Humor's Edge: Cartoons by Ann Telnaes*. San Francisco: Pomegranate, 2004.

———. *Dick*. Cartoonist Group, 2006.

Theiss-Morse, Elizabeth. *Who Counts as an American? The Boundaries of National Identity*. New York: Cambridge University Press, 2009.

Tholas-Disset, Clémentine, and Karen A. Ritzenhoff. *Humor, Entertainment, and Popular Culture During World War I*. New York: Palgrave Macmillan, 2015.

Thurston, Michael. "'Bombed in Spain': Langston Hughes, the Black Press, and the Spanish Civil War." In *The Black Press: New Literary and Historical Essays*, edited by Todd Vogel, 140–58. Piscataway: Rutgers University Press, 2001.

Tillery, Alvin B., Jr. "Black Americans and the Creation of America's Africa Policies: The De-Racialization of Pan-African Politics." In *The African Diaspora: African Origins and New World Identities*, edited by Isidore Okpewho, Carole Boyce Davies, and Ali A. Mazrui, 504–25. Bloomington: Indiana University Press, 1999.

Tougas, Shelly. *Birmingham 1963: How a Photograph Rallied Civil Rights Support*. Mankato: Compass Point, 2011.

Trout, Steven. *On the Battlefield of Memory: The First World War and American Remembrance, 1919–1941*. Tuscaloosa: University of Alabama Press, 2010.

Tulis, Jeffrey K. *The Rhetorical Presidency*. 2nd ed. Princeton: Princeton University Press, 2017.

Turley, David. "David Low and America, 1936–1950." *Journal of American Studies* 21 (1987): 183–205.

Twain, Mark. *Letters From the Earth*. Edited by Bernard DeVoto. New York: Fawcett Crest, 1966.

"2 Klansmen Face Charges in Clash." *New York Times*, January 20, 1958.

US Committee on Public Information. *The Creel Report: Complete Report of the Chairman of the Committee on Public Information 1917; 1918; 1919. 1920*. Reprint, New York: DaCapo, 1972.

Varisco, Daniel Martin. *Reading Orientalism: Said and the Unsaid*. Seattle: University of Washington Press, 2007.

Vogel, Todd. Introduction to *The Black Press: New Literary and Historical*

Essays. Piscataway: Rutgers University Press, 2001.
Von Eschen, Penny M. "Who's the Real Ambassador? Exploding Cold War Racial Ideology." In *Cold War Constructions: The Political Culture of United States Imperialism, 1945–1966*, edited by Christian G. Appy, 110–31. Amherst: University of Massachusetts Press, 2000.
Vonnegut, Kurt. *Deadeye Dick*. 1982. Reprint, New York: Dial Press, 2010.
W., H. "Slick, Downing, Crockett, Etc." *London and Westminster Review* 32 (December 1838): 136–45.
Waldstreicher, David. *In the Midst of Perpetual Fetes: The Making of American Nationalism, 1776–1820*. Chapel Hill: University of North Carolina Press, 1997.
Wallace, David Foster. "Just Asking." *Atlantic*, November 2007. https://www.theatlantic.com/magazine/archive/2007/11/just-asking/306288.
Walters, Ronald W. *Pan Africanism in the African Diaspora: An Analysis of Modern Afrocentric Political Movements*. Detroit: Wayne State University Press, 1993.
Wanzo, Rebecca. *The Content of Our Caricature: African American Comic Art and Political Belonging*. New York: New York University Press, 2020.
"The War Against Women." *New York Times*, January 12, 2003. http://www.nytimes.com/2003/01/12/opinion/the-war-against-women.html.
"War in the Ruins of Diplomacy." *New York Times*, March 18, 2003. http://www.nytimes.com/2003/03/18/opinion/war-in-the-ruins-of-diplomacy.html.
Warner, Marina. *Monuments and Maidens: The Allegory of the Female Form*. Berkeley: University of California Press, 1985.
Washburn, Patrick S. *The African American Newspaper: Voice of Freedom*. Evanston: Northwestern University Press, 2006.
Watkins, Mel. *On the Real Side: A History of African American Comedy*. New York: Simon & Schuster, 1994.
Weaver, Simon. *The Rhetoric of Racist Humour: US, UK, and Global Race Joking*. Burlington, VT: Ashgate, 2011.
Westheider, James E. *Fighting on Two Fronts: African Americans and the Vietnam War*. New York: New York University Press, 1997.
Whitfield, Stephen J. *The Culture of the Cold War*. 2nd ed. Baltimore: Johns Hopkins University Press, 1996.
Willis, Susan. *Portents of the Real: A Primer For Post 9/11 America*. London: Verso, 2005.
Wilmes, John. "Dr. Seuss' Forgotten Anti-War Book Made Him an Enemy of the Right." Outline, July 30, 2018. https://theoutline.com/post/5601/dr-seuss-the-butter-battle-book-history.
Winokur, Mark. *American Laughter: Immigrants, Ethnicity, and 1930s Hollywood Film Comedy*. New York: St. Martin's Press, 1996.
Wolcott, James. "How Donald Trump Became America's Insult Comic in Chief." *Vanity Fair*, December 2015. https://www.vanityfair.com/culture/2015/11/wolcott-trump-insult-comic.

Wonham, Henry B. *Playing the Races: Ethnic Caricature and American Literary Realism*. New York: Oxford University Press, 2004.

Woods, Jeff. *Black Struggle, Red Scare: Segregation and Anti-Communism in the South, 1948–1968*. Baton Rouge: Louisiana State University Press, 2004.

Young, Iris Marion. "The Logic of Masculinist Protection: Reflection on the Current Security State." *Signs: Journal of Women in Culture and Society* 29 (2003): 1–25.

Zangwill, Israel. *The Melting-Pot*. New York: Macmillan, 1917.

Zarefsky, David. *President Johnson's War on Poverty: Rhetoric and History*. Tuscaloosa: University of Alabama Press, 1986.

Zieger, Robert H. *America's Great War: World War I and the American Experience*. Lanham, MD: Rowman & Littlefield, 2000.

———. *For Jobs and Freedom: Race and Labor in America Since 1865*. Lexington: University Press of Kentucky, 2014.

Zijderveld, Anton C. *Reality in a Looking-Glass: Rationality Through an Analysis of Traditional Folly*. London: Routledge, 1982.

———. "Trend Report: The Sociology of Humor and Laughter." *Current Sociology* 31 (1983): 1–60.

Zimmerman, Eugene. *This and That About Caricature*. New York: Syndicate Press, 1905.

Žižek, Slavoj. *First as Tragedy, Then as Farce*. London: Verso, 2009.

Zulaika, Joseba. *Terrorism: The Self-Fulfilling Prophecy*. Chicago: University of Chicago Press, 2009.

Index

Italicized page references indicate illustrations. Endnotes are referenced with "n" followed by the endnote number.

Adams, John, 151
African American humor, 112–14
Aguinaldo, Emilio, 39
Ahmed, Sara, 47
Ajax Cups, 75
Aked, Stark N., 46
Ambassadors, The (Holbein's painting), 16, 18
America First Committee (AFC), 70, 72, 80, 92, 94
America First ideology, 135, 138, 164, 167, 197, 201
American Civil War, 2–3, 6, 53
American exceptionalism, 3, 15, 71, 79, 103, 184
American flag
  in caricature, 38, 40, 45–46, 144, 163, 167, 181
  patriotic sentiment of, 146–47, 156
Americanism
  in caricature, depiction of, 21–22, 34, 39, 70–71, 91–92, 192
  cultural values of, 3, 4
  ethical failure of, 183
  flag as symbol of, 146, 147
  ideological grandeur of, 28
  militarization of, 36, 187
  moral righteousness of, 46
  Nazism as antithesis to, 71
  outsider's perspective of, 194–95, 207n69
  rhetoric of, 11
  Uncle Sam as embodiment of, 186
  World War I and, 31, 34, 36
American national character
  as caricature, 13
  comic images of, 12, 22–23, 82
  ethnocentrism of, 4
  evolution of idea of, 10–11
  follies of, 7, 131, 138
  formation of, 3–4, 29, 30
  ideas of *homonoia* and, 134
  isolationism and, 82
  masculine emblem of, 31–32
  principles of, 6, 21
  racism and, 24, 102, 116, 119, 120
  studies of, 15
  Trumpism and, 8–9, 149
  Uncle Sam as emblem of, 35, 39, 40, 49, 60–61, 63
  war as feature of, 7, 24, 68–69, 94, 137, 185, 187
  See also caricatures of national character
American Protective League, 31, 51
American Red Cross, 55
American Society of Newspaper Editors, 104
Amsterdam News (newspaper), 101, 111
anamorphosis
  concept of, 18–19
Anansi, the Spider (folklore character), 100
Anderson, Benedict, 12
Anderson, Gail, 16
animalism, 67, 77, 83, 210n34
Aristotle, 210n34
Ashanti folktales, 100, 135

Ashcroft, John, 155, 156–57
Attwood, Francis Gilbert, 179

Bacevich, Andrew, 136, 182
Badiou, Alain, 113
Bakhtin, Mikhail, 35
Bald Eagle (cartoon character), 4, 5, 69, 83–85
Baldwin, James, 110, 111, 134, 174
banal nationalism
　notion of, 11, 146
Bannon, Steve, 164
Banta, Martha, 15
Beard, Frank, 61
Beckett, Samuel, v, 20
Beerbohm, Max, 33, 61
Behind the Lines 2017: The Three-Ring Circus (Rowe), 195
Bell, Darrin, 21
Bergen, Edgar, 154
Bergson, Henri, 11, 148, 165, 167
Berlant, Lauren, 146
Bernays, Edward, 30, 42
Berryman, Clifford K., 45
　"Not in a Position to Give Up the Chase," 32, *33*
Bhabha, Homi, 185
Bierce, Ambrose, 10
Billig, Michael, 11, 146
Black children
　depiction of, 104–5, *105*, 116–21, *117, 122*
　as outsiders, 102–3, 112, 116, 130–32
　race relations and, 105–6, 121–23
　social conditions of, 23, 128–29
Black children of war, 115, 131, 133
Blackness
　comic images of, 103, 112–15
　double-consciousness of, 81, 113
　political culture and, 29, 102
　as presence, idea of, 113, 114
Black people
　activism of, 108–9
　citizenship of, 53, 107
　civil rights of, 54, 105–6, 108, 129

　G.I. Bill and, 109
　humor of, 112–14
　popular propaganda and, 53–54
　poverty of, 124–25
Black press, 109–10
blame
　rhetorical force of, 47, 50
Block, Herbert Lawrence. *See* Herblock
Bootsie (cartoon character), 101–2, 104, 109, 110–11, 115
Borowitz, Andy, 162–63
Boskin, Joseph, 20, 125, 195
Bowman, Rowland C., 3
Boyesen, H. H., 12
Braithwaite, William Stanley, 113
Bressler, Harry S., 21
Brey, Laura, 21
Brother Jonathan (cartoon character), 13, *14*, 38
Brown v. Board of Education, 104, 116, 124
bugs. *See* insects
Bulgakov, Mikhail, 66
Bureau of Cartoons, 42, 44
Burke, Kenneth, 16, 19, 59, 77, 184–85, 193
Burroughs, William S., 65–66, 68, 71
Bush, George W.
　American flag pin of, 146
　caricatures of, 139–40, 144–45, 149, 154, 163, 180
　foreign policy of, 136, 163
　War on Terror and, 138, 145, 150, 162, 181
Bush Doctrine, 139, 143

"Call of the Sex, The" (article), 30
Capozzola, Christopher, 35, 36, 47
Capra, Frank, 95
caricatures
　American exceptionalism and, 15
　bird imagery, 79–87, *81, 85*
　comic abstraction in, 77–79
　comic looking glass of, 16–20, 22, 28, 183, 188

compositional elements of, 19
as crucible, 33–34, 36, 61–62
definition of, 18–19, 198, 206n55
distribution of, 20
emphasis on failure, 48
ethnic, 4
ethos and, 14
exaggeration and distortions in, 61, 194, 206n33
grotesqueries of, 15
humor in, 12, 19, 20, 25, 85–86, 183, 190
insect imagery, 87–89, *88*, 90, 91
monstrous characters, 39, 107, 199, 202
power of, 11–12, 42–43
President Trump as, 194–95
of Puritans, 28
racism and, 11
as rhetorical art, 95, 181–82, 184, 196
rhetorical weight of, 16
rhetoric of, 6, 13
scholarly studies of, 16, 17
sexualized appeals of, 48
of survival, 199
theme of governmental folly, 200
truths of, 19
caricatures of national character
anamorphic associations in, 18, 19, 210n34
bird imagery of, 83, 86
Black children as, 188
as collective selfhood, 15, 17, 61–62
humor of, 13, 42, 183
influence of, 61
nationalistic belief and, 13, 192
politics and, 2
public engagements with war and, 21
rhetorical forces in, 2
sexualized imagery of, 59
war culture and, 6–7, 20–22, 42, 191
Carracci, Agosto, 17, 18
Carracci, Annibale, 18
Carroll, Lewis, 17, 66, 79, 136, 140, 183, 200, 202

Carson, Rachel, 88
Carter, Jimmy, 130–31
Caté, Ricardo, 21
cats
  in caricature, imagery of, 66–67, 77, 78, 87, 94–95
  Churchill and, 70
  human attachment to, 65
Cavalier (cartoon character), 13
Cheney, Dick, 143, 154–56, 180
Cheshire Cat, 66–67, 187
Chesterton, G. K., 26
Chicago Defender (newspaper), 109, 112
Chicago Tribune (newspaper), 23, 68, 91, 137
children
  in caricatures, 70, 112, 134
  as last hope for egalitarianism, 116
  See also Black children
children of war, 103, 104, 112, 127, 135
Chinese Exclusion Act, 4, 90
Christy, Howard Chandler, 21
  images of women, 55–57, 59
  "I WANT YOU FOR THE NAVY" poster, 55–56, *56*
Churchill, Winston, 70, 201
civic duty, 10, 21, 22, 35, 156
Civil Rights Act (1960), 105
Civil Rights Movement, 54, 105–6, 108, 129
Cold War
  civil rights movement and, 109
  imagery of, 24
  impact on American character, 23, 62, 130, 131–32
  impact on domestic politics, 137, 166
  public culture of, 103–4, 111, 123, 132–34
Columbia (cartoon character), 13, 40, 41, 48
comic looking glass of caricature, 16–20, 22, 28, 183, 188
Committee on Public Information (CPI), 29, 34, 53, 54, 73, 181
Communist Labor Party, 110

Connor, Eugene, 120
Connor, Walker, 10
Conservative Political Action Conference (CPAC), 146, 181
Consolati, Claudia, 59
Cooley, Charles Cooley, 16
Corral, O.K., 132
Cosmopolitan (magazine), 46, 57
Council on African Affairs, 109
Couture, Thomas, 153
COVID-19 pandemic, 138–39, 142, 163–64, 175–77, 190, 193, 197–98, 199
Creel, George
    career of, 29, 34, 44, 181
    on cartoon power, 49
    view of war, 36, 51, 61, 70
Crisis, The, 53
crucible
    caricatures as, 33–34, 36, 61–62
    definition of, 61
Crucible: Life and Death in 1918 (exhibit), 61

Daily Worker (later *Daily World*, newspaper), 23, 104, 110, 112, 125, 127
Davis, Elmer, 72
Davis, Jefferson, 36
death
    sexuality and, 40
Deleuze, Gilles, 16, 18, 79, 89, 178
democracy
    despotism and, 150, 151–53
    founding principles of, 12–13
    war for, 30–35
Dickinson, Greg, 169
Dies, Martin, Jr., 91
Dies Committee, 91
Division of Pictorial Publicity, 48–49
Dorinson, Joseph, 125
Douglas, William O., 105
Douglass, Frederick, 107
Dr. Seuss (Theodor Geisel)
    approach to race relations, 93–94
    career of, 22, 74–77, 95, 98–99
    cat as alter ego of, 66

    humor of, 77–78, 99, 187
    legacy of, 97–99
    machine imagery, 77
    "Manly Art of Self Defense" watercolor, 77–78
    as outsider, 67
    view of American national character, 22–23, 86, 92, 94
    view of Nazism, 71
    view of warfare, 67–68, 71, 73, 192
Dr. Seuss's cartoons
    in advertising, 75–77, *76*
    bird imagery in, 69, 80, *81*, 83–85, 88–89
    cat imagery in, 66–67, 87, 94–95
    "The End of the Nap," 84–85, *85*
    "The Guy Who Makes a Mock of Democracy," 94
    images of enemies in, 86–91, 92, 95, 187
    "In God We Trust (And How!)," 80
    insect imagery in, 87–89, 90, 91
    "Lindbergh Quarter," 80–81, *81*
    machine imagery, 92–93
    ostrich imagery, 80, 81–82, 83, 84, 86, 187
    "Our Big Bertha," 92–93, *93*
    portrayal of Lindbergh in, 80, 210n54
    publications of, 73, 74
    "Quick, Henry, THE FLIT!," 75, 77, *88*, 88–89
    race relations in, 23, 69, 94
    Sam-Bird character, 83–85, 88–89
    The Seven Lady Godivas, 74–75
    "Society of Red Tape Cutters," 96–98
    "The Tower of Babble," 74
    "The Veteran Recalls the Battle of 1943," 95, *96*
    wartime, 95–96, 99
    weird humor of, 66, 70–71, 209n9
Du Bois, W.E.B., 29, 53–54, 107
Dudziak, Mary L., 107
Duns Scotus, John, 160
Dunst, Larry, 102

Eco, Umberto, 6
Eisenhower, Dwight D., 104, 125
Eisenstein, Zillah, 162
Elizabeth II, Queen of Great Britain, 139
Ellison, Ralph, 112
Emerson, Ralph Waldo, 16
enemies
   animal imagery of, 86, 95
   insect imagery of, 87–90, 187
   as monsters, depiction of, 4, 92, 187, 202–3, 204n8
Engelhardt, Tom, 22, 118
Erikson, Erik, 10
"Expansion" (cartoon), 38

Fairfax Court House, 36
Fauset, Jessie, 113
Field, Marshall, III, 73
Filipinos
   in cartoons, portrayal of, 4, 32, 33
Fisher, Walter, 151
Flagg, James Montgomery
   "All in the Same Boat," 46
   American character in works of, 23, 26, 28–29, 102
   "Arrested as a Witch in Salem, 1692," 27
   "A CALL TO ARMS," 40, 41, 208n39
   career of, 28
   "The Cartoonist Makes People SEE THINGS!," 49, 49–50
   depiction of the Puritans, 27–29
   "GET OFF THAT THRONE!," 51, 52, 53
   If, A Guide to Bad Manners, 28, 46
   I Should Say So, 30
   It's Risky to Want Things, 28
   "A Jill for Jack," 58, 58
   "Limericks," 46
   "A Millennial Forevision," 33
   "Our Beginnings," 26–27, 29, 31
   sexual humor of, 29, 59
   "The Target," 58
   Tomfoolery, 28, 46
   Uncle Sam cartoons, 30–32, 34, 39–40, 42, 46–47, 50–51, 62–64, 73, 184, 186–87
   wartime artworks of, 28, 46, 69
   women images, 57–60
   Yankee Girls Abroad, 57
   See also "I Want YOU" poster (Flagg)
folly of war, 9, 11–12, 136–37
Foucault, Michel, 16
Franklin, Benjamin
   on American nation, 4
   career of, 7, 26
   caricatures of, 3, 7, 13, 191
   humorous tracts of, 1, 207n3
   on national emblem, 9, 45
   nation-building project of, 2
   view of war, 7
Frazier, Benjamin, 72
Freedom Riders, 120
Freedom to Display the American Flag Act (2005), 146
Freud, Sigmund, 42–43, 47, 103
Fuchs, Esther, 40

Gates, Henry Louis, Jr., 113
Geisel, Theodor. *See* Dr. Seuss
Gibson, Charles Dana, 44, 57
Gilbert, Sophie, 192
Gillam, Victor, 3, 4, 204n8
Gillray, James, 191, 200, 216n13
Gisbertz, Anna-Katharina, 214n46
Glass, Philip, 20
Glasser, Susan B., 200
Gombrich, Ernst, 206n33, 210n34
Gómez, Máximo, 39
Gramsci, Antonio, 188, 189
Griffin, Roger, 71
Griffith, D. W., 54
Griswold, Alfred Griswold, 85
Gronbeck, Bruce, 186
guilt
   rhetorical force of, 47–48, 50, 62–63
   of survivors, 97

Hamilton, Alexander, 151
Hamilton, Grant E., 204n8
Hansberry, Lorraine, 111
Harding, Warren G., 138
Harrigan, Edward, 32
Harrington, Michael, 127
Harrington, Oliver ("Ollie") Wendell
  career of, 23, 101–2
  as outsider, 106, 111, 194
  self-exile of, 23, 101, 111–12
  view on war, 185, 188
  "Why I Left America" essay, 112
Harrington's cartoons
  African American humor in, 114–15, 130
  "BIGGEST BANG, BANG, BANG, BUDGET EVER!," 131
  Black children in, 102–4, 106–7, 112, 115–18, 120–24, 128, 130–32, 188
  Bootsie character, 101–2, 104, 109, 110–11, 115, 212n73
  casualties of War on Poverty, 125
  critique of the bombing campaigns, 130
  Crow character, 135, 213n86
  Dark Laughter serial strip, 101
  "Funny how kids' games change with the times, ain't it?," 121–22, *122*
  "General Blotchit, you take your tanks and feint at Lynchville," 116–17, *117*
  "Hey, why don't somebody tell these damn starvin' brats that there ain't enough for me and them too!," 126–27, *127*
  Jive Gray series, 132
  kids at the war table, *128*
  Lady Liberty character, 124–25, 127
  little Luther character, 117, 212n73
  lynched school bus, *119*, 119–20
  Miss McCoy's comments on, 101
  "My daddy said they didn't seem to mind servin' him on the Anzio beach-head," 104–5, *105*

race relations in, 101–3, 111, 118–24, 131, 132
realistic aesthetic of, 128
Hart, Tony, 32
Hay, John, 5
Hazlitt, Henry, 70–71
Hecht, George J., 42, 45, 62
  The War in Cartoons, 31
Heller, Steven, 16
Herblock (penname of Herbert Lawrence Block), 21, 78, 79, 102, 190
Hervey, Mary F. S., 16
Himes, Chester, 111
Hirohito, Emperor of Japan, 83
Hofstede, Geert, 9
Holbein, Hans
  The Ambassadors, 16, 18
Holloway, Jonathan Scott, 23
Holmes, John Haynes, 98
Hopkinson, Francis, 48
Hopps, Harry Ryle, 21
Houston, Herbert S., 72
Hughes, Langston, 101, 111, 114
Hulme, Etta, 21
humor
  of Blackness, 112–15
  Burke on, 19
  as characteristic of warism, 2–8, 44, 138, 145–46, 186–92
  and comic abstraction, 77–79
  and cultural stereotypes, 4, 32, 92–94, 133–35
  Deleuze on, 79, 85–86, 90, 178
  drivers of Americanism, 1–2
  feeling of guilt and, 47
  and the human condition, 24, 199, 203
  post-9/11, 147–48
  in visuality, 6, 17–20, 34–35, 90, 190–92
  See also sexual humor
Hunt, Tristram, 143
Hunter, James Hunter, 133
hylomorphism, 77, 210n34

idiocy
  in caricature, portrayal of, 152, 162, 167, 168, 170–71, 172, 173, 180
  Greek notion of, 150
immigrants
  comic portrayals of, 32
  discrimination of, 54
Ingersoll, Ralph, 73
insects
  caricature images of, 87–89, *88*, 90, 91
Irigiray, Luce, 59
"I Want YOU" poster (Flagg)
  conception of civic duty, 22, 29, 32, 44, 48, 49, 186
  distribution of, 50
  image of, *43*
  impression on the public, 50–51, 53
  mocking humor of, 36, 39–40
  parodies on, 40, 52, 56, 60–61, 156

Jackson, Andrew, 165
Jackson, Robert H., 141
Japan
  in World War II, 83, 84, 86–87, 88
Japanese
  caricatures of, 8, 89–92, 95, 99
  treatment of, 73
Jarrett, Gene Andrew, 113
Jim Crow culture, 4, 15, 53, 101, 103, 109–10, 123
Johnson, Georgia Douglas, 115
Johnson, Lyndon B.
  "Daisy Girl" campaign, 116
  "Peace Without Conquest" speech, 125
  "Vietnamization" policy of, 125, 126
  war on poverty of, 124–25
Jones, Alex, 193
Judge (magazine), 2, 33, 40, 46

Kaiser (cartoon character), *49*, 49–50, 51
Kammen, Michael, 28, 123
Katz, Harry, 147
Kellner, Douglas, 145

Kennedy, John F., 106, 124
Khan, Shahnaz, 161
Kimball, Warren F., 85
Kim Jong-un, 143, 162–63, 165, 167–69, *168*
King, Martin Luther, Jr., 120, 124–25
  "I Have a Dream" speech, 106
Klein, Naomi, 143
Korematsu v. United States, 141
Ku Klux Klan (KKK), 111, 116, 120, 124, 169

Lamb, Chris, 147
Larsen, Nella, 111
Legman, Gershon, 29
Lenape Turtle Clan, 26
Leslie's Weekly (magazine), 2, 51, 52, 185
Levin, Harry, 113
Lewis, Sinclair, 140
Lieberman, Joe, 143
Life (magazine), 26–28, 46, 57, 72, 74, 121, 179
Lincoln, Abraham, 12, 36
Lindbergh, Charles A.
  in Dr. Seuss's cartoons, 68, 72, 80–81, 210n54
  political activism of, 72, 80
  support of American isolationism, 79–80
  trans-Atlantic flight, 79
Lippman, Walter, 61
Lock, Herbert. *See* Herblock
Low, David, 78–79, 201
Luccock, Halford E., 71
Luce, Henry, 72
Luedtke, Luther S., 10
Lyotard, Jean-François, 16, 18

machines
  in caricatures, depiction of, 92–93, *93*
MacLeish, Archibald, 73
Manifest Destiny, 7, 21, 28
Marcoci, Roxana, 78
Marx, Groucho, 178–79
Marx, Karl, 151, 152, 165
Masson, Tom, 26, 27, 28, 29

Mauldin, Bill, 21, 78, 102
Mayfield, Julian, 111
McCartney, Paul T., 4
McCay, Winsor, 29, 61
McConnell, Mitch, 175
McCormick, Robert R., 72, 91
McCoy, Miss (teacher of Ollie Harrington), 101
McDaniel, James P., 186
McKay, Claude, 111
McKibben, Bill, 197
McKinley, William, 179
Mead, George Herbert, 121
Mead, Margaret, 106
Meeker, Joseph, 199
"melting pot" concept, 32–34
Mencken, H. L., 150, 151
Minear, Richard H., 73
Moore, Charles, 120
Mueller Report, 166
Mussolini, Benito, 189

Nast, Thomas, 2, 37, 38
National Association for the Advancement of Colored People (NAACP), 53, 111
National Defense Act, 47, 53
Native Americans
  bald eagle as symbol of, 4
  cartoonists, 21
  portrayals, 32
  stereotypes of, 26, 27
Nazism
  in caricatures, 67, 70–71, 78–79
Nel, Philip, 66, 67
Nervy Nat (cartoon character), 46
New Deal politics, 73, 80, 84–85, 91, 94
"New Negro"
  discourses of, 105, 107, 113
"New Woman"
  concept of, 55, 57
New York Times (newspaper), 23, 72, 137
Niagara Movement, 29
Nib, The (online comics), 179–80
Nickels, Cameron, 15

Nimitz, Chester, 97
9/11 terrorist attack, 137, 138, 145
Nixon, Richard, 126, 129, 165
Ntikuma (folklore character), 100, 101
Nussbaum, Martha, 47
Nye, Gerald P., 72

Obama, Barack, 139, 145, 190, 213n9
Obama Doctrine, 143
O'Leary, Cecilia, 31
Ong, Walter J., 63
Operation Desert Shield, 137
Operation Enduring Freedom, 145
Osborn, Robert, 102
ostrich (cartoon character), 80–82, 84, 86, 187
Ott, Brian L., 169
"Our Beginnings" (cartoon artwork), 26, 28, 29, 31

Paine, Thomas, 178
Patterson, Eleanor M., 91
Patterson, Joseph M., 72
Peacock, Margaret, 116
Pearl Harbor attack, 72, 184
Peirce, C. S., 17
Penn, William, 26
Perez, Louis A., Jr., 3
Perkins, David, 198, 202
Pierce, Charles P., 150
Pillweather, Matthew J., 46
Pittman, John, 110
Pittsburgh Courier (newspaper), 23, 101, 104, 110, 111, 112, 117, 122
Plot Against America, The (Roth), 80
PM (newspaper), 22, 67, 73, 184
posters. *See* recruitment posters
Prattis, P. L., 109, 110
Prunepincher, Pearl, 46
Pryor, Richard, 114
Public, John Q., 97
Puck (magazine), 2, 39, 44
Puritans
  caricatures of, 26–28
  as "chosen race," 28

Quixano, David, 33

racism, 94, 105–7
   American national character and, 24, 102, 116, 119, 120
Raemaekers, Louis, 45
recruitment posters
   image of Uncle Sam, 60
   influence of, 51
   instigation of guilt, 47, 48
   nationalistic appeal of, 40
   rhetoric of war, 49, 50
   women images in, 40–41, *41*, 55–60, *56*, *58*
   See also "I Want YOU" poster (Flagg)
Rogers, W. A., 3, 39
Roosevelt, Franklin D.
   on caricature of ostrich, 82–83
   cartoons of, 85, 91, 96
   meeting with Churchill, 70
   military policy of, 71–72
   personality of, 85
   racism of, 84, 91
Roosevelt, Theodore, 3, 4, 38, 46
Roque, Frank, 158, 160
Ross, Alex, 64
Roth, Philip
   The Plot Against America, 80
Rourke, Constance, 15, 57
Rowe, David, 194–95, 198–201
Rumsfeld, Donald, 143, 155, 156
Russert, Tim, 163
Ryan, Paul, 141

Salem Witch Trials, 31
Sam-Bird (cartoon character), 69, 70, 83–85, 88–89
Sartre, Jean-Paul, 14
Saturday Evening Post (magazine), 67, 74
"say uncle" idiom, 35–36
Sedition Act, 51
Seldes, George, 91
Selves and Others
   caricature perspectives of, 4, 28, 66, 74, 92, 157, 160, 162, 186, 190, 202

sexual humor, 22, 29
"Sheet of Caricatures" (Carracci brothers), 18
Sherwood, Margaret, 53
Sinatra, Frank, 14
Sodhi, Balbir Singh, 158, 160
Sorel, Edward, 102
Soviet propaganda, 108
Spanish-American War, 3, 4, 39
"Spanish Brute," 4, 204n8
Sparrow, James T., 72
Stahr, Paul, 40, 41, 48
Stamp Act, 7, 10
Stanley, Joseph, 72
Steichen, Edward, 184
Steiner, Palph, 184

Telnaes, Ann
   career of, 23–24, 139
   comic imagery of, 24, 143, 153
   on editorial cartooning, 147–48
   exhibitions of, 23, 142
   mockery of presidentialism, 138, 139, 142–43, 149, 163
   as outsider, 142, 194
   political views of, 137, 142
   sketch on Twitter, 190
   style of, 149
   wartime cartoons of, 143, 153, 155–56, 161–62
Telnaes's cartoons
   of American democracy, 146, 153
   American flag in, 146, 147, 154–56, 157
   of American national character, 161–62
   of Americans of the decadence, *152*, 153–54
   of American tyranny, 192
   comic travesty of, 149
   of Donald Trump, 24, 139–41, 144, 149, 164–72, 177–78, 180–82, 185, 190, 201
   of George W. Bush, 139, 144, 154, 180

Telnaes's cartoons (*continued*)
   "Guide to identifying people by their headgear," 158–60, *159*
   images of women, 161
   "I Want YOU" parody, 156–57
   The Lyin' King series, 142–43, 170–71
   "The megalomania of Donald Trump," 172
   pissing contest, *168*
   publications of, 137, 163
   of Queen Elizabeth and King George, 139–40, *140*
   of Self and Other, 157–58, *160*
   "U.S. War Coverage," 148, *149*
   of War on Terror, 158, 161
   "You can see these guys wrapped in the flag on TV," *155*, 155–57
Tocqueville, Alexis de, 153, 158
Tōjō, Hideki, 83
Truman, Harry S., 97, 108
Trump, Donald J.
   admiration for military parades, 169, *170*
   as an actor, 172
   appeal to white supremacists, 144
   appearance at CPAC, 181–82, *182*
   authoritarianism of, 176, 181
   caricatures of, 24, 139, 150, 163, *168*, 171, 173, *173*, *174*, 174–75, 178, 180–82, 194–95, *195*, 198, 199–200
   electoral politics of, 166
   foreign affairs of, 150–51, 162–63, 167, 169
   ideology of, 138, 197
   idiocy of, 213n8
   impeachment of, 175
   as imperial president, 24, 140–41, 170–71, 173
   inauguration of, 171
   Kim Jong-un and, 162–63, 165, 167–69
   as King Trump, depiction of, 24, 140, 171, 175, 176, 184, 201
   media feud of, 171–72, 190
   megalomania of, 172
   mockery of, 185
   perception of democracy, 144, 165
   personality of, 166–67
   political agenda of, 138, 143, 151
   public affinity for the American flag, 146
   as Queen of Hearts, *141*
   racism of, 175
   response to COVID-19 pandemic, 138, 163–64, 175–77, 190
   as showman, 176
   tweets of, 169
   war rhetoric of, 164, 165–66, 168, 189–90, 191–92
   withdrawal from international organizations, 197
Trumpism, 8, 24, 140, 166, 175, 189–90
Trump @War (film), 164
Tulis, Jeffrey K., 151
Turkey (cartoon character), 9
Twain, Mark, 66, 67, 68, 129, 131, 179, 209n10
Two Bulls, Marty, Sr., 21

Uncle Sam
   burden of, 4
   cartoon images of, 30–32, 37–40, 44–46, 51, 73, 86, 90, 92, *93*
   in cartoon politics of World War I, 34–35, 42
   contradictions of, 38–39
   on cover of *Leslie's Weekly*, 185
   dual meaning of, 37
   as emblem of national character, 35, 40, 63, 186, 187
   as face of militarism, 46–47
   finger pointing, 36, 64, 185
   humor of, 39–40
   image of Black, 60–61
   as image of white male America, 31
   male-oriented humor of, 63
   masculinity of, 48
   as personification of the United States, 5, 13, 22
   pointing a gun, image of, 51, *52*, 53

political cartoons of, 3
popularity of, 44–45
precursors of, 13
projection of cultural anxieties, 55
as propaganda machine, 48
rhetorical mobilization of, 60, 62–63
with a rifle and a sword, 179
as *self*-caricature, 50
sexual appeal of, 40
Spanish-American War and, 37
war imagery and, 39, 40, 60–61
as white male, portrayal of, 54
United States
    foreign affairs, 21, 136, 150–51, 162–63, 167, 169
    hate crimes in, 158
    integration policies, 118, 120, 129
    isolationism of, 72, 81–82
    military-industrial complex, 108–9
    poverty in, 124–26, 132
    racial tensions, 105–8, 120–21
    victory culture, 22, 137
    "Vietnamization" policies, 125, 126, 129
    withdraw from the Paris Agreement, 197

Vann, Robert Lee, 110
Vietnam War, 106, 109, 111, 126, 131
Vonnegut, Kurt, 14

Waldstreicher, David, 10
Wanzo, Rebecca, 102, 103, 113, 128
war
    comic art of seduction to, 42
    images of national character and, 6–7, 20–22, 42, 191
    visualization of the follies of, 46
War on Drugs, 132
War on Poverty, 124–26, 132
War on Terror
    Bush's approach to, 150, 189
    in caricatures, 137, 138, 142, 161

collateral damage in, 158
declaration of, 145
nationalism and, 136, 161, 170, 181
Obama's approach to, 143
public views of, 145–46, 147
roots of, 144
struggles with pandemic as, 181, 193
War on Women, 160–62, 189
Washington, George, 12, 48
Watkins, Mel, 114
Wells, H. G., 146
Wheatley, Phillis, 107
Wheeler, Burton K., 72
Williams, Holly, 195
Williams, Raymond, 20
Wilson, Samuel, 37
Wilson, Woodrow, 5, 31
    address to Congress, 32
    "America First" slogan, 138
    Creel Committee of, 181
    doctrine of neutrality, 43
    fourteen points of, 62
    racism of, 54
    wartime policies, 34, 43–44, 47
women
    and gender politics, 39–40, 54–59, 148, 161–62
    in recruitment posters, images of, 40–41, *41*, 55–60, *56*, *58*
Women's Land Army, 55
Wonham, Henry B., 10
Woodward, Bob, 169
Wounded Knee Massacre, 4
Wright, Richard, 111

Xi, Jinping, 199

Yankee (cartoon character), 15, 57, 58
Yankee Notions (periodical), 13, 14

Zangwill, Israel, 33, 34
Zijderveld, Anton, 17

www.ingramcontent.com/pod-product-compliance
Lightning Source LLC
Chambersburg PA
CBHW022047290426
44109CB00014B/1011